P9-DVA-306

"The noted Scripture scholar Fr. Raymond Brown has chosen a rich and representative selection from his published articles of the past ten years for inclusion in the present book. In each of the essays, which number fourteen in all, Fr. Brown invariably views his difficult subject matter in its broadest context and manages to clarify it by thorough but unobtrusive scholarship. *New Testament Essays* is, then, at once learned and eminently readable."

Herder Correspondence

Father Brown's "essays embody a wide range of scholarly interest, power to penetrate to the cardinal issues, thorough acquaintance with current research, lucidity in literary style, and cogency in scholarship."

Paul S. Minear, Yale University

"The two words that occurred most often to this reviewer as he read the collection were candor and competence."

Catholic Biblical Quarterly

"Perhaps most characteristic of his essays is his unfailing ability to present a balanced position. One may disagree with some technical points, but the thrust of his work is toward both a scientific and religious appreciation of the New Testament."

Commonweal

Father Brown's work "shows an admirable combination of close textual study and theological analysis."

R. A. F. McKenzie, S.J.,
Rector of the Pontifical Biblical Institute

"Anyone weary of reiterated introduction and eager for more than a passing acquaintance with the sacred text will rejoice in this collection of Father Brown's essays . . . This book is distinguished not only for the depth of its author's scholarship but also by the readability of its prose."

The Catholic World

New Testament
ESSAYS

New Testament
ESSAYS

Raymond E. Brown, S.S.

IMAGE BOOKS

A Division of Doubleday & Company, Inc.
Garden City, New York

Image Books edition 1968
by special arrangement with The Bruce Publishing Company
Image Books edition published October 1968

NIHIL OBSTAT:
JOHN A. SCHULIEN, S.T.D.
Censor librorum

IMPRIMATUR:
✠ WILLIAM E. COUSINS
Archbishop of Milwaukee
July 12, 1965

© 1965 The Bruce Publishing Company
All Rights Reserved
Printed in the United States of America

To
ST. MARY'S SEMINARY, BALTIMORE
The oldest and largest
of American Catholic seminaries
on the 175th anniversary of its foundation
(1791–1966)

PREFACE

The essays in this book represent a selection made from articles published by the author in various biblical journals over the past ten years. They have been edited in the sense that passages affected by later biblical research have been modified and corrected, but no need was felt to rewrite them completely. It is indeed comforting to an author to know that his brain-children are not destined to die in the pages of periodicals, but have been found worthy of a longer life and a larger family. The selecting of the articles to be included was a difficult task, but what is presented here is a good cross section; for not only "lighter" articles but also studies in depth have been included.

The Catholic biblical movement of the postwar period has produced a hunger for modern works on Scripture. Up to now what has been offered to the Catholic public has in large part been by way of an introductory nature. This was very necessary, but then one can be introduced to Scripture only a limited number of times. We are now reaching the second stage of development where the public that has been introduced to Scripture wants to know in more detail about the individual books and passages of the Bible. This writer is convinced that there is an audience, religious and lay, that will respond to a more serious level of writing on Scripture and especially on the New Testament. He is grateful to The Bruce Publishing Company for the opportunity to test this conviction.

By way of introduction for the general reader, we may say that the choice of essays was guided by the desire to develop harmoniously certain themes of importance. The essays in Part One, for instance, deal with a more general topic, namely, the motivation and orientation of modern Catholic biblical research. To some extent they answer the questions of "why?" and "to what purpose?" The opening essay makes it clear from the very first page of the volume that author is committed, heart, mind, and soul, to the modern biblical movement that for Catholics had its origins in Pope Pius XII's great encyclical *Divino Afflante Spiritu* (1943). This scientific approach to the Bible is the only approach that can make sense to the men of our time. The essay has as its purpose to explain to all who are open to conviction that the modern biblical movement is solidly grounded in science, has received the approving patronage of the Church, and is a thoughtful and necessary Christian response to contemporary culture.

The next two essays in Part One exemplify one direction that this response can take by exploring the ecumenical possibilities of the biblical advances. It is no secret that since its beginning in 1943 the Catholic biblical movement has been heavily dependent on the work of Protestant scholars. Between the Modernist crisis at the beginning of this century and 1943 there was a period in which the authorities of the Catholic Church, made cautious by the Modernist extravagances, frowned on the free application of scientific historical criticism to the Bible. When Pope Pius XII changed this position and insisted on the importance of scientific criticism, Catholic scholarship had fallen seriously behind. Fortunately, Protestant scholarship, which had gone through its own problems with the liberal and fundamentalist extremes, was at this particular time producing much solid work that could motivate and inform the revitalizing of Catholic biblical studies. Only in the past few years has Catholic scholarship reached a sufficient maturity in modern techniques to begin to repay the debt by making *substantial* contributions of its own in the New Testament field.

Because of the way in which this development has taken place, Catholic and Protestant biblical scholars have come to know and trust one another and to appreciate one another's work. Indeed, there exists a rather broad consensus in biblical interpretation—a consensus that cuts across denominational lines—and one can often read a biblical article without knowing whether the author is Protestant or Catholic. This does not mean that the respective authors are in any way disloyal to their own confessions, but that they recognize in Scripture a common heritage which should be able to be interpreted objectively by all Christians. No Christian Church worthy of the name should have to bolster its theology by an interpretation that is not an honest reflection of the sacred writer's intent. Most of the differences that separate Christians stem from the evaluation given to postbiblical developments in Christian thought and practice. The second and third essays attempt to show in practice what contributions the modern biblical movement is making in a study of the scriptural material relevant to some of the differences between Christians. One essay, in particular, addresses itself to the concept of "the Church" in the New Testament.

The essays in Part Two constitute the major portion of this volume. Here we progress from the general to the particular and try to show modern biblical technique at work in the field of the Gospels. The author's own research in these past years has been largely in the study of the Fourth Gospel, and so the majority of the essays deal in one way or another with John. Many of the readers will already be familiar with the writer's popular commentary on John in the Collegeville *New Testament Reading Guide.* Very often the essays presented here show how the conclusions briefly mentioned in that commentary were reached.

In the first section under Part Two there are five essays dealing with various points in the Fourth Evangelist's theology and background. It is commonly thought that one of the major purposes in the writing of the Fourth Gospel was a desire to show the relation between Church life and the ministry of Jesus. As he lived late in the first century, the Evangelist seems to have been impelled to recall to the Christians of his time that the mainstays of their life in the Church, e.g., the sacraments, were intimately connected to what Jesus had done in Palestine some forty to sixty years before. It is curious that we find this same need in our own time and that in this century theologians are finding it necessary once more to stress that the sacraments cannot be divorced from the action of Jesus. Symbolism was John's tool in accomplishing this purpose. The Evangelist (Chap. 9) tells the story of how Jesus opened the eyes of a man born blind so that the man came not only to see physically but also to see spiritually and to believe in Jesus. He uses such a story to symbolize the effects of baptism, which leads the Christian from the sin and darkness into which he was born into the light and life that is Jesus. In a similar manner the Evangelist shows that in multiplying the loaves and in speaking of Himself and His revelation as the bread of life Jesus was preparing the way for the Eucharist. Two of our essays are concerned with this sacramental theme in the Fourth Gospel. The Johannine emphasis on sacramental symbolism is closely related to John's theology of the Incarnation whereby, having become man, Jesus uses the things of this world both to explain His thought and to sanctify men. The short essay on the Incarnation in Johannine theology is really a challenge to live up to the implications of such a Christian worldliness in our own lives.

The last two essays under the first section deal with the background of the tradition found in the Fourth Gospel. It is immediately obvious that in John Jesus speaks in an abstract language and a dualistic outlook (e.g., a world divided between light and darkness, truth and falsehood) that is not characteristic of His speech in the first three Gospels. The failure to find a good parallel for these patterns in contemporary Jewish usage made many scholars of the past suspect that the Evangelist had placed on Jesus' lips the language of second-century Greek thought. The discovery of the Dead Sea Scrolls has challenged this assumption. We now find abstract language and dualistic thought very similar to John's in the writings of a Jewish community who lived in Palestine in Jesus' time. One of the major obstacles to treating John as a serious witness to the historical Jesus has been removed. Yet, of course, that does not mean that John is simply a history of Jesus' ministry. Rather, a body of historical tradition which served as a source for the Fourth Gospel has been developed through preaching and teaching until in the form of a written Gospel it conveys the Evangelist's own appreciation of Jesus' significance. The essay on John the Baptist is meant to demonstrate the difference of insight between the written Gospel and the original historical tradition. Thanks in part to the Dead Sea Scrolls, we are now able to fit John the Baptist into an intelligible milieu. In studying the sayings that Fourth Gospel attributes to John the Baptist, we can see, on the one hand, how in their original meaning these sayings fit into that milieu, and how, on the other hand, they have undergone theological development so that they fit smoothly into the perspective of the Evangelist.

The essay on John the Baptist also shows how, when properly understood, John's tradition about the Baptist is reconcilable with the picture of the Baptist in the Synoptic Gospels. Thus this essay serves as a bridge leading the reader to Section 2, which discusses the relations between John and the Synoptic Gospels. Today almost all scholars agree that John was not written to fill in the lacunae of the Synoptic Gospels, but some tend to treat John as totally dependent on the Synoptic Gospels for any historical material pertaining to the ministry of Jesus. The whole case for Johannine historicity depends on the existence of independent historical material as a source for the Fourth Gospel. Three essays are devoted to a very close comparison of the Johannine and Synoptic traditions to show the similarities and the differences in the basic material behind each and the different ways in which that material is developed. The conclusions hopefully do justice both to the wealth of historical material in the Fourth Gospel and to the Evangelist's theological genius at developing this material in his own way.

Section 3 shows how biblical research can be applied to some very familiar passages in the Synoptic Gospels. It is the writer's hope that, after reading the essay on the Lord's Prayer, the reader will have seen new depths of meaning in this frequently recited formula. The parables of the Gospels are familiar Sunday fare in the readings at Mass, and one essay is devoted to reclaiming the authenticity of some features in the parables from an overcritical exegesis. The volume closes on the well-known theme of the beatitudes, but the beatitudes seen in a light that many will find quite different. Perhaps this final short essay in the volume is the one best adapted to show the reader that the modern biblical movement not only supplies nourishing intellectual fare, but also opens up some fascinating possibilities for deepening one's spiritual insight.

The author is quite aware of his own limitations as scholar and writer; he makes no pretense that the views he proposes will be acceptable to all his fellow workers in the biblical field, nor even to all Catholic scholars. (Disagreement among Catholic scholars is a good sign; too often in the past uncritical consent to a particular view as "the Catholic view" has led us to grief.) But he does hope that these essays will exhibit to the reader how much wealth can be discovered in Scripture if we use the modern tools available to us.

ACKNOWLEDGMENTS

The author and publisher are grateful to the following for permission to reprint:

The Midwestern Institute of Pastoral Theology and *Guide,* for "Our New Approach to the Bible";

The Journal of Ecumenical Studies for "Ecumenism and New Testament Research";

Novum Testamentum for "The Unity and Diversity in New Testament Ecclesiology" and "Parable and Allegory Reconsidered";

Theological Studies for "The Johannine Sacramentary" and "The Pater Noster as an Eschatological Prayer";

The Bible Today for "The Theology of the Incarnation in John," "The Beatitudes According to Luke," and "The Date of the Last Supper" (included as part of Chapter IX);

The Catholic Biblical Quarterly for "John the Baptist in the Gospel of John" (originally "Three Quotations from John the Baptist in the Gospel of John"), "The Problem of Historicity in John," "John and the Synoptic Gospel: A Comparison" (originally "Incidents That Are Units in the Synoptic Gospels but Dispersed in St. John");

The Catholic Biblical Quarterly, Harper & Row, and Krister Stendahl for "The Qumran Scrolls and the Johannine Gospel and Epistles" (the essay originally appeared in the CBQ and was reprinted in slightly modified form in Dr. Stendahl's work, *The Scrolls and the New Testament,* Harper & Row, Inc., 1957);

Herder & Herder and St. Mary's College, Kansas, for "The Gospel Miracles" which appeared originally in *The Bible in Current Catholic Thought,* edited by John L. McKenzie, S.J., Herder & Herder, 1963;

Proceedings of the Society of Catholic College Teachers of Sacred Doctrine, for "The Eucharist and Baptism in John."

CONTENTS

Part One

BIBLICAL RESEARCH TODAY
AND
ITS ECUMENICAL POSSIBILITIES

I

Our New Approach
to the Bible

That there is something new afoot in Catholic biblical circles has become obvious to all: to the hierarchy, to theologians, to priests in the ministry, to teachers, and to the ordinary laity. Some are enthusiastic; some are opposed; some are afraid; and some are just confused.

In all the discussion of the "new" biblical movement, however, there is one question that does keep coming up, namely, why a new movement? The Christian Church has been in possession of the Bible for nearly two thousand years. Naturally there are always new insights. But the notion that there can be a new approach to the Bible seems to imply that either the Church has been on the wrong track in the past, or has been neglecting its duty. It is this mistrust of the "newness" of the biblical movement that leads many to suspect that it is just a passing fancy or something worse.

We think that a great deal of confusion can be cleared away by carefully answering this question of newness. We would like to go into the background of the new biblical movement to show why it has come about now and not before. We would like to make it clear that there is no question of any sort of reproach to the Church of the past, for the material that has given rise to the new biblical movement could not possibly have been known before our own time. Rather, the very fact that there is a new biblical movement is a witness to the eternal vitality of the Church and to God's providential plan for its growth. In short, the newness of the biblical movement is not a dangerous novelty gained by wanton uprooting, but the freshness of organic growth.

The modern Catholic biblical movement is the result of a grafting of the past one hundred years of scientific discovery on to the tree of Christian knowledge. In the past other grafts have been made on this tree; and each time, with proper pruning, the tree has borne ever richer fruit. In the early centuries Greco-Roman culture with its laws, ethics, organization, and philosophical imagery was grafted on to the basic teachings of the Galilean Rabbi; and the result was the flowering of the patristic period. In the Middle Ages there was a graft of Aristotelian philosophy, transmitted through the Arabic commentators; this gave its life to the splendid flowering of Thomism and the revival of the *philosophia perennis*. In the period of the Renaissance a graft from the new classical and scientific insights flowered in the great theological and spiritual advances of the Counter-Reformation.

So now in the past hundred years there has been a growth in scientific knowledge unparalleled in the history of mankind; and this knowledge, too, has its role to play in the growth of Christianity. The wise men of today must bring their gifts to the God-Man, as did wise men of the past. To turn our backs on this new knowledge of our times and to claim that it has nothing to offer to religion would be a denial of history, and a blasphemous confession that Christianity is dead because it can grow no longer. To fear this new knowledge and to hide from it is a denial of faith, for "the refusal to face facts in the name of piety is not the evidence of faith but of the lack of it."[1]

The biblical movement is but one phase of the contribution of science to religion, but it is a very active phase. In discussing the scientific origins of the new biblical movement let us consider the contributions made in the past hundred years by language studies, by history, and by archaeology to the growth of biblical knowledge.

LANGUAGE STUDIES

First, language studies. It is difficult to realize today that up to one hundred years ago the Bible was really the only firsthand witness to the great civilizations that preceded Greece and Rome. True, there were echoes in the Greek historians (especially in reference to Persia), in Josephus and Eusebius, but they were often badly garbled. The Bible was our chief source of knowledge of the Egyptians, the Assyrians, the Babylonians, the Aramaeans, and of a host of other kingdoms that had flourished and died in the ancient Near East. And we must remember that the foreign empires figured in the Bible only incidentally, i.e., as a background for the story of God's dealings with an insignificant Semitic tribe known as the *Benê Israel.* This isolation of the Bible presented all sorts of difficulties. Many parts of the historical books remained virtually incomprehensible because of a lack of background. And for the more literary parts of the Bible, e.g., its sapiential poetry, no intelligible standards of comparison had survived from the civilizations contemporary with Israel.

Then the picture changed radically. In the first half of the nineteenth century Champollion deciphered hieroglyphics and Rawlinson deciphered (Persian) cuneiform. It took

[1] Bruce Vawter, "Genesis and the College Teacher of Sacred Doctrine," *Proceedings of the Sixth Annual Convention of the Society of Catholic College Teachers of Sacred Doctrine* (1960), 31.

time before these decipherments could be fully used in giving us the grammar and vocabulary of the respective languages, but by the end of the century Egyptian, Babylonian, and Assyrian records could be read accurately. The Bible was no longer alone in its witness to the past.

The historical contributions of these records we shall discuss later; let us mention here just a few examples of their literary importance. The Egyptian records, for instance, give us a whole body of wisdom literature very close in concept to the wisdom literature of the Bible. In fact, it seems clear that part of the Book of Proverbs was dependent on the sayings of the Egyptian Amen-em-ope, and that there is a close parallel in Psalm 104 to the Egyptian hymn to the sun-god Aton. The Assyro-Babylonian records and those of their forerunners, the Sumerians, have given us even richer material. The Babylonian flood story (ultimately of Sumerian origin) and its hero Utnapishtim are identical in many details with the biblical story of Noah. This shows us that some of the stories of Genesis 1–11 were not the peculiar property of the Hebrews but were drawn, with modifications, from the common traditions of the Near East. The great law codes of the Sumerians and Akkadians (e.g., Hammurabi) have made us realize that the Mosaic code reflected the legal traditions of neighboring peoples.

These nineteenth-century linguistic discoveries were only the first in a series. More recently (1930), the discovery and decipherment of the tablets found at Ugarit have made a tremendous impact on biblical studies. When Abraham and, later Joshua came into the promised land, they found a flourishing civilization, that of the Canaanites. They borrowed the language of this civilization (for Hebrew is just a Canaanite dialect) and many of its customs. But until 1930 we knew of no literary records left by the Canaanites. The decipherment of Ugaritic (ancient Canaanite written in a cuneiform alphabet) made available the poetic myths which dealt with the gods of Canaan. The language itself was of interest; for, more ancient than Hebrew, it gave us the meanings of words and constructions in Hebrew poetry which had long been forgotten. But more than that, this ancient Canaanite poetry was of basically the same form as biblical poetry; and so we now realize that the Hebrews borrowed not only their language but also their poetry and music from the Canaanites. Many expressions of the Psalms appear word for word in the Ugaritic literature, and it seems clear that some of the praises sung of Yahweh were borrowed from those once sung of Baal. None of this is shocking: the God of Israel was a God of history, and the people that learned to worship Him used familiar materials in fashioning their religion, although they infused these materials with an entirely new spirit.

Even more recently than Ugarit, the discovery of the Dead Sea Scrolls (1947) has thrown light on the Bible. This is the first large body of Palestinian literature from the period after the Maccabees and before the fall of Jerusalem (c. 130 B.C. to A.D. 68). The Scrolls are useful in giving us an idea of the type of Hebrew and Aramaic being written in the period before and during Jesus' lifetime. For the standard books of the Hebrew Bible the Scrolls have given us a text almost one thousand years earlier than that hitherto available. For the first time we can see a deuterocanonical book like Tobit and apocryphal books like *Jubilees* and *Enoch* in their original Semitic form, without having to depend on Greek and Ethiopic translations.

The linguistic discoveries we have mentioned thus far have affected Old Testament studies (although, as well known, the Dead Sea Scrolls are of importance for New Testament background). But there have been equally important discoveries with regard to the New Testament. True, Greek was well known long before the past one hundred years. Yes, classical Greek, but not New Testament Greek. Indeed, there were scholars who thought New Testament Greek so strange that they suggested that it was a dialect peculiar to the New Testament. It was only at the end of the past century with the discovery of the Greek papyri in

Egypt that there were made available some examples of the everyday (*koine*) Greek spoken in New Testament times. Here were business contracts and letters—the documents of the ordinary man written in the ordinary Greek that he spoke. This Greek, not classical Greek, was the language of the New Testament; and any modern New Testament Greek dictionary shows the great influence of the papyri on New Testament studies.

More recently the discovery of papyri fragments of New Testament books has given us Greek biblical texts hundreds of years earlier than the great codices like Vaticanus. The Rylands fragment of Jn (P^{52}, published in 1935), for instance, dates to A.D. 125–150. The Bodmer papyri of Jn (P^{66}, published in 1956, and P^{75}, published in 1961) give us relatively long texts of the Gospel from the late second century. These papyri discoveries, both in the Gospels and Epistles, are of great importance for studies of the biblical text.

All of these discoveries that we have mentioned belong to the past one hundred years, many to the past few years. The knowledge that they have supplied for interpreting and translating the Bible was not available to earlier centuries. We might remember, by way of comparison, that for the seven hundred years between the time of St. Jerome and that of the School of St. Victor (twelfth century) Hebrew was virtually an unknown language in the Western Church. Hence we can understand how this tremendous increase of linguistic knowledge in the short period of one hundred years has produced a more rapid advance in the biblical field than all of the past centuries put together.

HISTORICAL DISCOVERIES

Second, we may turn now, more briefly, to the contributions of another science, that of history, to biblical knowledge. The ancient records, whose discovery we have mentioned, have filled in the background of the history of Israel and put that history on a scientific basis. Even today, a close knowledge of the history of a period enables us to determine whether a modern author is writing real history or only using historical details as a backdrop for fiction or parable. The same is true of the knowledge gained of the biblical period. What we have learned of ancient history in the past hundred years has enabled us, in part, to determine whether the author of a sacred book intended to write history or not. A knowledge of ancient records has convinced many Catholic authors that books like Jonah and Daniel were never intended as scientific history by their authors.

It might be interesting to look at a few examples of how historical discoveries have thrown light on Israel's history. The Egyptian records have clarified the Joseph story, for now we know more about the Hyksos period (seventeenth century B.C.) in Egypt when the country was ruled by foreigners, and when a Semitic nomad like Joseph might well have made his way to power. The centralization of property attributed to Joseph in Gn 47:11–26 fits in very well with the Hyksos period. Again our knowledge of the Egyptian building activities in the delta under the first pharaohs of the Nineteenth Dynasty (late fourteenth, early thirteenth centuries) now enables us to date the exodus under Moses to the thirteenth century. The complicated foreign affairs of the monarchies of Judah and Israel are only intelligible now when Egyptian, Assyrian and Babylonian documents have traced for us the struggle for power between the neighbors of Israel. Only a few years ago the annals of Nebuchadnezzar were discovered, annals which enable us to pinpoint the first capture of Jerusalem to March 16, 597 B.C. For the subsequent Babylonian captivity of the Jews there have been found the actual Babylonian records dealing with the provisioning of the royal house of Judah.

We could go on and on with these historical finds that have clarified the Bible. A whole world has opened before our eyes—forgotten peoples who were previously only biblical names have come to life, like the Hittites and the Hurrians. Their customs, laws, and treaties have explained de-

tails in the patriarchal narratives. Light on even such a
basic thing as the Ten Commandments has been received
from the categorical imperatives in Hittite treaties. There
the agreement to keep certain commandments marked the
signing of a covenant, just as Israel's agreement to keep
God's commandments marked the Old Covenant.

And once again these historical discoveries are not confined to the Old Testament. How many times the records
of the Roman Empire in Greece and Asia Minor have confirmed information given to us by Luke in Acts, information
that was once doubted. Needless to say, all this historical
knowledge was unavailable to previous generations. Its
availability to our generation has been the backbone of the
biblical movement.

ARCHAEOLOGICAL DISCOVERIES

Third, and last, let us turn to the contributions of the
science of archaeology, a science which is itself the product
of the past one hundred years. Here there is a question not
only of the archaeology of Egypt and Babylonia, but of the
archaeology of Palestine itself. Beginning in the 1890's, the
archaeology of Palestine has been put on a scientific basis;
and, thanks to ceramic chronology, we have, independently
of the Bible, the material for a history of the Holy Land
and of its peoples.

The archaeological discoveries pertaining to the Middle
and Late Bronze periods (roughly 2100 to 1200 B.C.) have
unfolded before our eyes great Canaanite cities like Jericho,
Beth-shan, Megiddo and Hazor. The public and private
buildings of the Canaanites, their temples, defenses,
weapons, chariots, artifacts, are all there for us as they were
in the times of the patriarchs—from the idols that Rachel
hid under her saddle to the Hazor destroyed by Joshua.
And the discoveries go on. Only in the past ten years Jewish
archaeologists have traced the ancient settlements and travel
routes in the Negeb, the southern desert of Israel, and thus

clarified the travels of two of its ancient citizens, Abraham of Hebron and Isaac of Beersheba.

After the Canaanite period, archaeology has unfolded the Iron Period, Iron I being roughly contemporary with the Judges, and Iron II with the monarchy. The excavations of settlements at Megiddo and Taanach have helped fix the date of the song of Deborah, celebrating the victory at Taanach by the waters of Megiddo (Jgs 5:19). Saul's unpretentious fortress has been excavated at Tell el Ful, as have Solomon's tremendous economic and military constructions throughout the land. The history of the divided monarchy has been vividly illustrated both in battle-scarred ruins and in magnificent building projects (such as those at Samaria, the capital of the northern kingdom). And its dramatic end has been spelled out in the letters excavated at Lachish where a desperate official describes the ever-tightening noose drawn by the Babylonian advance on Jerusalem.

Scarcely a detail of life as portrayed in the Bible has not been elucidated by the archaeological discoveries of these past years. And this includes the New Testament period. For instance, the mention of the pool of Bethesda with its five porticoes (Jn 5:2) has been confirmed by the discovery of this pool in Jerusalem near the Sheepgate of the Temple, exactly where John said it was. Once more none of this material was available in the past, when it lay covered by the dust of centuries.

And so whether the new biblical information has come from language studies, or from history, or from archaeology, there can be no question of blaming biblical scholars of earlier generations for not using it; it was not theirs to make use of. The only possible blame could be on our own generation if we seek to ignore it because of preconceived ideas.

Nor in this catalog of modern biblical advances do we mean to undervalue the biblical insights of earlier periods, especially the theological insight which the Fathers gained from the Bible. (In fact, today's biblical scholars have revived interest in patristic exegesis.) God has always seen to it that in each period the Church profits from the Bible according to her needs. The present biblical advances are in a scientific direction which was closed to past ages but which peculiarly fits the needs of the Church today. And, naturally, from this scientific advance there has been an ever deeper theological perception of the wealth of the Bible.

CATHOLIC USE OF NEW MATERIAL

The observations made thus far should explain the origins of the new biblical movement, but they do not explain why this movement has arisen so recently in Catholic circles. After all, the new Catholic movement is a product of the postwar period, after 1945. Yet, some of the scientific discoveries we have been mentioning were available before 1900. While there may have been limited Catholic use of this material before the Second World War, its free employment is something recent. Why? The answer is *Divino Afflante Spiritu*.

At the end of the past century many non-Catholic scholars were using the new scientific material. Often, however, their approach was guided by rationalistic philosophy. The result, seen in such schools of biblical criticism as that of Wellhausen, was a radical and basically irreligious approach to the Bible. Often their facts were correct, e.g., Moses did not personally write the whole Pentateuch; but the interpretations were wrong, e.g., when they claimed that there was nothing Mosaic in the Pentateuch. In the same era some Catholic scholars, too, began to use the scientific material at times with splendid results, e.g., the works of Père Lagrange. Other Catholics, however, fell under the spell of the rationalists, and failed to distinguish between fact and interpretation. Their misguided steps ultimately led them into the Modernist heresy. This unhappy finale had the unfortunate extraneous result of casting an aura of suspicion on attempts to employ modern scientific material in biblical research. Thus, in the years between 1910 and 1940 Catholic biblical research continued to feel the impact of the Modernist troubles.

Then in 1943 came the encyclical *Divino Afflante Spiritu* and its redirection of Catholic biblical studies. Pope Pius XII praised the type of scientific discoveries of which we have been speaking (No. 11).[2] He pointed out that, while the criticism at the beginning of the century had misinterpreted this material, biblical science was now much more secure (No. 18). And so the Pope ordered Catholic scholars to go ahead and use the new scientific material in interpreting and translating the Bible (No. 15, No. 16, No. 19). Particularly in the field of translation he insisted that Catholics should no longer confine themselves to the Vulgate but should use the original Hebrew and Greek.[3]

The Pope's encyclical implied a radical change in the Catholic approach to Scripture. Naturally time was required for its commands to be put into effect, and so it is that only in the 1950's was the new Catholic biblical movement set in motion. Part of the glory of this new movement is that it has sprung up under Church auspices, and that some of its leaders are found on such eminent Catholic faculties as that of the Pontifical Biblical Institute in Rome and the magnificent Dominican School of St. Stephen in Jerusalem.

CURRENT FACTS

Before we close this explanation of the "newness" of the new Catholic biblical movement, we might add a few remarks to assure any who may have felt uneasy about the movement. Sometimes the term "Modernism" is used by

---

[2] All paragraph (No.) references are to the edition of the encyclical in *Rome and the Study of Scripture,* 4 ed. (St. Meinrad: Grail, 1946).

[3] We are now receiving the fruit of this wise counsel in such Catholic translations as the Jerusalem Bible and the American Confraternity translation.

the adversaries of the movement; and more than one opponent has triumphantly remarked of some idea expressed by a biblical scholar: "That is just what the Modernists said." As we have pointed out, the Modernists did make use of some scientific facts which they *interpreted* wrongly. The fact that a modern Catholic biblical scholar will occasionally accept some fact that the Modernists accepted fifty years ago proves nothing regarding his heterodoxy. The important question is how does he interpret his facts. And you can be sure that the erroneous and heretical presuppositions that were the backbone of Modernism are held by no modern Catholic biblical scholar. It is interesting to take a problem like the first eleven chapters of Genesis and compare the modern Catholic views with the errors of Loisy and those of his predecessors, like Wellhausen. Starting from the same facts, the two groups arrive at totally different interpretations. Above all, the modern Catholic biblical scholars submit their opinions to the Church's teaching authority, something that was anathema to the Modernists. Thus the charge of resembling Modernism is based purely on appearances and lacks any foundation in fact.

We stress, too, that the Church *continues* to encourage the biblical movement. The Pontifical Biblical Commission was set up to watch over Catholic biblical studies and insure their safety (*Vigilantiae* of Leo XIII, 1902). It has been regarded as the upholder of very conservative positions. Yet, in face of the new biblical movement, the secretary of the Biblical Commission stated that Catholic biblical scholars now have "full liberty" in investigating matters touched on by the past decrees of the Commission, except where there is a question of faith or morals.[4] Thus, on such points as the unity of a biblical book or its authorship, Catholic scholars now enjoy much greater liberty. This is why many Catholics now freely hold such views as the

[4] The text is published in the *Catholic Biblical Quarterly*, 18 (1956), 23–29.

existence of deutero-Isaiah, the priority of Mark, etc., even though there are past decrees of the Commission to the contrary.

All well and good, it may be answered, but have not Catholic scholars gone too far? What about the recent Roman *monitum* (Holy Office, June 20, 1961)? It is unfortunate that this *monitum* was so poorly presented in much of the Catholic press as if it were a warning to biblical scholars alone.[5] Many newspapers did not even stress that the *monitum* opens with *praise* for the fervor of today's biblical studies. And, again, if one reads the *monitum,* one will find that it is directed, not to biblical scholars alone or as such, but to all "who deal with the Sacred Books whether in writing or speaking." The special target of the *monitum* is the "circulation of opinions which endanger the genuine historical and objective truth of Sacred Scripture." The *monitum* is most anxious that such opinions be not allowed to disturb the faithful. Thus it would seem that the *monitum* is directed principally against popularizations which are transmitting dangerous and, often, garbled opinions to the faithful. Undoubtedly there are scholars (few, we hope) who have been imprudent; but a real and, perhaps, greater danger flows from the overzealous popularizers—seminarians who have not understood their professors, or who exaggerate one aspect of the professor's teaching; young priests with a desire to shock parishioners or older pastors; educated laity with a desire to lord it over a poorly informed priest. Yet these are a hazard in any Church movement whether it be liturgical, catechetical, social, or biblical, and are part of its growing pains.

Catholic biblical scholars have long been conscious of

---

[5] We recommend highly "The Wayward Press," by Bruce Vawter, C.M., in *America* (August 5, 1961) which shows how poorly the press handled the *monitum.* He says (p. 592): "That a paternal admonition such as that of the 20th of June should be willfully or unthinkingly distorted into a cease-and-desist order against the biblical movement is the worst thing that could happen to the cause of Catholic truth."

this danger of incorrect generalizing and overzealous popularizing, and are only too happy to have it pointed out clearly by the Holy Office. They are especially grateful for the very cautious wording of the *monitum* which shows that the Holy Office is quite sensitive to the views of this biblical movement whose fervor it praises and has no desire to crush them. Notice that what is condemned are opinions that endanger the *genuine* (or "proper"—*germanam*) historical truth of Scripture. As Father Fitzmyer[6] has pointed out, this is an implicit reference to different literary forms, each having its own purpose and standards of historical truth. (This is the very doctrine that was the key teaching of *Divino Afflante Spiritu*, Nos. 35–39.) Thus there is no sign that the *monitum* was designed to reverse the biblical movement or to return to the days before the encyclical when some treated the whole Bible, outside of the Sapiential Books, as if it were nineteenth-century scientific history written by moderns.

CONCLUSION

The biblical movement has greatly interested large numbers of the Catholic laity in the Bible, as the tremendous sale of the pamphlet *New Testament Reading Guide* (Liturgical Press) has shown. Catholic biblical articles and books are being received with real appreciation and interest in non-Catholic circles, for non-Catholic scholars recognize that Catholics are using the latest scientific data (thanks to *Divino Afflante Spiritu*) and are holding positions that are scientifically tenable. In the ecumenical and liturgical movements our "new" approach to the Bible has rendered great service.

In conclusion, we hope that our remarks have made it

---

[6] "Recent Roman Scriptural Controversy," *Theological Studies* 22 (1961), 444. He cites Cardinal Bea's dictum: *"Sua cuique generi literario est veritas"*—"Every literary form has its own truth." This article is essential for an understanding of the opposition to scriptural studies today.

clear why there is a certain "newness" about the Catholic biblical movement today. We firmly believe that with the proper precautions this biblical movement can make a tremendous contribution toward the growth of the Church in our times precisely because it is a logical development of our times. Can we fail to see the workings of the Holy Spirit in this movement which holds as its *magna carta* the encyclical of a great and saintly Pope?

POSTSCRIPT: *This paper was delivered in 1961 when the modern biblical movement was facing considerable opposition and, indeed, was fighting for its life. It is a great joy that now a few years later the clouds have lifted and the hopes of the writer for tolerance and acceptance have been granted beyond expectation. Vatican II has adamantly refused to approve any statement on Revelation which would set the biblical movement back. Teachers in Rome who were under a cloud of suspicion have been restored to their chairs of biblical studies. Above all, the Pontifical Biblical Commission issued a magnificent instruction (April 21, 1964) pertaining to the Gospels. Not only does this instruction permit the Catholic scholar to make use of what is valuable in the method of form criticism; but also it very clearly outlines the development that has taken place in the formation of the Gospels. The instruction shows how the apostolic preachers interpreted the words and deeds of Jesus according to the needs of their listeners, and then how the sacred authors adapted this material passed down from the primitive instruction by selecting, synthesizing, and "explicating" (note well), according to the purpose they had in writing and the situation of the churches which they were addressing. The instruction of the Biblical Commission was taken over substantially into the Second Vatican Council's constitution on revelation (1965). As far as the writer knows, no Protestant community possesses an official statement on biblical criticism so progressive in tone as the one now given Catholic scholars by Rome.*

II

Ecumenism and
New Testament Research[1]

It has become a commonplace of the ecumenical movement that biblical studies, which in Reformation days divided Christianity, are now serving to bring Christians together. Recently this writer has been in a favorable position[2] to evaluate this maxim and would consequently

[1] The scope of this essay is confined to Protestant and Roman Catholic perspectives. Modern biblical research has not yet had its full impact on the writings of Eastern Orthodox theologians. We might note that for convenience we have had to include the Anglican communion under the title "Protestant"; otherwise the titles of the two sides would be rather cumbersome.

[2] On such occasions as: speaking with the Protestant observers at Vatican II; delivering the Roman Catholic paper in the biblical section of the Harvard Colloquium where Catholic and Protestant scholars were brought together for dialogue; addressing the Faith and Order Conference of the World Council of Churches at Montreal in July, 1963; as a participant in the national Catholic-Lutheran discussions; as the only American Catholic member of the theological discussions between the World Council of Churches and the Vatican Sec-

make at least one important limitation in its application. Modern *critical* biblical studies[3] are very fruitful in an ecumenical way among those Christian bodies whose theology allows such influence. It would be hopelessly romantic to forget that there are large groups of Christians of fundamentalist or ultraconservative leanings upon whom modern biblical studies have made no impact. For them the Bible remains a divisive factor.

It may be true that occasionally a fundamentalist Protestant work will quote a conservative Roman Catholic work approvingly, for instance, because it interprets Genesis so as to rule out evolution, or because it treats many of the Old Testament prophecies as if they were exact predictions concerned exclusively with the distant future. Yet such a meeting of minds is deceptive. When more basic questions arise, e.g., the role of the Church in transmitting divine revelation, such ultraconservative theologians will revert to customary and often polemic positions which allow little if any common ground for discussion.

Critical biblical studies, on the other hand, may seem impious to some because they disturb former positions on date, authorship, and meaning of biblical books; and in this they apparently create greater division by allowing latitude where once there was uniformity. Yet an objective criticism tends to see the gray as well as the black and the white, to evaluate the elements of truth in other positions, and, above all, to recognize that past theological debates by their very "either-or" approach often missed a third

---

retariat for Christian Unity on the topic of the apostolicity and catholicity of the Church.

[3] We are not speaking of rationalistic biblical criticism. To a great extent the rationalism and liberalism that so dominated scriptural studies at the end of the nineteenth and the beginning of the twentieth centuries have disappeared from the scene. The Bultmannian movement, for instance, even though it may employ biblical criticism in a manner that alarms more conservative Christians, is honestly religious and antiliberal in its orientation.

possibility which could capture the essential truth of both positions. It is clear that, despite their indefatigable use of the Bible in argumentation, at the time of the Reformation many theologians in both the reformed and counter-reformed traditions were still the children of a late scholastic age[4] which was ill-equipped to meet the Bible on its own terms. Argument and rebuttal vehemently pressed home on the basis of biblical texts not infrequently concerned points which were really quite foreign to the biblical mentality itself.[5] Modern biblical study, by ascertaining clearly what the Bible has to say for itself, has pinpointed how many of the traditional divisions among Christians really flow from the Bible and how many are the products of postbiblical theological development.

Such critical study has had its effect on the theological thought of large segments of the classical Protestant churches; it is having an increasing impact on Roman Catholic theology. In parts of Europe this has been more obvious than in the U. S. A. for several reasons. First, those churches most favorable to such research (stemming

---

[4] In the classical scholastic period in the twelfth and thirteenth centuries the Bible had more influence on theology than it did in the decadent scholasticism of pre-Reformation times. St. Thomas' commentaries on the Pauline epistles have withstood well the test of time.

[5] For instance, in previous eras of the Protestant-Roman Catholic debate, the question of Purgatory would be discussed on the basis of biblical evidence or the lack thereof. Some Protestants would reject Purgatory because of the lack of biblical evidence; Catholics would appeal to 2 Maccabees and some obscure references in the New Testament. Behind the whole argument would be the tacit assumption that the Bible contained a sufficiently complete revelation concerning the fate of the soul after the particular judgment. Today we recognize more clearly that the Bible itself is confined in its perspective, with rare exception, to the general judgment and to the resurrection of the body. The destiny of the separated soul belongs more to the growth of doctrine in the postbiblical period and is not really a question answered in a purely biblical theology.

from Lutheran, Calvinist, and Anglican origins) dominate the European religious scene, whereas in America fundamentalist churches and sects have an important voice. Second, rationalism and liberalism in scriptural research lost their influence in European Protestantism under the impact of Barth and Bultmann more quickly than did liberalism in American Protestant religious thought. Third, the decisive reorientation of Roman Catholic scriptural studies effected by Pope Pius XII in his encyclical *Divino Afflante Spiritu* (1943) [6] made its influence felt among French and German Catholic scholars more swiftly than among Americans. [7] Until the past few years evidences of a new biblical movement in American Roman Catholic circles were confined to the pages of a few technical journals; now first-rate books on the subject have begun to appear. [8] Today,

[6] An interesting fact that became obvious at the Harvard Colloquium is that the *Hofstil* of papal encyclicals often obscures their real import from Protestants who have not been trained in the requisite arts of interpreting. This particular encyclical, although it begins by emphasizing previous papal documents of a more conservative bent, was really a radical about-face in the Roman Catholic approach to the study of the Bible. The Pope made clear that scientific criticism, previously regarded with suspicion because of its rationalistic tendencies, had now reached a state of maturity in which it could and should be used by Catholics.

[7] One reason for this is that the leading Roman Catholic biblical schools, where one would expect the impact to be felt quickest, are of Central European origin, thus the École Biblique in Jerusalem, the Catholic University of Louvain, and most recently the Pontifical Biblical Institute in Rome. (In the latter, however, it has been the importation of young American professors that has changed the orientation.) Nevertheless, the Semitics Department of the Catholic University of America has maintained a very fine record in critical studies.

[8] Lest we bask in euphoria, however, it is worth recording the sobering thought that as of 1968 there is no completed full-scale scientific commentary by an American Catholic on a single book of the Bible. Nor, as of 1968, did the American Catholic

as the recent Harvard Colloquium showed, American Protestant and Roman Catholic scholars can meet on a relatively equal basis.[9] Both sides have advanced scientifically to the stage where they recognize value in the other's work; and joint projects of translation and commentary give promise of drawing on the best efforts of scholars of both groups.[10]

Thus, at the moment modern biblical studies give great ecumenical promise. But a fear for the future is often expressed by Protestants: will the present Roman Catholic scriptural renaissance continue? Or is the movement in danger of sudden repression by Church authorities? That there is a hostility to critical biblical studies in certain areas of Roman Catholicism is well known.[11] Yet the predominant attitude of the overwhelming majority of the hierarchy was made evident at the first session of the Second Vatican Council when almost two thirds of the bishops expressed their dissatisfaction with the proposed schema *"De Fontibus Revelationis."*[12] This vote and the subsequent

---

public yet have a completed official Bible from the original languages (although the *New* Confraternity Translation was reaching completion).

[9] Mutual recognition has been slow to come in print. *The Interpreter's Dictionary of the Bible* (1962), a truly prodigious Protestant effort, painfully ignores worthwhile Catholic literature in most of its bibliographies. Until the late 1950's the articles in the *Journal of Biblical Literature* showed few references to important Catholic (European) contributions. A survey of the *Catholic Biblical Quarterly* reveals that at the same period Catholic scholars were making better use of Protestant literature.

[10] One example is the Doubleday Anchor Bible.

[11] See Joseph A. Fitzmyer, S.J., "A Recent Roman Scriptural Controversy," *Theological Studies*, 22 (1961), 426–444. William S. Schneirla, *"Roma locuta . . .?"* St. *Vladimir's Seminary Quarterly*, 6 (1962), 79–92.

[12] The debate on this schema is found in gossipy fashion in Xavier Rynne, *Letters from Vatican City* (New York: Farrar, Straus, 1963), pp. 140–173. The wording of this schema *could*

papal directive to have the schema rewritten may be interpreted as an assurance that the modern Catholic biblical movement which began under papal auspices will continue to enjoy official patronage despite the inevitable unfavorable reaction upon the part of the more conservative. Another very important testimony to this is found in the recent attitude of the Pontifical Biblical Commission in Rome. This is the commission officially entrusted with the supervision of biblical scholarship in the Roman Catholic Church. Its carefully worded decrees in the early part of the century were criticized, often unjustly, by Protestants[13] as the epitome of fundamentalism (e.g., the Mosaic authorship of the Pentateuch; unicity of Isaiah; priority of Matthew). Recently the secretary of this commission[14] himself made it clear that Catholic scholars have "full liberty" with regard to such decrees except where they concern faith or morals (a rare exception). After a long silence during the Scripture controversies of 1960–1963, on April 21, 1964, the Biblical Commission issued an instruction concerning Gospel exegesis. The instruction is positive in content, guaranteeing the right of Catholic exegetes to use form criticism in interpreting the Gospels. With such encourage-

---

have been interpreted as a repudiation of modern scriptural advances, in the judgment of many of the biblical scholars who saw it. Moreover, the schema seemingly would have canonized doctrinally the separation of Scripture and Tradition as *two* sources of divine revelation—a relatively recent theory of Counter-Reformation origins that would be entirely unacceptable to both Protestants and Orthodox. Since this first form of the schema (the title was later changed to *De Revelatione*) has never been published, information about its contents is not scientifically verifiable.

[13] At times Protestant scholars have tended to treat these decrees as if they were Catholic dogma. While they required obedience, the decrees were really prudential decisions in view of the Modernist dangers of the time; they were never presented as either infallible or irrevocable.

[14] Text and discussion in *Catholic Biblical Quarterly*, 18 (1956), 23–29.

ment the Roman Catholic biblical movement should make even greater progress in years to come and offer many ecumenical possibilities.

Having commented in general on the ecumenical import of biblical studies, we should like now to illustrate this by three examples.

A. FORM CRITICISM AND THE CHURCH'S RELATION TO THE GOSPELS

A common Protestant-Roman Catholic disagreement could be (over)simplified thus: The Catholic believes what the Church teaches him about Christ, whereas the Protestant believes the direct evidence of Scripture. Faulty as it is,[15] such a summation does underline traditional emphases. Recent critical analysis of the formation of the Gospels has put the whole question in a better focus.[16]

In the latter part of the nineteenth century, at least Mark's Gospel was looked on as a rather direct, untouched report of the deeds and sayings of the historical Jesus, a report which the later Evangelists (Matthew, Luke) had adapted to specific theological themes. Therefore, it was assumed that through Mark it was possible to reach a truly objective view of Jesus. However, further study, especially W. Wrede's careful analysis of the way Mark emphasizes Jesus' messianic secret, convinced scholars that even Mark's Gospel is a highly theological composition.

A new approach to the Gospels was opened through form criticism, a technique already applied to the Old Testament by H. Gunkel. It was pointed out that the Gospels consist of various smaller literary units ("forms"),

[15] Obviously Roman Catholics also believe the evidence of the Scriptures, and Catholic Tradition is closely related to Scripture. On the other hand, many Protestants have a strong theology of the Church and a strong appreciation of Tradition.

[16] A readable account of what follows may be found in V. Taylor, *The Formation of the Gospel Tradition* (London: Macmillan, 1953).

such as miracle stories, parables, passion accounts, resurrection narratives, etc., each with its own well-delineated characteristics. The German form critics, like K. L. Schmidt, Dibelius, and Bultmann, maintained that these units were passed on orally for years until they were joined together into groups and finally into the written Gospels. In the final or Gospel stage, in order to make a consecutive story, the Evangelist had to adopt a sequence and supply connectives. The way he presented these units in his Gospel shows how they were interpreted in the Christian community of his time (and, indeed, in the earlier years of pre-written existence, local church interests had already greatly modified these units, eliminating some and preserving others). The English scholar, C. H. Dodd,[17] carried this analysis further by pointing out that the outline of the ministry in Mark is basically that of the Petrine sermons in Acts (especially Acts 10:37–40). This means that apostolic preaching supplied the backbone for unifying the various units handed down orally in the Christian churches.

This general approach, formulated chiefly by German Protestant critics, met with opposition on the part of more conservative Protestants (especially in England) and Roman Catholics. Part of this opposition was quite understandable, for form critics often went beyond their evidence concerning the literary composition of the Gospels to make judgments on the historical truth of Gospel ma-

---

[17] "The Framework of the Gospel Narrative," *Expository Times,* 43 (1932), 396–400. This suggestion has been attacked by D. E. Nineham, "The Order of Events in St. Mark's Gospel —an Examination of Dr. Dodd's Hypothesis," *Studies in the Gospels* (Lightfoot Festschrift; Oxford: Blackwell, 1957), 223–240. He maintains that the sermons in Acts are Lucan constructions and the influence could be the other way around— Luke borrowed the outline for these sermons from the Marcan Gospel. However, there is very primitive language in some of these sermons (e.g., Acts 2:23, 36) indicating that Luke drew his material from early sources. Also there is evidence for a similar outline in the Pauline sermons.

terial. It is one thing to hold that the Christian community and its leaders helped to shape the Gospel units in the valid sense that the Christians preserved and transmitted the stories narrated and preached by the apostolic witnesses. It is another thing to hold that the Christian communities created many of the stories about Jesus as answers to contemporary problems. It is because of this latter tendency that some form critics claimed that we could know very little with certainty about the historical Jesus.[18]

But when it was realized that such aberrations are not essential to the core of the theory, many Roman Catholics[19] as well as Protestants came to accept the basic principle that the Gospels took their origins in the preaching and teaching of the Apostles, preserved by the Christian churches, and assembled by the Evangelists to provide a theological understanding of Jesus Christ. The picture of the Evangelists as impartial observers writing a strictly chronological and biographical history of Jesus was recognized as an eighteenth- and nineteenth-century projection of a modern ideal of historiography. The most ancient and traditional approach to the Gospels,[20] recovered in modern

[18] One tends to associate the name of Rudolf Bultmann with such a minimalist approach. However, recently there has been a serious debate between Bultmann's followers about the master's view of the historical Jesus. For details see "After Bultmann, What? An Introduction to the Post-Bultmannians," *Catholic Biblical Quarterly,* 26 (1964), 1–30.

[19] One of the earliest Catholic attempts to sift the theory and preserve what was valid, instead of condemning the whole approach, was that of P. Benoit, O.P., "Réflexions sur la 'Formgeschichtliche Methode,'" *Revue Biblique* (1946), 481–512. Today, Catholics like Malevez, Marlé, Theunis, and Hasenhüttl are first-class authorities on Bultmann.

[20] It is interesting to evaluate the information gathered by Papias in the early second century about Mark's Gospel in the light of our modern theory of Gospel formation (*Ancient Christian Writers* VI, 118): "When Mark became Peter's interpreter, he wrote down, though by no means verbatim, as much as he remembered of the works and words of the Lord, for he

times, was that they were written records of the good news of salvation, heralded by the Apostles to the world.

The recovery and common acceptance by scholars of this understanding of the Gospels has had its impact on the Protestant and Roman Catholic positions given in simplified form at the beginning of this section. One can no longer contrast belief in the Gospels with belief in the Church, for the Gospels themselves came out of the Church.[21] If they had their origins in the preaching and teaching of the Apostles and were constructed of units preserved and formed into shape by the local Christian churches, this means that he who bases his faith on the Christ of the Gospels is really basing his faith on what the early Church taught about Christ. From Pentecost on it has been impossible to approach Christ except through the

---

had neither heard the Lord nor been in His company, but he subsequently joined Peter, as I said. Now, Peter did not intend to give a complete exposition of the Lord's ministry, but delivered his instruction to meet the needs of the moment. It follows, then, that Mark was guilty of no blunder if he wrote, simply to the best of his recollections, an incomplete account." Lack of verbatim accuracy, lack of chronological sequence, oral transmission, adaptation to the needs of the Church—all are included by Papias. And Papias concludes with a very valid qualification: "For of one matter he [Mark] took forethought —not to omit anything he had heard nor to falsify the account in any detail."

[21] Strangely enough ultraconservative Roman Catholics who have resisted even a moderate application of form criticism to the New Testament do not seem to recognize that in its essence this theory is well adapted to Roman Catholic emphasis on the Church. The strictly biographical approach to the Gospels, which they often defend, is far less favorable to the Catholic position. In this connection the following statement of Bultmann is worthy of note (*Das Verhältnis der urchristlichen Christusbotschaft zum historischen Jesus* [3 ed.; Heidelberg: Winter, 1962], 26): "There is no faith in Christ which is not at the same time faith in the Church in as much as she was bearer of the kerygma. . . ."

Church's preaching. Thus the Protestant-Roman Catholic debate becomes more a difference of degree than of kind. The real difference is seen to lie not so much in dependence on the Church but in the importance attributed to post-biblical Church teaching. Here the Catholic would allow a wider latitude than the Protestant.

To sum up then, the modern approach to Gospel formation[22] has brought the Church and Tradition into greater focus in current Protestant thought. At the same time the close tie between Tradition and Scripture has come into greater focus in Roman Catholic thought. The Dominican Yves Congar has made this statement:[23] "There is not a single dogma which the Church holds by Scripture alone, nor a single dogma which it holds by Tradition alone." Such a view, it would seem, holds far greater ecumenical possibilities than the polemical positions of the past.

[22] In the past few years we have even newer developments in the post-Bultmannian movement in Germany. This involves a healthy reaction to overskepticism about our ability to know the historical Jesus. By use of the existential historical approach developed by Dilthey and Collingwood, the post-Bultmannians maintain that we can learn a great deal about the significance of Jesus for our own existence. In *A New Quest for the Historical Jesus* (London: SCM, 1959), James M. Robinson maintains that there are two ways to find what Jesus Christ means to us: (*a*) through the Church's preaching of the salvific meaning of Jesus as found in the Gospels; (*b*) through historical research which penetrates beyond the primitive preaching to reveal how Jesus presented Himself to men during His life. And he says (105, 125) that by either way the selfhood of Jesus is *equally* available to us as a possible understanding of our own existence. We have discussed and evaluated this whole movement in detail in the *Catholic Biblical Quarterly,* 26 (1964), 1–30. Let us say here only that, with some of Robinson's Bultmannian colleagues, we doubt the equality he stresses.

[23] *Informations Catholiques Internationales* (December 1, 1962), p. 2.

B. THE DEAD SEA SCROLLS AND CHURCH
ORGANIZATION

The question of a hierarchical or nonhierarchical structure of the Church has continued to be one of the prominent divisive problems in Christianity.[24] That a hierarchy passed on through ordination came into existence at an early stage in the history of Christianity is generally admitted. However, many Protestant critics relegate this "early Catholicism" to a postbiblical era and consider it as a corruption of the original charismatic, democratic constitution of the Church. More recently, some of the Bultmannian scholars, like Ernst Käsemann,[25] have admitted that "early Catholicism" is found in the New Testament itself, e.g., in the Pastorals, 2 Peter, and perhaps even in Acts. But these works are looked on as belonging to the last stages of New Testament theology, and as not having the same normative value as the earlier books of the New Testament. In particular, the Pastoral Epistles are treated as deutero-Pauline and are sharply contrasted with the real epistles of Paul. While Roman Catholic scholars are quite pleased to see this gradual recognition that the roots of the hierarchy and of sacerdotal ordination are already present in the New Testament, they are not content (and neither are many Protestant scholars) to have differences in the

[24] Recently there have been two important books on the subject, respectively by a Protestant and a Catholic: Eduard Schweizer, *Church Order in the New Testament* (London: SCM, 1961); Rudolf Schnackenburg, *The Church in the New Testament* (New York: Herder, 1965).

[25] In articles collected in *Essays on New Testament Themes* (Studies in Biblical Theology; London: SCM, 1964). For the view of his Catholic colleague at Tübingen, see Hans Küng, *Structures of the Church* (New York: Nelson, 1964), 151–169. A superb summary article, "The New Testament is Catholic," by the Lutheran scholar John H. Elliott is found in *Una Sancta* 23 (1966), 3–18.

theological outlook of New Testament authors hardened into contradictions. The principle that some parts of the New Testament can be considered less normative means that the evidence of the whole New Testament is not being accepted.

Germane to this whole discussion is the theory that the episcopate is a development of a later period (whether late New Testament or postbiblical) and marks an intrusion of Hellenistic organization on the original free structure of the early Church. According to this theory, Luke's picture in Acts, which shows organization in the closely knit Jerusalem church ruled over by the apostles[26] and presbyters, is to be regarded as an anachronism. However, recent evidence has called into question such a sketch of the history of the episcopate. The best analogy for the Christian bishop is now found not in the Greco-Roman world, but in Palestine itself. The Dead Sea Scrolls, discovered in the caves near Wadi Qumrân near the northwest corner of the Dead Sea, have given us the library of a Jewish sect of Essenes who flourished there from c.130 B.C. to A.D. 68.[27] The documents which pertain to the organization of this

[26] In this section we shall distinguish between "apostles" and "Apostles." We use "apostles" for those sent out by Christ to preach the Resurrection—thus, in a larger sense than the Twelve Apostles. The term "apostle" includes the Twelve (who are the Apostles par excellence), but is a wider term embracing such leaders as James, "brother" of the Lord. This use of "apostle" is accepted by most critics, including such eminent Catholics as Cerfaux, Dupont, and Wikenhauser.

[27] We knew something of Essene organization from Josephus and Pliny, but these documents greatly increase our knowledge. Very little Jewish literature has survived from the first century B.C. and the first century A.D., whence the importance of the Dead Sea Scrolls: they fill in an important background area for Christianity. The most carefully done translation of this material is *Les Textes de Qumran* by J. Carmignac and P. Guibert (Paris: Letouzey et Ané, 1961). See also G. Vermès, *The Dead Sea Scrolls in English* (Pelican, 1962).

community stem from different periods in its life span,[28] and so we must allow for a certain variation and development.

In general, the important elements in the organization of the Qumran community are as follows: (*a*) a cabinet of twelve or fifteen men within the community council.[29] This cabinet seems to have been a body with some legislative authority. (*b*) The Assembly of all the mature members of the community. This Assembly, called the "Session of the Many," had judicial and executive authority and seems to have been the instrument by which the community governed itself. (*c*) The priest who presided over the Assembly who is called the "Supervisor or Inspector of the Many" (*mebaqqer* or *paqid*).[30]

[28] The two most important documents are the *Community Rule* (1QS) and the *Damascus Document* (CD). The former, 1QS, is one of the earliest compositions of the community (even though our copy may be later), probably from before 110 B.C., and is perhaps the work of one of the great figures of the group, the Teacher of Righteousness. CD is a later production but still pre-Christian.

[29] 1QS 8:1: "In the Council of the Community there shall be twelve men and three priests. . . ." The picture is not totally clear: some think these men constitute the whole council; others that they constitute a cabinet within the council. Some think that there are fifteen men involved; others that there are twelve of whom three are to be priests. Some think that "council" here really means deliberations ("counsel") rather than a select body. Personally the writer agrees with Frank M. Cross, *The Ancient Library of Qumran*, 2 ed. (Doubleday Anchor, 1961), 231: this is a higher and authoritative body within the general assembly.

[30] The arrangement in CD seems to be different, perhaps because this was composed to regulate a different form of community life. CD speaks of a "Session of all the camps" (14:3—seemingly equivalent to the 1QS "Session of the Many") and of a *mebaqqer* over all the camps (14:8–9). Whether the latter is a layman or a priest, and whether the terms *mebaqqer* and *paqid* are interchangeable are disputed questions.

Is it sheer coincidence that all of these governmental structures are found in the nascent Christian Church? Let us compare:

a) There was the group of the Twelve, mentioned both in Acts and the Pauline Epistles. The Twelve Apostles, just as the twelve officials at Qumran, are patterned in number on the Twelve Tribes of Israel; they are to be the leaders of a renewed Israel. The Qumran literature pictures its cabinet-council under the imagery of foundation walls (1QS 8:7–8), the same imagery the Apocalypse uses of the Twelve Apostles (Ap 21:14). Qumran describes its cabinet-council as having a role in the judgment (1QS 8:6), even as the Christian Twelve are promised such a role (Lk 22:30).

b) There was an assembly of the "multitude" (Greek: *plēthos*)[31] in the Jerusalem church which exercised a certain authority, even as did the Qumran "Session of the Many." We see this Christian assembly in action in Acts 6 where it is summoned by the Twelve[32] and makes the decision to select seven Hellenist leaders. Again, in Acts 15:12 the "multitude" under the direction of "the apostles and elders"[33] hears the case concerning the circumcision or noncircumcision of Gentiles. Acts 15:31 speaks of an assembly of the "multitude" at Antioch. In these executive and judicial activities the resemblance between the Qum-

[31] There is obviously a terminological similarity between the "multitude" and the "many" (*rabbim*). However, in describing the Essenes, Josephus (*Bell.* II, 9: #146) speaks of their obedience "to the elders and to the many (*pleiones*)." Thus he did not use *plēthos* as the Greek equivalent of *rabbim*. Some believe that in 2 Cor 2:6 *pleiones* has the meaning of an assembly, in which case its function as a court of last correction is the same as that of the Qumran *rabbim* (1QS 6:1).

[32] As we pointed out in n. 29, the Qumran cabinet of twelve (or fifteen) seems to have some authority in the Assembly.

[33] The "elders" are mentioned at Qumran too as having second place in seniority in the assembly (1QS 6:8). See the quotation from Josephus in n. 31.

ran "many" and the Christian "multitude" is quite obvious. Acts 4:32 describes the spiritual life of the Jerusalem "multitude," and one of its characteristics is the common possession of goods. A community of goods, at least to some extent,[34] is one of the distinguishing marks of Qumran life.

c) Several books of the New Testament[35] speak of the bishop (*episkopos*). The verbal stem *episkopein* is used in the Greek Old Testament to translate the Hebrew roots *pqd* and *bqr* from which come the Qumranian titles *mebaqqer* and *paquîd*. Greek *episkopos* and Hebrew *paqîd* both mean "overseer" or "supervisor."[36] And there are interesting similarities in the duties of the two offices. 1 Pt 2:25 uses the imagery of the shepherd in connection with the term "bishop";[37] CD 13:9–10 says that the function of the *mebaqqer* in each camp is like that of the shepherd of the flock tending to the sheep in distress. The Qumran *mebaqqer* is responsible for the community property; Ti 1:7 refers to the bishop as a steward (*oikonomos*), and 1 Tim 3:2–7 stresses that the bishop must be an efficient manager of his own house. That an ability to handle prop-

---

[34] Scholars at first believed that all goods were held in common at Qumran. Recently the absoluteness of this practice has been challenged by Matthew Black, *The Scrolls and Christian Origins* (London: Nelson, 1961), 32–39.

[35] Acts, Philippians, 1 Timothy, Titus, 1 Peter.

[36] Actually the Greek term used by Josephus in reference to Essene official is *epimelētēs* ("manager") (*Bell*. II, 3: #123); Philo speaks of *epitropos* ("governor").

[37] Also Acts 20:28 "Take heed . . . to all the *flock* in which the Holy Spirit has made you *episkopoi* to *feed* the Church of the Lord." Mt 18:10–14 sets the parable of the shepherd and the lost sheep in the framework of a discourse on the duties of the authorities of the Christian Church. Jn 21:15–17 makes Peter a shepherd. Since in Christian tradition the Twelve, besides their special role, were also bishops (Acts 1:20 refers to their office as an *episkopē*), some of their functions have parallels in the duties of the Qumran *mebaqqer* or *paquîd*.

erty was expected of the Christian bishop may be indicated by the very Greek term used, for in Hellenistic literature *episkopos* was the title of an official responsible for the financial affairs of a cultic organization. Another similarity is that just as the *Didache* 15:1 says that the churches chose (by the raising of hands; *cheirotoneō*) bishops, so Josephus (*Bell.* II, 3: #123) tells us that the Essenes chose (*cheirotoneō*) their supervisory officers. Just as the Christian bishop is responsible for the sound doctrine of his subjects (Ti 1:9), so the *mebaqqer* is the authority for settling questions concerning the traditional lore of Qumran (CD 13:5).

There are other, more subtle allusions that could be given to fortify these parallels,[38] but enough has already been said to illustrate the close similarity between the Qumran community and the Christian Church of the New Testament from the aspect of organization. The closest parallels are to the Jerusalem church of Acts. (Yet we should notice that no "bishops" are mentioned in the New Testament descriptions of the Jerusalem or Palestinian churches, but only in the descriptions of the Gentile churches. James is a ruler in the Jerusalem church, but he is never called a bishop.) Such parallels are very difficult to explain on the presumption that the description of this church is anachronistic and that its organizational features pertain more to the ecclesiastical situation of the eighties than to that of the thirties, and that these features are Hellenistic rather than Palestinian. Such parallels are very easy to explain if we accept the solution that the early Church in Palestine very soon appropriated and modified offices and institutions of

[38] H. Braun, in *Theologische Rundschau,* 29 (1963), 147–176, goes through Acts verse by verse listing all the possible Qumran parallels. For a sober evaluation see J. A. Fitzmyer, "Jewish Christianity in Acts in Light of the Qumran Scrolls," in *Studies in Luke–Acts,* edited by L. E. Keck and J. L. Martyr (Nashville: Abingdon, 1956), 233–257.

groups like the Qumran sect in developing its own organizational structure.[39]

The latter conclusion has ecumenical import for the Protestant-Roman Catholic dialogue. Modern Catholic theologians with a developed historical sense have come to recognize the growth of church organization through the centuries and the gradual clarification and specification of papal and episcopal powers. Therefore Roman Catholics now recognize anachronisms in an oversimplified identification of external features of the later Church with the organization of the primitive Church. On the other hand, thanks to this new evidence, Protestant scholars are coming to recognize that the idyllic simplicity and charismatic freedom which some of their forebears pictured as characteristic of the primitive Church simply do not fit the contemporary evidence. Thus there seem to be possibilities of a widening theological consensus on the constitution of the Church in New Testament times.

C. THE LIMITED POSSIBILITY OF A "COMMON BIBLE"

Our last example differs from the first two in that it extends beyond the New Testament and in that it emphasizes some of the sobering limitations in ecumenical possibilities. No subject of an ecumenical nature attracts more attention in the press than that of a "common Bible."[40] No subject

[39] Cross, *op. cit.,* 234. It is Roman Catholic doctrine that Jesus Christ instituted the essential organization of the Church. However, the commands and powers He gave to those who followed Him had to be made efficacious in some recognizable format. This outward format seems to have been adopted from a format already found effective in contemporary Jewish communities. To recognize this is simply to say that the institution of the Church, like all other things associated with Jesus, was subject to a procedure consonant with the Incarnation: a divine use of the things of this world.

[40] The newspaper summations of the situation often are quite inaccurate. This writer has been cited twice in the press on the

is more frequently raised in the question period after a biblical lecture. Evidently, although it is not a frequent subject of discussion among scholars, many people are interested in this topic. And certainly, as the ecumenical movement grows, so does the need for a scriptural translation officially acceptable to the religious bodies involved in the dialogue. The feasibility of such a project, however, needs careful discussion in a more realistic manner than has been evident in recent journalism.[41]

The first question that needs to be raised is this: a Bible common to whom? (I confine myself here to the American scene. Common Bibles for missionary situations are feasible and necessary, and recently the Vatican has taken initiatives in this direction.) Publicity about this Bible seems to presume that it will be common to all English-speaking Christians (and perhaps the Old Testament will be common to Jews as well). The idea that in the foreseeable future all English-speaking Christians will accept a single Bible is a romantic dream. There are large groups of fundamentalist Protestants who are emotionally attached to the King James Version (KJV). Despite its critical shortcomings, the KJV is for them *the* Bible; and attempts to replace it with the Revised Standard Version (RSV) led to book-burnings in the Bible Belt. On the Roman Catholic side, although for the first time in 1943 Pope Pius XII recommended translations from the original language, there remains a preference among more conservative Catholics for translations made from the Latin.[42] No one can estab-

---

subject: once as adamantly against a common Bible (this false impression was created by cutting one of his sentences in half), the other time as wholeheartedly for the common Bible.

[41] The article in *Time* (September 27, 1963), 48, is more realistic than most.

[42] The Vulgate is the official Bible of the Roman Catholic Church. Pope Pius XII made clear, however, that its strength lies in its doctrinal orthodoxy, not in its critical witness to the inspired text. The apostolic constitution *Veterum Sapientia* (February 22, 1962) stresses that Catholic students for the

lish a Bible common for all over such opposition in both camps.

Nor would it be desirable that a Bible be so common that it replace all other translations. Bibles have different purposes. A Bible written in colloquial style may be perfect for home reading but sound vulgar in a pulpit or in a solemn religious ceremony. A Bible that is quite literal may be very useful for study purposes but not make attractive continuous reading. We need to have various translations of the Bible to bring out the many facets of God's word.

If, for the reasons given, one must rule out a common Bible suitable for all English-speaking Christians and all purposes, one cannot deny that one legitimate purpose for a Bible is ecumenical use. And indeed, a common Bible in this limited ecumenical framework may be feasible. It is certainly a divisive factor that one branch of Christians often tends to distrust the Bible used in other branches. At one time such a distrust was based on the well-substantiated fear that Bible translations and notes were slanted in an apologetical way.[43] The better known translations made in our own day, however, are objective and should not inspire such distrust. Nevertheless, the fact of the distrust remains. It could be overcome if a Bible were approved as objectively correct by representative authorities in both the Protestant and Roman Catholic communities.[44]

---

priesthood should possess a Vulgate. It is reported that the proposed Vatican II schema *De Fontibus Revelationis* (above, n. 12), gave much more attention to the Vulgate than to texts of Scripture in the original languages. The final form of *De Revelatione,* however, reiterated and reinforced the position of Pius XII.

[43] Today this lack of objectivity is found chiefly in Bibles translated by the smaller sects; e.g., *The New World Translation* is definitely phrased in terms guided by Jehovah Witness belief. In Reformation times apologetic translations and notes were much more frequent; the marginal notes in Tyndale's (1525) New Testament are a famous example.

[44] It has been proposed that the National Council of Churches could be the agent for the major Protestant groups, while the

This approved Bible would be for use in all ecumenical activities (discussions, prayers, etc.). Such a step would have great symbolic value as well; yet it should arouse a minimum of opposition since there would be no attempt to replace official Bibles already in use within the various religious groups.

If we allow the usefulness and desirability of this *ecumenical* common Bible, there are still obstacles to its becoming a reality. We see two ways in which such an ecumenical common Bible might come into existence. *First*, there could be mutual recognition by the proper authorities of a Bible or Bibles already in use. Among the current translations we might mention the following as scientifically accurate:[45]

RSV: the Revised Standard Version which is complete with the Apocrypha. This latest revision in the King James tradition was sponsored by the National Council of the Churches of Christ. It is very literal and the English is somewhat stiff.

Chicago Bible: the American Translation of Smith and Goodspeed which is complete with the Apocrypha. This

---

Episcopal Committee of the Confraternity of Christian Doctrine could act for the American Catholic hierarchy. The American Bishops have recently approved a number of different translations (including the RSV) from which the priest may choose the alternative weekday readings at Mass. In 1967 the General Convention of the Episcopal Church authorized the *Jerusalem Bible* for use in public worship.

[45] We give only translations made from the original languages, omitting translations from the Vulgate, such as the Ronald Knox translation and the 1941 Confraternity New Testament. Certainly any common Bible for ecumenical use should be from the original languages. We shall not discuss the popular *Jerusalem Bible* for similar reasons: although the English translators consulted the original languages, basically the project is a translation from the French. For a survey of the present situation in English Catholic Bibles see R. E. Brown, "Recent Roman Catholic Translations of the Bible," *McCormick* [Seminary] *Quarterly,* 19 (1966).

Bible has no official religious standing. It is in good modern English.

NEB: the New English Bible of which only the New Testament is complete. This Bible has official status in England. It is in modern, often breezy English; it is very British and even freer than the Chicago Bible.

Conf.: The Confraternity Catholic translation is (as of 1968) in its final stages of completion—the 1941 New Testament is being replaced with an entirely new translation from the original languages. This is the closest thing to an official Roman Catholic Bible in America, since the translation was commissioned by the Episcopal Committee of the Confraternity of Christian Doctrine. The parts already published are in modern English, closer to the Chicago Bible than to the RSV.

One of these Bibles might be approved for ecumenical purposes. Already the RSV as it appears in the Oxford Annotated Bible[46] has received an *imprimatur* from Cardinal Cushing. There is also a "Catholic RSV," originating in England where changes were introduced into the New Testament text of the RSV by Catholic scholars in order to make the translation eligible for an *imprimatur*. The present writer disapproves strongly of this latter project, for most of the changes sacrifice the ambiguity of Scripture in favor of the imposition of later theological insights. Moreover, such changes are almost an implicit admission that Catholics and Protestants have to translate the Bible in different ways! A better solution would be to have Catholic authorities recognize the RSV without changes, and to have Protestant authorities, like the Protestant National Council, recognize the Conf.—thus two Bibles recognized as accurate and usable for ecumenical purposes. The differ-

[46] The Oxford Annotated Bible, as approved, meets two conditions required by Roman Catholic Canon Law: (1) the Apocrypha or Deuterocanonical Books of the Old Testament are included; (2) there are explanatory notes—in this instance they are of a factual rather than of a theological nature. The text of the RSV is unchanged.

ences between the two translations could be quite instructive in discussing biblical questions. Of course, such a move would not be possible until the Conf. is completed.

There is a *second* way in which an ecumenical common Bible might become a reality in the English-speaking world. A new translation might be made just for this purpose by a duly appointed, mixed body of translators. (It is this enterprise that seems to have attracted the greatest journalistic enthusiasm.) Presumably biblical books would be translated by individuals; and then collectively these Protestant and Roman Catholic translators would serve as a committee to supervise and correct the individual work until finally they could recommend a commonly accepted translation to the appropriate authorities for approval. The amount of work on such a translation would require at least ten years and, perhaps, considerably longer.

While this suggestion seems to be ideal, there are practical obstacles that immediately occur to one familiar with the biblical situation in the respective churches. Problems of religious preferences for certain expressions, of explanatory notes, etc., would be thorny but could be overcome with goodwill. A much more practical and difficult problem is the availability of highly qualified translators for such a project. Many of the best scholars are already engaged in other projects, like the Doubleday Anchor Bible. Most of the experienced Roman Catholic translators, having at last brought to a conclusion the Conf. translation, will be unwilling to turn from this thirty-year-long project to still another effort at translation. Remember that a common Bible is not a need felt by scholars for their work; they recognize that the Bibles already existing are objective. The ecumenical common Bible is a need for a hesitant public, and scholars would be impelled only by a Christian sense of ecumenical responsibility.

Some have thought that they have found a way out of this difficulty by suggesting that a Bible translation already under way might be turned into a common Bible (presumably for ecumenical purposes). Father Walter Abbott of *America* has suggested that the above-mentioned Doubleday Anchor Bible could serve this purpose. This is a translation (and commentary) being done in individual volumes by scholars of different faiths under the editorship of W. F. Albright and D. N. Freedman. This translation was never planned as a common Bible, and Professor Albright has insisted that it will be nothing remotely resembling a common Bible. We should have to add that in our own judgment this type of translation would be very unsatisfactory for a common Bible. It is being done by individuals; there is no translation committee to level out peculiarities. The translation of each book of the Bible will have the benefit of the genius of the individual translator, but also the burden of his idiosyncrasies. From the viewpoint of scholarship, this is stimulating; but such strong individualism can scarcely contribute to making a translation serve as a unifying factor between the great Christian communities.

A more practical solution was to "ecumenize" a Bible already under way. In the last stages of the completion of the Conf., the American bishops invited the cooperation of distinguished Protestant scholars. However relatively few books were affected by this cooperation, because of the already advanced stage of the project.

Thus in giving an honest estimate of the chances of producing a common Bible for ecumenical use in the English-speaking world, one has to realize that even if the appropriate religious authorities were to give their endorsement of the project, there remain formidable difficulties. Nevertheless, great difficulties in ecumenism have been overcome in recent years. Who could have dreamed in 1958, at the beginning of Pope John's pontificate, that we would have been this far in a few short years? And who can foretell how fast the modern advances in biblical study will bring receptive Christians to milestones along the road to unity?

III

The Unity and Diversity
in New Testament Ecclesiology[1]

Biblical studies are emerging now from their perilous journey between the Scylla of blind literalism and the Charybdis of liberalism (or, in Roman Catholic circles, modernism); and today critical studies of Scripture have a great deal to contribute to the ecumenical movement. Perhaps such critical biblical studies seem to offer an obstacle. The divergence of critical views may seem only to constitute more disunity, especially in comparison to the monolithic simplicity of a fundamentalistic biblical interpretation.

[1] This was an address given in July 1963 at Montreal to the Fourth World Conference on Faith and Order. (The Commission on Faith and Order is the theological organ of the World Council of Churches, and Father Brown was the first Catholic ever to address such a conference.) This conference gave particular attention to the concept of "the Church" in the ecumenical movement, and so it was thought desirable to have at the general session two papers on the Church in New Testament times. These papers were to focus on what bound first-century Christianity together and what divided it. The Protestant speaker who shared the platform with Father Brown was Professor Ernst Käsemann of Tübingen.

Yet true critical studies demand a humble submission to evidence and a willingness to accept truth no matter where it may be found. In the long run this humility and docility to truth serve the ecumenical movement better than do the hidden presuppositions of an over-literalistic approach to the Bible.

That there are differences among critics in their interpretation of New Testament ecclesiology is quite obvious from a comparison of the two recent works on the subject by E. Schweizer and R. Schnackenburg.[2] Perhaps before beginning my observations on the unity and diversity in New Testament ecclesiology, I might point out three areas of New Testament criticism which are vigorously discussed by biblical scholars and which have a very important bearing on ecclesiology.

1. *The Gospels as a Witness to Jesus' Own Attitude Toward Church, Church Order, Sacraments, etc.*

Granting that the essential Gospel structure is the *kerygma* and *didache* of the primitive Christian preachers and teachers, we are faced with the critical question of distinguishing Jesus' own position from that of the later Church. It seems that much of the latest exegesis, e.g., the post-Bultmannian exegesis in Germany, is moving away from an ultraskepticism which would maintain that we cannot penetrate beyond the kerygma to Jesus Himself. Nevertheless, there still remains a sharp cleavage among the critics concerning many of the ecclesiastical and sacramental sayings attributed to Jesus in the Gospels, e.g., the passages in Mt (16:18; 18:17) where "church" is mentioned. For some, these sayings are creations of the Palestinian community; others think there is evidence for evaluating them as genuine sayings of Jesus, but recognize that the insight of the Evangelist into the theology of these sayings is much richer than the understanding possible to the audiences to whom they were originally addressed. Thus, in seeking the

[2] See above, Chap. II, n. 24.

ecclesiology implicit in such statements, one would have to ask a series of questions: What did they mean when uttered by Jesus of Nazareth? What did they mean in the earliest stage of the apostolic preaching? What did they mean to the communities that preserved them? What did they mean to the Evangelist who recorded them in the sequence we now find them? Such an approach would respect both the theological nature of the Gospels and the stages of their composition without needlessly undermining their value as witnesses to Jesus of Nazareth.

In particular, the evaluation of the Fourth Gospel and its sacramentalism is a much disputed question. For Professor Bultmann the original Gospel of John was antisacramental before it was retouched by the ecclesiastical redactor; for others Jn is nonsacramental or not specifically sacramental (why less so than Mk or Lk?); for Barrett and Cullmann Jn seems to be the most sacramental of all the Gospels. Now obviously the theology concerning baptism and the Eucharist in a late Gospel such as Jn is of extreme importance for any theory of the historical development of New Testament ecclesiology. I might summarize by saying that I do not believe that Jn is an attempt to correct the obvious sacramentalism of the Church; I believe it is an attempt to show how this valid sacramentalism is rooted in the words and deeds of Jesus. Therefore, as I see it, Jn presupposes sacraments in the Church.[3]

2. *The Value of the Book of Acts*

In his two-part theological treatment of Christ and the Church, Luke shows a remarkable ability to synthesize material from many sources into a unified picture. It is true that among scholars today there is less tendency to split the Book of Acts into sharply defined sources, each maintaining its own characteristics; today we recognize that all that has passed into Luke's work bears the mark of his

[3] For a more detailed study of the Gospel of John and sacramentality, see Chap. IV.

theological outlook. Nevertheless, we must admit that Luke did have sources; his material is not invented. The parallels with Qumran have convinced many of us that the Lucan picture of the Jerusalem church, its organization, its ideals of community life and poverty, is perfectly at home on the Palestinian scene of the thirties.[4] If Luke organized the Book of Acts from the viewpoint of a more fully developed theology of the latter half of the first century, this theology was not an *ex nihilo* creation. It requires a careful critical study to uncover the earlier theological insights that are preserved for us in this book.

3. *The Pastorals*

The assumption that the Pastorals are post-Pauline remains an assumption, with strong arguments both for and against. It should be remembered that there are first-rate Pauline scholars who still consider Paul as the author (in the broad biblical sense of "author," not necessarily in the current, restricted sense of "writer"). And this is my own view. But even if the Pastorals should prove to be pseudepigraphical (*Datum sed non concessum*), their unknown composer must have felt that their theology was close enough to Paul's to warrant the assumption of the Pauline mantle. A study of pseudepigrapha in the Bible seems to indicate that generally a pseudepigraphical work is attributed to an author because it is a continuation of his thought, style, or spirit, rather than because it is designed to correct his theology. Therefore we must proceed with care in drawing a sharp line of demarcation between Pauline theology and that of the Pastorals.

After these prolegomena let us now turn to the general question of unity and diversity in New Testament ecclesiology. The *first* question that should be discussed concerns continuity in the theology, and specifically in the ecclesiology of the New Testament. Too often continuity

[4] See the treatment of this above, Chap. II, Part B.

is pictured in an oversimplified manner: Jesus left to the Twelve a detailed blueprint for a Church, and the Apostles simply had to follow His specific directions. Such a theory will not withstand biblical criticism. I do not mean that Jesus never spoke of a Church, but there is no evidence that He indicated in detail the where, the how, the when of ecclesial development. Even the Book of Acts, wherein, as Professor Käsemann has pointed out, the "one, holy, and apostolic" viewpoint is most clear, does not present this type of continuity. In Acts the great steps in ecclesiastical life and organization are presented as responses to novel challenges, responses guided by the Spirit. No one can read the story of Cornelius or of the Council of Jerusalem and not see that the question of admission of the Gentiles to the Church was a difficult problem that had to be worked out by the Apostles themselves under the guidance of the Spirit of Christ. This does not mean that we must deny the authenticity of all the Gospel sayings whereby Jesus allots the nations a place in the Kingdom of God. But Jesus' sayings were in the prophetic-apocalyptic context of the Kingdom; and the connection of these sayings to the admission of uncircumcised Gentiles to the *qahal* of the new Israel was something that had to be clarified for His followers.

Thus, if we are to speak of continuity in New Testament theology, it must be in terms of the Spirit of Christ which constantly brought out the meaning of Jesus, His words and works, for the new circumstances, times, and places in which His followers found themselves. Certainly there are new stages and new concepts in New Testament ecclesiology that become apparent in a critical study of the various books, but for the New Testament authors each of these stages or concepts was rooted through the Spirit in Jesus Himself. Such an awareness of continuity finds its most eloquent statement in Jn 16:13: "When the Spirit of Truth comes . . . he will not speak on his own authority: whatever he hears he will speak . . . he will take what is mine and declare it to you." The gradual working of the Spirit of Jesus must be taken into account when we consider questions of Christ's institution of Church order or of the sacraments.

A *second* question that we must ask concerns uniformity in New Testament theology: Is there a linear development in the theology and ecclesiology of the New Testament? That there is development is obvious: after all, it is an ancient axiom in theology that revelation closed only with the end of the apostolic era. Many of the developments found in the New Testament are complementary, filling in a larger picture of the Church.

But New Testament theology is not simply a picture of linear progress toward a uniform position. There are strong differences in outlook found among the various New Testament writers, a fact often neglected in past theological discussion. For instance, the attitude toward the Law preserved in Mt (5:18; 23:2–3) is different from the attitude toward the Law found in Gal and Rom. (It is not sufficient to explain that Mt is giving us the attitude toward the Law that was prevalent during Jesus' lifetime; such sayings would not have been preserved if they did not have enduring value for the community to which Mt was addressed). In ecclesiology, Luke in the Book of Acts makes no attempt to suppress the information that the Hellenist Christians objected to the type of organization prevalent among the Jewish Christians.

Thus, to ask us to believe that there was absolute *uniformity of theology* among the different groups or theologians represented in the New Testament is to ask us to deny obvious evidence. (Indeed, has there ever been absolute uniformity in any stage of Christianity?) The Church of the New Testament was broad enough to include the Judeo-Christian (diaspora?) Church for which St. Matthew's Gospel was written and the Pauline churches. However, and this should not be forgotten, the Church was not broad enough to include the later exaggeration of Judeo-

Christianity that was Ebionitism, nor the later exaggeration of Pauline opposition to the Law that was Marcionism.

Yet, if New Testament ecclesiology cannot be oversimplified in the direction of theological uniformity, neither can we neglect a *unity in belief* that is present in all stages of New Testament thought about the Church. (As we know, there is a difference between unity and uniformity, between faith and theology.) If with justification we can speak of the theologies present in the New Testament, we must recognize that each of the New Testament theologians was conscious of belonging to the one Christian Church. There are common elements found in all the ecclesiologies of the New Testament, and to neglect them in favor of diversity would be to fail to give a complete picture of the New Testament concept of the Church. For the sake of example I shall select and discuss three.

A. CONTINUITY WITH ISRAEL

From one end of the New Testament to the other there is a deep consciousness that the Church, whether predominantly Jewish or Gentile, is deeply rooted in the Israel of the Old Testament. Undoubtedly in the first days when the community consisted exclusively of converted Jews, the concept of a *renewed* Israel was stronger. We see this in the many parallels between the Christian community and Israel: the settling of the primitive Church in Jerusalem; the symbolism of the Twelve; the Jesus-Moses parallelism; the very title *ekklēsia* (whether it reflects *qahal* or *'edah*). The Jerusalem community was the Church of God as Israel had been the "church of God" in the desert.

In the course of time, as the percentage of Gentiles increased, there may have been a shift toward the concept of a *new* Israel, although it is interesting to note that it is not in the New Testament but in the *Epistle of Barnabas* (5:7) that we find for the first time an explicit mention of "the new people"—Paul is content to say that the Christian is a new man. Yet the shift of emphasis from a renewed

Israel to a new Israel is almost imperceptible, and I am not certain that we can really speak of two different New Testament concepts. The very fact that the Gentile communities call themselves "churches" shows a conscious self-patterning on the mother *ekklēsia* in Jerusalem with its deep roots in Israel, a patterning that Paul encourages with his unifying collection for the Jerusalem church.

It is true that the Hellenists[5] seem to have gone quite far in their tendency to separate from Judaism, but this may well have been because of a peculiar sectarian opposition to certain religious institutions, like the Temple. And the Hellenists were not the spokesmen for Gentile Christianity. It is important that in 58, long after the Gentiles had begun to flock into the Church, Paul could still maintain (Rom 11:2) that God did not reject the people Israel whom He foreknew, and that the wild olive had to be grafted on to the cultivated olive tree. The complicated Pauline explanation of how all Christians are true descendants of Abraham shows that Paul believed that continuity with Israel was something to be clung to. 1 Pt (2:9), which many consider to be an echo of one of the oldest baptismal liturgies, uses a battery of terms identifying the new Christians with the Israel of the Sinai covenant (Ex 19:5–6). A late work like the Apocalypse, addressed to the churches of Asia, insists that the foundations of the new Jerusalem are the Twelve Apostles.

To sum up, from the beginning of its history the Christian community was conscious of a continuity with Israel, as well as of a newness in Christ. Throughout the New Testament the various theologians seek to balance these two aspects of continuity and newness; at times the scales will tip one way; at times, the other. There will be different explanations of what constitutes the continuity with Israel (but Paul is by no means the first to insist that carnal descendance from Abraham is not enough—Mt 3:9; Jn

[5] See the account in Acts 6 and the attitude toward the Temple evinced by the Hellenist Stephen in Acts 7.

8:39–40). There will be a gradually increasing opposition
to the unbelieving mass of Jews (an opposition which began in the ministry of Jesus Himself). Yet, the basic notion
of continuity with Israel is a common factor in all stages
of New Testament ecclesiology.

B. APOSTOLICITY

It has become customary today among critical scholars
(including such Roman Catholics as Cerfaux and Dupont)
to distinguish between *the Twelve,* who accompanied Jesus
throughout His ministry, and *the apostles,* the wider group
of those "sent" to preach the resurrected Jesus.[6] It is hypercriticism, however, to deny the evidence that the Twelve
were among the apostles, and indeed played a special role
as the Apostles par excellence (so that in the later New
Testament compositions we find by simplification *the
Twelve Apostles*). Paul himself, writing in the fifties (Gal
1:17), recognized the privileged position of "those who
were apostles before me." It is interesting that the Synoptic
Gospels and the Acts preserve lists of the Twelve—a testimony to the continuing import of the concept of the
Twelve in the Church in the second half of the first century. (Naturally as the membership of the Twelve dwindled
through death and churches were founded by other apostles like Paul, the vital memory of the personal identity of
the original Twelve grew dim, whence the difference of
names in the various lists.) As we have mentioned, the
Apocalypse (21:14) still portrays the Twelve Apostles as
the foundations of the heavenly Jerusalem.

It is true that Jesus promised the Twelve an eschatological role in the Kingdom (Mt 19:28; Lk 22:30), and undoubtedly the eschatological aspect of the Twelve was more
prominent in the early days of the Christian community
when the return of Christ in judgment was eagerly anticipated. But from the very beginning there is evidence

[6] See above, Chap. II, n. 26.

that the role of the Twelve was not confined to final judgment. There are simply too many witnesses in the New Testament that manifold power (to preach, to teach, to heal, to baptize, to forgive sins) and authority was committed to the Twelve and exercised from the start. Peter, for instance, appears as a man of great authority, not only in the sayings preserved in Mt, Lk, and Jn, but also in the echoes of community life preserved in Acts and Paul.

Thus the older critical picture of an original "spiritual" Church being fossilized into a later authoritarian, hierarchical Church will simply not stand examination. There is every reason to accept the thesis that the Church possessed organization from the beginning, an organization not without its parallels in the Qumran community. The constant insistence throughout the New Testament that those who are placed over others must humbly serve speaks eloquently for the thesis that the concept of a Church without human authority would have been strange at any period of New Testament ecclesiology. Some may insist that the Christian community is a flock in which Christ has the unique shepherdship. Yet there are good testimonies from such diverse witnesses as Jn (21:15–17), 1 Pt (5:2–11); and Acts (20:28) that in the early Church the duty of carrying on the shepherdship of Jesus was entrusted to men. That authority in the New Testament period lay in the hands of the Twelve and of the apostles in general is seen in other works besides Acts. When Paul is called on to defend his authority, he appeals to his status as one sent by the resurrected Christ (Gal 1:16). He tells the Corinthians (1 Cor 12:28) that in community life God has appointed first apostles. Eph (2:20) with all its developed Christology still sees the apostles as the foundation of the household of God.

We shall not raise in detail the question of how the ministry exercised by the Twelve and the apostles in general was subsequently communicated to others. The Pastorals speak of an office communicated by the laying on of hands (seemingly also Acts). For those who believe that the

Pastorals are post-Pauline such ordination, along with the episcopate, is simply one of the latest developments in New Testament ecclesiology. Besides the provisory character of such judgment on the Pastorals, there are many other objections to such an oversimplification. With regard to the episcopate we mention here only the remarkable resemblance between the Qumran *mebaqqer* (*paqid*) and the New Testament portrait of the *episkopos* (in Acts, Phil, 1 Pt, as well as the Pastorals), a resemblance which suggests that the origins of the Christian episcopate belong more appropriately in Palestine than in the churches of Asia Minor.[7]

C. BAPTISM AND THE EUCHARIST

That the Christian community from its very inception practiced baptism is quite clear. Christian baptism set men off as belonging to the people of God who had been saved through Jesus Christ. Beyond this initiatory value, the Book of Acts associates the remission of sins with baptism; John associates the idea of spiritual rebirth with baptism; Paul sees baptism as immersion into the death and Resurrection of Christ. Are these different views of the effects of baptism evidence of really different ecclesiologies? Was baptism originally a simple initiatory sign which only in later theology acquired the spiritual effects attributed to it in various parts of the New Testament?

Even from the most critical viewpoint there seems to be no real proof that Christian baptism was ever administered without some concept of spiritual renewal. Repentance as a present necessity was characteristic of John's baptism as well as of Christian baptism. The background of baptism, as we see it in the Old Testament prophets (Is 4:4; Ez 36:25–27) and in Qumran, is that of a communication of a new spirit and of cleansing from impurity, in short, "a

---

[7] See above, Chap. II, Part B.

baptism with a holy spirit and fire."[8] Likewise, Lk 12:50 where Jesus speaks of His death as a baptism with which to be baptized indicates a very early connection between baptism and the death of Jesus (see also Mk 10:38). Thus, while the great theologians of the New Testament like Luke, John, and Paul may have brought out more clearly the relationship between baptism and the forgiveness of sin, spiritual rebirth, and the death of Jesus, there are traces of these ideas in the earliest picture of baptism.

Another vital factor in the ecclesiology of the New Testament is the Eucharist. Indeed, Paul bases his concept of Church unity on the model of the unity of those who eat the same Eucharistic Bread (1 Cor 10:17). In Acts, as well as in the Gospels, we hear the eschatological and joyful overtones of the earliest Eucharistic breakings of the bread. Yet the two-Eucharist approach of Lietzmann which would separate the eschatological Jerusalem meal from the Pauline memorial feast does not really account for all the evidence. The eschatological and joyful element is found in the Eucharistic banquets of the Pauline churches too: Paul's understanding of the Eucharist is that it proclaims the death of the Lord *until He comes;* the Eucharistic banquets at Corinth were joyful to a fault. On the other hand, there is no real evidence that even the most primitive form of the Jerusalem Eucharist lacked a connection with the death of the Lord. The echoes of anticipation of death at the first Eucharist, the Last Supper, are too strong in all the accounts of the Institution to be dismissed as a later accretion. And the basic notion of memorial or *anamnesis* is not confined to the Hellenistic world. The ceremony of the renewal of the covenant which has emerged as a key factor in Old Testament studies offers an excellent pattern for understanding the remembrance of the death of Christ which in the new covenant is effected in the Eucharistic *anamnesis.*

We are not at all denying that eschatological anticipation

---

[8] See below, Chap. VIII on Jn 1:33.

was stronger in the early days of the Church. And the fact
that the example of Greek mystery religions had some influence on later Eucharistic theology is seen in the patristic
period. Yet, even if there were different emphases in different periods, both the eschatological and the *anamnesis*
elements of the Eucharist were present from the beginning
and run through all phases of New Testament ecclesiology.

To sum up our very brief treatment of the New Testament theology of the Church, we have rejected an oversimplified picture of the continuity and uniformity of New
Testament ecclesiology; but we have also rejected an overemphasis on the diversities found in New Testament
thought, as if there were no common elements that bound
the various stages of New Testament ecclesiology together.
We have given but three examples of these common elements; others could be pointed out.

In evaluating this type of biblical criticism, we should
recognize that biblical criticism is but one avenue of research into the Church of the first century. I believe that
the subsequent history of the Church in the postapostolic
period is also a witness to the Church of the New Testament since the Spirit of Christ did not cease to work when
the New Testament was completed, and this Spirit in the
Church guarantees continuity in essentials. Also we must
recognize that no form of purely scientific research can
hope to unravel entirely the mystery of the Church, for
the Church and what pertains to it is an object of faith.
Nevertheless, it is incumbent on us to use all the means at
our disposal, including the science of biblical criticism, to
know and understand what the Church of the New Testament was and was not as a guide to our understanding
of what the Church must be today. (This must be done
honestly; for, as I think we are all agreed, minimizing of
doctrinal difficulties and differences cannot aid ecumenism.) The importance of this task cannot be overesti-
mated; for as Schnackenburg has put it, "Faith in Christ,

union with Christ, life in Christ has been found only in the bosom of a community bound to Christ." This community of those bound to Christ, the Church, is constitutive for Christian existence.

Part Two

EXAMPLES OF MODERN
BIBLICAL RESEARCH INTO
THE GOSPELS

Section 1
The Theology and Background of the Fourth Gospel

IV

The Johannine
Sacramentary

he question of sacramentality through symbolism is one
which deeply affects the interpretation of the Fourth Gos-
el. Yet, in approaching this question, one encounters two
ery different scholarly evaluations. On the one side, there
the antisacramental (or at least nonsacramental) school
d by Bultmann and most of the German scholars. On
e other, there is a type of ultrasacramentalism which sees
symbolic reference to some sacrament or other in vir-
ally every chapter of Jn. This view is championed by
ullmann[1] and by many of the French and British scholars.
o see how far this trend has gone, the reader need only
onsult the list that we have placed at the end of our essay,
list of the Johannine passages that have been interpreted
acramentally.

[1] His *Urchristentum und Gottesdienst*, which appeared in
944, has had tremendous influence through its translations.
Ve shall cite it as *Early Christian Worship*, tr. by A. S. Todd
nd J. B. Torrance (London, 1953). Cullmann's pupil, L.
ouyer, has popularized a sacramental view in *Le quatrième
vangile*, 3 ed. (Tournai, 1956).

Our purpose in this essay is to reexamine the method
ological principles behind the theory of Johannine sacra
mentality and, in particular, to distinguish relatively well
founded examples of sacramentality from the less defensibl
suggestions. We believe that there is true sacramenta
symbolism in Jn; nevertheless, unproved applications o
this symbolism have served only to bring the whole prin
ciple of symbolism into disrepute.

We recognize, of course, that in pursuing such an in
vestigation we are to some extent dealing in categories and
precisions that may be foreign to Jn. Whether we confine
our study to baptism and the Eucharist, or include the
complete sacramentary, we may be overprecise in the ques
tion we are asking, namely, are there references to the
sacraments in Jn? For would the author of Jn have dis
tinguished precisely between sacraments and sacramen
tals?[2] His was a general insight that the lifegiving powe
of Jesus was effective through the material symbols em
ployed in the deeds and discourses of the public ministry.
Now we know that in the course of time some of thos
material symbols were recognized by the Church as per
manently valid signs communicating Christ's grace (the
sacraments), while others were recognized as having only
a lesser or temporary significance. We shall take advantage
of this distinction and confine ourselves to the sacramen
tary in the strict sense; yet we must recognize that thi
precise delineation is more our own than the Evangelist's

[2] Henri Clavier, "Le problème du rite et du mythe dans le
quatrième évangile," *Revue d'histoire et de philosophie religi
euses*, 31 (1951), 287, thinks that in Jn we have a generalization
of sacramentalism in the direction of sacramentals. He think
that the Evangelist did not want to confine sacramental refer
ences to two particular rites like baptism and the Eucharist.

[3] The Johannine concept of miracle as a "sign" border
closely on this. If men could really see and believe the revelatio
of Jesus portrayed in a material "sign," they could receiv
life eternal.

THE NONSACRAMENTAL VIEW OF JN

Those scholars who see a minimal sacramental interest in Jn have based their case on literary criticism. Bultmann[4] finds in Jn three clearly sacramental passages: 3:5 with its reference to water, 6:51b–58, and 19:34–35 (passages referring respectively to baptism, Eucharist, and to both sacraments together). Otherwise Jn does not mention the institution of the sacraments, and places all emphasis on a personal union with Jesus. For Bultmann,[5] then, Jn basically ignores the sacraments and serves as a corrective to that tendency in the early Church which would see the sacraments as a means of salvation. The three sacramental passages are additions made by the ecclesiastical redactor, a censor postulated by Bultmann who made corrections in the Gospel to conform it to the Synoptic tradition and Church usage.

While many have rejected Bultmann's view of Jn as basically antisacramental, there has been a wider acceptance of at least a nonsacramentality or of a peripheral sacramentality. Eduard Schweizer[6] doubts whether or not one can prove that the three sacramental passages are redactionary. In any case, their sacramentality is merely anti-Docetic and only helps to show the reality of the Incarnation. In Jn there is no stress on the sacraments in themselves, but only as witnesses to Jesus, and sacraments are

[4] *Das Evangelium des Johannes,* 16 ed. (Göttingen, 1959). See also *Theology of the New Testament,* 2, tr. by K. Grobel (London, 1955), 3–14.

[5] *Das Evangelium,* 360: "Although the Evangelist tolerated the Church's use of baptism and the Eucharist, he remained suspicious of it because of the misuse to which it was subject, and therefore he did not speak of it. In truth the sacraments were superfluous for him."

[6] "Das johanneische Zeugnis vom Herrenmahl," *Evangelische Theologie,* 12 (1952–1953), 341–363.

not a central thought. Helmut Köster[7] maintains that even if 6:51b–58 and 3:5 ("water") are secondary, there is already a cultic and sacramental element in the other parts of chaps. 6 and 3. Yet the Evangelist is interested in sacramentality only insofar as it leads back to the reality of Jesus. In Jn there is nothing like the metaphysical viewpoint that characterizes the sacramentality of Ignatius of Antioch.[8] Eduard Lohse[9] agrees with Bultmann that the three sacramental passages are redactionary and that the original Gospel had no sacraments. But this does not mean that the Evangelist was antisacramental. Rather the Evangelist's interest was centered on *martyria:* he wished to emphasize contact through witness with Jesus, and this main purpose did not call for any sacramental stress.

Despite certain disagreements, most of the above-mentioned discussions[10] are focused on the three sacramental passages singled out by Bultmann. The question of wider

[7] "Geschichte und Kultus im Johannesevangelium und bei Ignatius von Antiochien," *Zeitschrift für Theologie und Kirche* 54 (1957), 56–69.

[8] Gunther Bornkamm, "Die eucharistische Rede im Johannes-Evangelium," *Zeitschrift für die neutestamentliche Wissenschaft* 47 (1956), 161–169, maintains, on the other hand, that the interpolation 6:51b–58 is much more sacramental than the rest of chap. 6 and much more Ignatian. Wilhelm Wilkens "Das Abendmahlszeugnis im vierten Evangelium," *Evangelische Theologie,* 18 (1958), 354–370, tries to refute Bornkamm's arguments and to show that the passage is truly Johannine and not an interpolation. Yet he agrees with E. Schweizer on the anti-Docetic, peripheral character of Johannine sacramentality.

[9] "Wort und Sakrament im Johannesevangelium," *New Testament Studies,* 7 (1960–1961), 110–125.

[10] Köster, *art. cit.,* 66–67, treats of the possible sacramental significance of (*a*) the foot washing in chap. 13, in which he sees no baptismal significance but only a symbol of unity through love—the failure of Judas shows that there is no magical union with Jesus by sacramental means; (*b*) the vine passage of chap. 15. Here there may be Eucharistic significance, but the primary unity with Jesus is still a moral one (15:7, 10).

sacramental symbolism is, for the most part, regarded as unproved and almost unworthy of detailed rebuttal. The underlying methodological principle seems to be that if the Evangelist had intended sacramental significance, he would have expressed it more clearly.

THE ULTRASACRAMENTAL VIEW OF JN

This school approaches Jn from another standpoint. Albert Schweitzer[11] maintained that the exegete had to consider the whole New Testament ethos. The theory that Old Testament prophecy had a fulfillment in the New Testament created a sensibility to typology. Therefore, it was natural for Jn to present Jesus' words and actions as prophetic types of the Church's sacraments, and the significance of these types would be easily recognizable to the Christian readers of the Gospel. Schweitzer began a trend; it was for Cullmann to go through Jn in detail and establish the case for sacramentality. Cullmann stresses that we know something of baptism and the Eucharist as essential parts of early Christian worship. Therefore, he maintains, both the Evangelist and his audience must have been familiar with these sacraments. Since the Evangelist's purpose was to ground the community's faith in the historic Jesus, what more natural than for him to show a basis for the sacraments of baptism and the Eucharist in Jesus' words and works? Of course, this sacramental reference would be understood only in the postresurrectional period in which the Evangelist and his audience were living. As Cullmann proceeds through Jn incident by incident, he seeks to find some internal indication that sacramental symbolism was intended by the Evangelist. In fact, however, he often seems to fall back on the principle that since a passage could have been understood sacramentally, it was intended sacramentally. His treatment was answered incident by in-

---

[11] *Die Mystik des Apostels Paulus* (Tübingen, 1930), 345 ff.

cident by Wilhelm Michaelis,[12] who maintained that in virtually every case Cullmann had not proved the existence of sacramental symbolism.

The Swedish scholar Alf Corell[13] also takes a deeply sacramental view of Jn, although he does not see as many sacramental references as Cullmann does. Corell believes that just as there is a strong influence of the Jewish festal liturgy on Jn (in the direction of replacement), so there is influence of the Christian sacramental litugy, i.e., baptism and the Eucharist. As Protestants, Cullmann and Corell would confine the sacramental references to just two sacraments; the Catholic scholar Bruce Vawter[14] would enlarge the sacramentary. He suggests the possibility of a reference to a sacramental anointing, similar to extreme unction, in the anointing of the feet (Jn 12), and to matrimony in the Cana scene (Jn 2).

The British commentaries on Jn have tended to be more prosacramental than the German. Edwyn Hoskyns[15] presents some interesting researches into Church history and liturgy to back up the sacramental interpretations of the narratives of the healing of the blind man (Jn 9) and of the washing of the feet (Jn 13). Even the more critical

---

[12] *Die Sakramente im Johannesevangelium* (Bern, 1946). This excellent work, since it appeared in mimeographed form due to postwar conditions, never got the attention in American circles that it deserved. A similar skeptical view of Cullmann's arguments was taken by Philippe-H. Menoud, *L'Evangile de Jean* (Neuchâtel, 1947), 53–56: "In its details, this exegesis of O. Cullmann is not convincing."

[13] *Consummatum Est* (Swedish ed., 1950; English ed., London, 1958).

[14] "The Johannine Sacramentary," *Theological Studies,* 17 (1956), 151–166. David M. Stanley, S.J., has also shown himself very favorable to ultrasacramentalism in his series of articles in *Worship,* 32–35 (1957–1961).

[15] *The Fourth Gospel,* 2 ed. (London, 1947), esp. 363 and 443. R. H. Lightfoot, *St. John's Gospel* (Oxford, 1956), also accepts much sacramental symbolism in Jn.

commentary of C. K. Barrett[16] states ". . . there is more sacramental teaching in John than in the other Gospels." He traces this to several Johannine categories of thought which are favorable to sacramentalism, e.g., symbolism and emphasis on the material circumstances of Jesus.[17]

Paul Niewalda[18] has given us the most recent and complete defense of sacramental symbolism in Jn. He frankly admits that by the ordinary tools of exegesis one cannot prove that the Evangelist intended to refer to the sacraments by means of material symbols. And so he suggests a different exegetical approach. Niewalda shows that a dependence on some type of symbolism or deeper meaning was in vogue in all types of literature at this time, and that our earliest Christian records (liturgy, Church art, the Fathers) witness to the use of fixed symbols for the sacraments. Therefore, he maintains that when these traditional symbols are encountered in the New Testament and, in particular, in Jn, they should be interpreted as references to the sacraments. The author of Jn was a child of his time: symbolism would have been part of his literary technique, and he would have used the same symbols as his contemporaries. Rudolf Schnackenburg[19] objects to this principle on the grounds that most of the early Christian witnesses are later than Jn and may represent a more developed symbolism. Water, for instance, certainly plays a more symbolic and sacramental role in Tertullian than it does in Jn. Schnackenburg, who is a moderate sacramentalist, has his own method of procedure; first he studies the clearly sacramental texts in Jn and establishes from

[16] *The Gospel according to St. John* (London, 1958), 69.

[17] Clavier, *art. cit.*, 287, has the same view; for, he asks, how could Johannine thought ignore sacramentalism (i.e., the use of exterior forms as a means of grace) when it makes a fulcrum of the Incarnation?

[18] *Sakramentssymbolik im Johannesevangelium* (Limburg, 1958).

[19] "Die Sakramente im Johannesevangelium," *Sacra Pagina*, 2 (Paris, 1959), 235–254.

them an estimate of the sacramentality of the Evangelist with which to approach the more obscure texts.

CONSIDERATION OF THE METHODOLOGY OF THESE VIEWS

The study of all the arguments for and against Johannine sacramentality suggests that a balance may be achieved through a better methodological appreciation on both sides.

First, the literary criticism of the nonsacramentalists should not be neglected. This pertains chiefly to the three definitely sacramental passages stressed by Bultmann: 3:5; 6:51b–58; 19:34b–35. Too often, if we take Jn 6 as an example, supporters of the sacramental position satisfy themselves by proving that the chapter is a unity. Against Bultmann, and quite correctly, they point out Eucharistic indications in the earlier part of chap. 6.[20] To some this would prove that the Eucharistic section belongs to the rest of the chapter. Yet why could it not have been added to the chapter by someone desiring precisely to clarify the Eucharistic undertones of the rest of the discourse? The unity could be purely a literary or logical one.

What the recognition of Eucharistic elements in other parts of chap. 6 does prove is that Bultmann's concept of the ecclesiastical redactor is false. There is every evidence that the sacramental section has a certain harmony with the rest of the discourse and was not simply superimposed by an act of ecclesiastical censorship to make Jn conform to sacramental ideas.[21] Nevertheless, while we may rule out

[20] This is admitted by Bornkamm, *art. cit.,* 162, and Köster, *art. cit.,* 62, and is a commonplace among Catholic writers. For an excellent summary of Catholic views, see Cyril Vollert, S.J., "The Eucharist: Quests for Insights from Scripture," *Theological Studies,* 21 (1960), 404–415.

[21] Clarence T. Craig, "Sacramental Interest in the Fourth Gospel," *Journal of Biblical Literature,* 58 (1939), 32, pointed this out a long time ago. He stressed that we cannot discover a

such a theory of arbitrary redaction, we cannot exclude editorship in the history of the composition of Jn. E. Schweizer and Ruckstuhl,[22] by the use of stylistic characteristics, have devastated the source theory of Jn as posited by Bultmann and others. There is too much literary homogeneity in Jn to posit the simple combination of totally distinct sources. Yet this homogeneity cannot rule out subsequent editorship *within* the Johannine tradition. The Last Discourse is, perhaps, the best example of this: it is all quite Johannine, but it certainly shows signs of editorial modifications.

With this in mind, we cannot dismiss the possibility that some sacramental sections in Jn (e.g., 3:5 and 6:51–58) are editorial additions of Johannine material, designed to bring out the real sacramental undertones already present.[23] This would account for the surface unity of the sections, and yet allow for the startlingly deeper sacramentality of the specific additions. Thus there would be truth in the remarks of the nonsacramentalists that certain specific sections do have clearer sacramental emphasis than the rest of the Gospel. In our view, this theory weakens Schnackenburg's criterion of using the clearly sacramental sections as a canon for judging the sacramental symbolism and interest of the rest of the Gospel.

Second, we must discuss the claim of the nonsacramentalists that Johannine sacramentality is of a peripheral character, or introduced only as part of anti-Docetist apologetic.

---

redactor's addition by isolating ideas that seem to us to contradict the main position of the Evangelist. "It is quite another thing to demonstrate that they were contradictory to him."

[22] Eduard Schweizer, *Ego Eimi* (Göttingen, 1939); Eugen Ruckstuhl, *Die literarische Einheit des Johannesevangeliums* (Freiburg, 1951).

[23] We have given a preliminary sketch of our personal views on these sections in our pamphlet commentary on Jn in the *New Testament Reading Guide*, 13 (Collegeville, Minn., 1960). Also see Chap. V below.

This peripheral sacramentality is contrasted with "Hellen-istic" or "Ignatian" sacramentality, which gives independent value to the sacraments.

Here, too, there is a methodological difficulty. Most of those who hold this view (see above) have confined their study to the three so-called clearly sacramental passages of the Gospel and to 1 Jn 5:6–8. Now there probably is an anti-Docetist emphasis in 1 Jn 5:6–8 and in Jn 19:34b–35;[24] the author is stressing the bloody death of Jesus as the Christ. The water and blood bear witness to the humanity of Jesus. Another section, 6:51b–58, may have some claim to be considered as anti-Docetist, although this seems less clear to us.[25] Yet it is only in these two or three sacramental passages that there is any emphasis on the connection between anti-Docetism and sacramentalism. The many other sacramental passages claimed by Cullmann, Niewalda, and others have no such particular bent. Thus, if any truth can be granted to even a part of the claims of the ultrasacramental school, this very specialized aspect attributed to Johannine sacramentality would disappear, and anti-Docetism would become merely one aspect of a larger sacramental picture.

As for "peripheral sacramentality" in general, a great deal depends on the definition of terms. No exegete with a sense of history expects to find a fully developed Scholastic

[24] See E. Schweizer, *art. cit. (supra, n. 6)*, 344–352. The two passages, however, do not have exactly the same emphasis in their sacramental symbolism. As Schnackenburg, *art. cit.*, 249, points out, the blood and water of 19:34 stress the origins of the Eucharist and baptism in the death of Christ, whereas the water and blood of 1 Jn stress the place of baptism and the Eucharist in the work of the Church. Thus, even here the anti-Docetist element is not the exclusive sacramental interest.

[25] The stress on "Feeding on" Jesus' flesh may help to prove His humanity, but 6:55 ("My flesh is a real food, and my blood a real drink") seems to put more emphasis on the true nourishing value of the flesh and blood, rather than on any anti-Docetist motif. There is nothing particularly anti-Docetist about 3:5.

sacramentalism in Jn. And it is probably true that even between the time of Jn and that of Ignatius of Antioch there was some development of sacramental theology.[26] Yet, in evaluating Johannine sacramentality, we must remember that the purpose of the Evangelist was different from that of an author like Ignatius. The Evangelist cannot treat of the sacraments as such, but only inasmuch as they are reflected in the words and works of Jesus.[27] Therefore the claim that in Jn the sacraments are emphasized only insofar as they help unite the Christian to the historical Jesus is a bit naïve. What other role could the sacraments play in *a gospel?* Any reference to the role of the sacraments in the postresurrectional Church can only be through prophetic typology or some other secondary sense, if the author is to maintain his purpose of telling the significance of what really happened between the baptism of Jesus and His resurrection. Thus, most of the exegetes who interpret Jn sacramentally are quite correct methodologically in seeing any sacramental reference as the second of a twofold meaning present in the words and works of Jesus. For example, if we posit some historical tradition behind the Nicodemus incident, then we must allow a primary, nonsacramental meaning to Jesus' words, a meaning which Nicodemus could have understood. The reference to Christian baptism can only be secondary, at least chronologically. Johannine sacramentality fits into the Gospel's

[26] The picture is not totally clear. The reason for the rejection of the three sacramental passages is because often they are regarded as Ignatian rather than Johannine (so Bornkamm). Yet Köster distinguishes carefully between the sacramentality of these passages and that of Ignatius.

[27] Schnackenburg, *art. cit.*, 253–254, says that for Jn the sacraments take the work of salvation once performed by Jesus, re-present it, and apply it to all believers after the coming of the Spirit. The self-revelation of Jesus as the source of truth and life stands in the foreground of the Gospel; the Church and the sacraments stand in the background as a continuation of that work.

oft-repeated confession that the deeper meaning of these things was not understood until afterward. In this sense, then, Johannine sacramentality is "peripheral," but such a description tends to be misleading.

Nor does the fact that Jn omits the institutions of baptism and the Eucharist mean that the Evangelist was not interested in the sacraments. That Jesus Christ instituted the sacraments is a dogma of the faith. But there is nothing of faith about when He instituted baptism. St. Thomas connects the institution of baptism to Jesus' own baptism in the Jordan, a scene which Jn does not narrate but at least implies (1:33). Estius connects the institution of baptism to the Nicodemus scene (3:5), in which case Jn would be the only one to have recorded the institution. More frequently, perhaps, theologians follow Tertullian and Alexander of Hales in connecting the institution of baptism to Mt 28:19, "Go . . . baptizing them in the name of the Father and of the Son and of the Holy Spirit," words not recorded by Jn (nor by Mk, nor by Lk—are these also non-sacramental?). Many scholars today, however, suggest that the Trinitarian formula as given by Mt came into the Gospel from liturgical usage.[28] Therefore, in not connecting the institution of baptism to any precise words, but in seeing references to baptism in many of the words and works of Jesus, Jn may be representing the original, imprecise outlook of the earliest Christian theology.

The Eucharist presents a more complicated problem. Tradition places the institution of the Eucharist at the Last Supper. But did the early Church preserve the precise words of Jesus as words of institution? Behind the four accounts in Mt, Mk, Lk, and 1 Cor, scholars see two basic traditions, that of Paul (Lk) and that of Mk (Mt), both with claims to antiquity.[29] And while Jn does not record the scene of institution at the Last Supper, the words of

[28] For example, D. M. Stanley, S.J., in his pamphlet commentary on Mt in *New Testament Reading Guide*, 4 (Collegeville, Minn., 1960), 92.

[29] For bibliography see Vollert, *art. cit.*, 416 ff.

6:51, "The bread that I shall give is my own flesh for the life of the world," may stand quite close to the Semitic original of Jesus' words at the Last Supper, since many claim that Jesus probably spoke of His flesh rather than of His body. Thus the argument against Johannine sacramentality from the failure to record institutions is not as impressive as might first seem, and probably reflects more of modern theological interests than of those of antiquity.[30]

Third, we must consider the methodology of the sacramentalists and answer the fundamental question: Is it necessary to have some internal indication that the author himself intended a symbolic reference to the sacraments? As we have said, most of the ultrasacramentalists approach the problem from the viewpoint of what the Evangelist's audience could have understood. Yet that is a very delicate instrument of exegesis, or rather an instrument that is used with much more ease in eisegesis.

A few considerations seem in order. We grant that we cannot approach Jn with the idea of accepting only the symbolism that is clear to us today. Certainly Niewalda is correct in pointing out that some type of symbolism (typical sense, secondary sense, *sensus plenior,* or whatever hermeneutical tag we may give it) was in more general vogue in New Testament times than it is in our own. And there are indications all through Jn that the author was

---

[30] Barrett, *op. cit.,* 71, says that Jn never refers explicitly to sacramental institutions because the sacraments do not hang from any one moment but from the whole fact of Christ. This is an attractive explanation, but we suspect that the whole problem is a modern creation, as Craig holds, *art. cit.,* 33–34. Of course, if one is really interested in finding institutions in Jn, the Council of Trent (*DB* 894) says that the principal institution of the sacrament of penance was in the scene recorded exclusively in Jn 20:22–23. (Probably this does not mean that penance is the exclusive object of the verse. The power to forgive sins through the reception of the Spirit is a wide power exercised in baptism—see Lk 24:47; Acts 2:38—and in penance.)

prepared to carry his symbolism quite far. Who would have dared to interpret 21:18 and its vague reference to Peter's stretching out his hands as a symbol of his crucifixion, if the sacred writer did not make it specific? Or, if one prefers to avoid chap. 21, the same may be said of the equation of the Temple and the body of Jesus (2:21), and of the Spirit and water (7:39).[31]

Now it may be objected that these symbols show that the Evangelist can and does explain symbolism when he employs it, and that therefore we should confine ourselves to just those symbols that he explains. But is there anyone who believes that "the Lamb of God," which Jn does not explain, does not have some symbolic reference, whether it be to the Suffering Servant or to the paschal lamb, or both? And since the water-Spirit equation is not specified until chap. 7, are we to believe that in none of the earlier passages water refers to the Spirit?[32] Thus it might be more precise to say that the symbols the Evangelist explains are precisely the very difficult ones that might otherwise have been overlooked. To confine the Gospel's symbolism to them would be arbitrarily to prejudice our exegesis.[33]

Niewalda's investigation of the symbols used in the early Church for the sacraments can serve as a negative criterion in exegeting Jn. If there is no clear indication in the Gos-

[31] We might add the comparison of the crucified Christ to the brazen serpent (3:14), of the multiplication of the loaves to the gift of manna (chap. 6), and the symbolism of 12:32–33. See Vawter, *art. cit.* (*supra*, n. 14), 165.

[32] We do not suggest that every mention of water refers to the Spirit; but since the Spirit gives life (6:63), we would find difficulty in dissociating the "living water" of chap. 4 from the Spirit.

[33] This is the basic objection that we would bring against Michaelis' work (*supra,* n. 12). Many of his objections against Cullmann are perfectly valid, but on the whole he seems to demand from the Evangelist a type of indication that we might expect in a twentieth-century writer. This is to narrow overly the symbolic import of Jn.

pel itself that a passage has symbolic reference to a sacrament, and if there is no evidence in the early Church that the passage was understood sacramentally, then we may well rule out a sacramental exegesis. A sacramental symbol that the Evangelist intended to be easily understood without explanation should have left some trace in art or in liturgy or in the writings of the Fathers. Without such assurance, we may suspect that we are dealing with modern imaginative eisegesis.

Let us consider, for instance, Cullmann's[34] interpretation of the foot-washing scene in chap. 13 as a symbol of the Eucharist. Jesus specifically holds up the foot washing as an example of humble and loving service to one's brethren (13:15). Nevertheless, in this scene many have seen a symbolic reference to a sacrament or sacraments. Verse 10 reads: "He who has bathed does not need to wash, except for his feet." The first clause, says Cullmann, "can surely have only this meaning; he who has received Baptism, even when he sins afresh, needs no second Baptism." While we would not attribute to this exegesis the certainty that Cullmann gives it, we believe that some symbolic reference to baptism is solidly probable, and it was well known in antiquity.[35] But Cullmann goes on to maintain

[34] *Op. cit.*, 105–109.

[35] In our pamphlet commentary (*supra*, n. 23), 67–68, we have listed our reasons for seeing a reference to baptism. But this symbolism must be interpreted loosely (we certainly do not mean that this scene is the baptism of the disciples). It is a secondary symbolism, perhaps gained by the fusion of two accounts; in the primary significance we have an example of love, and that is what must be repeated. But the washing, considered as bathing (v. 10), also symbolizes baptism in the sense that it flows from the power of Jesus (compare 13:3 with Mt 28:18–19) and is necessary if we are to have a share with Him in the next life (13:8). The arguments against all sacramental symbolism proposed by Johann Michl, "Der Sinn der Fusswaschung," *Biblica*, 40 (1959), 697–708, fail to appreciate any subtlety in the proposed symbolism. Schnackenburg's treatment, *art. cit.*, 249–251, is much more nuanced.

that the clause "except for his feet," which is of doubtful authenticity,[36] is a symbol of the Eucharist, a sacrament which is meant to be repeated. This is a view shared by Goguel, Loisy, W. Bauer, and Macgregor, who point out the connection between the washing of the feet as a symbol of love and the Eucharist as the sacrament of love. Now antiquity may have seen a reference to penance in this text, but not to the Eucharist. The lack of external support makes the exegesis suspect, especially since foot washing is scarcely a natural symbol for the Eucharist. The statement in v. 14 that the disciples must wash one another's feet would be an exceedingly strange form of a command to repeat the Eucharist. And so, on the basis of our criteria, we would reject this interpretation.

Fourth, if thus far we have accepted some of the criteria of the sacramentalists, and if, in particular, we can employ Niewalda's criterion of traditional symbolism as a negative check, we cannot accept it as the sole positive criterion that he makes it. We agree that the author need not have explicitly explained a symbol, but can we rule out the need for some indications in the text or context?[37] Exegesis is still the determination of the author's intent, and not

---

[36] See M.-E. Boismard, *Revue biblique,* 60 (1953), 353–356. Verse 10 should probably read: "The man who has bathed has no need to wash; he is clean all over." The excision of a reference to the feet delivers us from the exegesis proposed by H. von Campenhausen, "Zur Auslegung von Joh 13, 6–10," *Zeitschrift für die neutestamentliche Wissenschaft,* 33 (1934), 259–271, and championed by Craig, *art. cit.,* 37. These authors have suggested that the idea in v. 10 is that foot washing is valid baptism and that one need not wash the whole body (perhaps a polemic against the disciples of the Baptist). For completeness, we might add that E. Lohmeyer, "Die Fusswaschung," *Zeitschrift für die neutestamentliche Wissenschaft,* 38 (1939), 74–94, saw in the foot washing a symbol of apostolic ordination.

[37] So Niewalda, *op. cit.,* 165: "The logical context is of little or no import, for the association of images is of more import to the man of antiquity than the train of thought."

primarily the determination of the audience's understanding. We agree fully with Schnackenburg that the examination of how others understood the Gospel a century later cannot serve as a sole criterion of interpretation. (On that principle, could we not determine the literal meaning of the Old Testament through its usage in the New Testament?) Such a criterion is especially open to question when we are dealing with something like symbolism, which lends itself to imaginative development.

Let us take an example. For Niewalda,[38] both the healing of the man at Bethesda in chap. 5 and the healing of the blind man in chap. 9 are symbols of the cleansing and healing wrought through baptism. There is good patristic and liturgical evidence for this interpretation of both.[39] Yet, what a difference of internal indication!

a) The main theme of chap. 9 is the opening of the man's eyes to what Jesus really is, in contrast to the blindness of the Pharisees (9:35–41). That baptism was spoken of as "enlightenment" (*phōtismos*) is seen in the New Testament (Heb 6:4; 10:32) and in the earliest patristic evidence.[40] If we turn to chap. 5, we find that the main theme concerns the Sabbath. The dramatic role of the man who was healed is reduced to a minimum. He recovers his

---

[38] *Ibid.*, 166–167. Cullmann, *op. cit.*, 84, 102, accepts both; Corell, *op. cit.*, 62, 67, rejects the first and accepts the second; Michaelis, *op. cit.*, 19, treats only the first and rejects it. D. M. Stanley, S.J., "The Mission of the Son," *Worship*, 33 (1958–1959), 30, seems favorable to the baptismal interpretation of chap. 5.

[39] Niewalda marshals the evidence. Both scenes are connected with baptism in catacomb art. For chap. 5, Tertullian and Chrysostom are among those who see baptismal reference; for chap. 9, Irenaues and Chrysostom. For the lectionary evidence, see Hoskyns, *op. cit.*, 363 ff.

[40] Justin, *Apol.* 1, 61: "This bath is called enlightenment." Notice that the New Testament references are from Heb, an epistle with strong Johannine affinities. See C. Spicq, *L'Epître aux Hébreux*, 1, 2nd. ed. (Paris, 1952), 109–138.

health, but he receives no particular gift of understanding. His healing is simply the occasion for the Sabbath dispute.

b) In chap. 9 there is a specific connection between blindness and sin. The disciples think that physical blindness is an index of sin (9:2). Jesus denies this, but points out (9:4–5) that the healing of this blindness will demonstrate how, as the light of the world, He overcomes night, which is certainly a symbol for Satan's power. At the end (9:41) we hear that the Pharisees are spiritually blind and remain guilty of sin. Thus the whole context lends itself easily to a symbolism of baptism removing sin.[41] On the other hand, the only reference to sin in the Bethesda story is the direction to "sin no more" in 5:14. This direction merely establishes the same connection between Jesus' power over sickness and His power over sin that is common to many miracles in the Synoptics. No figurative aspect of the healing is brought out as in chap. 9. True, the discourse that follows is concerned with the power to give life, but this is in the light of the rabbinic theology that God continues to give life *on the Sabbath.*

c) The man in chap. 9 is healed by washing in water (9:7). The man in chap. 5 is healed by the command of Jesus. In fact, this healing is contrasted with the healing that might have been accomplished by washing in the pool.

d) A symbolism is specified in 9:7 which connects the healing waters with Jesus. Siloam means "sent," and in Jn Jesus is the one sent. There is no such definite symbolism in chap. 5. Some have pointed out that the name of the pool is "Bethesda," which means "place of mercy." Actually, we now know that the Hebrew form of the name was *byt 'šdtyn,* which does not refer to mercy. It is true that there could be a play on the Greek form of the name, but the manuscript evidence is very uncertain as to which

---

[41] Whether or not "blindness from birth," so often mentioned in chap. 9 (vv. 1, 2, 13, 18, 19, 20, 24, 32—the only case in the Gospels) is a deliberate reference to original sin, is more difficult to say.

is the real Greek form (Bethesda, Bezatha, or Bethsaida). In any case, the man was *not* healed in this pool. Another symbolism, suggested by Tertullian, labors under similar difficulties. A reference to baptism is seen in the angel's stirring of the waters and giving healing power to them (even though these waters do not heal the man!). It is well known that the verse that concerns the angel (5:4) is not found in any early Greek manuscript and is probably not authentic.

And so, while Niewalda's external criterion may fit both chap. 5 and chap. 9, there is no parity in the internal indications pointing to sacramental symbolism. It is quite plausible that the Evangelist may have intended a secondary reference to the healing and enlightening power of baptism in chap. 9, but he has left no real indication of a similar intention for chap. 5. Therefore, in our judgment, we should reject the claim for baptismal symbolism in chap. 5.

These observations have led us to two relatively clear criteria for judging the presence of sacramental symbolism in Jn. While there need be no clear identification of the symbolism, there should be some internal, contextual indication. This should be corroborated by the external criterion of good attestation for the sacramental interpretation in early Church art, liturgy, or literature. Now, of course, the combination of these two criteria will give us varying degrees of certitude in our exegesis. At times, as in chap. 9, the evidence may be strong enough to be reasonably probative. At other times, the internal evidence will be somewhat elusive, and the most we can have is a probability. If either criterion is totally unfulfilled, we should reject any sacramental symbolism, rather than allow ourselves to be victimized by accommodation.

APPLICATION OF THE CRITERIA

We shall not attempt to apply these criteria to every example of sacramental symbolism that has been proposed for Jn; some examples would obviously meet the criteria, some would obviously not. Let us take, however, some of the more difficult examples.

First, the baptism of Jesus in the Jordan (Jn 1:19–34). In this scene Cullmann[42] sees the historical origin of Christian baptism and "a pointer to the baptism of the Christian community." This is fairly evident. Jesus' baptism by John marked the beginning of the public proclamation of God's dominion. For His followers, baptism was the means by which men were incorporated into this dominion. The two baptisms were joined because the apostolic kerygma, which began its narrative with the baptism of Jesus, put a demand on the listener to be baptized. The question we wish to decide here, however, is whether *in Jn's account* there is any special baptismal symbolism beyond that which is the common heritage of all the Gospels. We should point out from the start that the external criterion is difficult to apply here, for references to the baptism of Jesus will not always specify Jn's account as the precise source of the symbolism.

The suggestion that Jn's account, in particular, specifies that Christian baptism will be a baptism communicating the Spirit is not too impressive. This is far clearer in the Synoptics (Mk 1:8; par.), where a baptism with a Holy Spirit is directly contrasted with a baptism with water. This contrast is not found in Jn, since 1:33 stands by itself.

Cullmann maintains, however, that Jn 1:26 really presents a deeper insight than the Synoptic contrast, for Jn contrasts John's baptism in water and the person of Jesus: "I am only baptizing in water, but there is one among you whom you do not recognize." The true significance of Christian baptism, Cullmann maintains, is achieved in the person of Jesus Himself—a truth foreshadowed in Jn. Actually, the supposed contrast in v. 26 does not exist. The contrast there is between John the Baptist and the one to come after him. The interrogators have demanded to know

---

[42] *Op. cit.,* 60 ff. Also Corell, *op. cit.,* 55–56; Niewalda, *op. cit.,* 166.

what the exact role of the Baptist is and why he is baptizing. He tells them that they should not worry about him, but about the more important one-to-come who stands in their midst.[43]

Does the fact that Jn 1:33 says that the Spirit rested on Jesus symbolize that Christian baptism will communicate a permanent gift of the Spirit? Jn 1:33 is a reminiscence of the Suffering Servant passage in Is 42:1; and the Suffering Servant theme in the baptism of Jesus is found in all the Gospels (Mk 1:11 also echoes Is 42:1). We might add that the descent of the Spirit on Jesus at the baptism, as described in the Synoptics, is also permanent (see Mt 4:1, where the Spirit conducts Jesus into the desert). Again there is no distinct sacramental symbolism in the Johannine account.

According to Cullmann, Corell, and Niewalda, Jn like Paul connects Christian baptism with the death of Jesus, for the Baptist points Him out (1:29) as "the Lamb of God who takes away the world's sin." Thus, in a baptismal context, Jesus was marked out as one to die for sin. We admit that the Evangelist thinks of the baptism as revealing Jesus to be the Suffering Servant, the Lamb of God (even though Jn does not specifically draw this causal relation, for Jn does not describe the baptism of Jesus as such). Likewise, we admit that the designation of Jesus as the Lamb, at least in its Gospel sense, refers to His death. But how does the fact that Jesus' baptism pointed to His death also signify that from His death would flow Christian baptism? It is true that the Lamb of God who will die for sin (1:29) will also baptize with a Holy Spirit (1:33), but one must admit that there is no hint in Jn of the connection of the two ideas. Is there any more or less connection in the Synoptics between Jesus as the Suffering Servant (Mk 1:11) and baptism with a Holy Spirit (Mk 1:8)?

Thus the special baptismal symbolism attributed to Jn's

[43] Michaelis, *op. cit.*, 2–4.

account of the scene lies in extremely complicated exegesis —exegesis which finds little support in the Gospel itself.

Second, the Cana scene (Jn 2:1–11). Fr. Vawter[44] suggests for this scene a symbolic reference to the sacrament of matrimony, or at least to marriage as a sacred institution in the sense of Eph 5:25, which compares it to the union between Christ and the Church. Vawter stresses the presence of Mary at Cana as the "woman" and draws on what is, in our opinion, the very plausible relation to the figure of the "woman" at the cross (Jn 19:26) and in Ap 12. He thus sees Mary as a symbol of the Church. "The presence of Mary-the-Church at this wedding forecasts the sacramental nature of Christian marriage once the glorification of Jesus is accomplished." Jesus and the Church are present at this marriage, the two terms of the comparison in Eph 5.

In applying our external criterion to this suggestion, we find that most of the ancient evidence connects Cana with the Eucharist or baptism.[45] However, a few of the Fathers[46] do see in the Lord's presence at Cana a tacit attestation of the sanctity of marriage against any encratitic extremes. By way of internal support, Stanley[47] reminds us of the wedding symbolism present in the Old Testament, where marriage symbolizes the relations between God and Israel. Thus, for him, the mention of the wedding at Cana could symbolize the relations of Christ and the Church, which in turn could point to Christian marriage.

In our judgment, neither the external nor the internal evidence for a symbolic reference to matrimony is strong.

---

[44] *Art. cit.* (*supra,* n. 14), 164.

[45] Niewalda, *op. cit.,* 137–138.

[46] For references to Tertullian and Cyril of Alexandria, see M. F. Wiles, *The Spiritual Gospel* (Cambridge, 1960), 42–43. The Fathers mentioned this scene in their treatises on marriage, but that is not exactly the same as seeing the scene as a symbol of Christian matrimony. As Wiles remarks, marriage is never suggested as the essential meaning of the sign.

[47] "Cana as Epiphany," *Worship,* 32 (1957–1958), 83–89.

The wedding is only the backdrop and occasion for the story, and the joining of the man and woman does not have any direct role in the narrative. In the Vawter-Stanley hypothesis we still have an obvious difficulty: Jesus and Mary-the-Church are only present; there is no union between them to symbolize matrimony as in Eph 5. Perhaps our objections smack too much of modern logic, but the proposed symbolism does not seem to have made any particular impression in antiquity either, at least in the form proposed by Vawter and Stanley. We cannot allow, then, any more than a remote possibility to the symbolism.

The Eucharistic reference of changing the water into wine[48] is better supported. Niewalda[49] points out its early occurrence in a fresco in an Alexandrian catacomb, where it is linked to the multiplication of the loaves. St. Irenaeus says that "Mary was hastening the wonderful sign of the wine and wanted before the [appointed] times to partake of the cup of recapitulation."[50] Internally, too, there are many possible hints of Eucharistic symbolism. The changing of water to wine occurs before Passover (2:13), as does the multiplication of the loaves (6:4) and the Last Supper. Thus before Passover we have a wine miracle and a bread miracle; these might be seen as taking the place of the Eucharistic institution, which Jn does not mention.

There is a probable connection with the death of Jesus

[48] Cullmann, *op. cit.*, 66–71 (he sees it as a complement to the baptismal reference proposed for chap. 1); Corell, *op. cit.*, 56–58; Stanley, "Cana," 88; Niewalda, *op. cit.*, 166 (he would not exclude a baptismal reference as suggested by Ephraem the Syrian).

[49] *Op. cit.*, 137 (second or third century).

[50] *Adv. haer.* 3, 16, 7: ". . . conpendii poculo," i.e., as F. Sagnard, O.P., explains it (*Sources chrétiennes*, 34, 295–297, n. 1), the cup "which sums up and concentrates in it the mysteries of salvation, in a striking 'epitome' of the marvels of grace . . . it is the cup of the Eucharist, 'the wonderful sign of the wine' of which Cana is the figure . . . in intimate connection with 'the hour of His passion.'"

in the mention of the hour that was to come (2:4) and would only begin at the Last Supper (13:1). The water becomes wine, as the wine would become blood. The wine at Cana is praised as "the quality wine," the wine of the new dispensation kept until now; and this wine is the means of Jesus' manifesting His glory (2:11 and 17:5). All of these indications, though far from conclusive, do have special significance when we realize that, for the Jew, wine was the blood of the grape.[51] Thus, on the basis of our criteria, we would allow a good probability for the Eucharistic symbolism of Cana.[52]

Third, the cleansing of the Temple (2:13–22). Cullmann[53] suggests this as the other half of the Eucharistic symbolism that we have seen at Cana: there the blood, here the body, of Christ. The Temple does stand for the body of Jesus (2:21); nevertheless, scarcely the Eucharistic body, which in Jn is referred to as "flesh." That this ingenious theory proposed by Cullmann has no real internal support is obvious, nor is there an echo in tradition for Eucharistic symbolism in the cleansing of the Temple.

Also to be rejected is A. Schweitzer's[54] suggestion that the Temple scene is a reference to baptism because it is a fulfillment of Ez 47:1–12, where water flows out from the Temple. While the threatened destruction of the old Temple and its replacement with a temple of messianic nature may have been a fulfillment of a whole battery of Old Testament passages, there is no reason to single out Ez 47 in particular, or to think that the stream of water mentioned there was in the Evangelist's mind.

[51] Gn 49:11; Dt 32:14; Sir 50:15.

[52] Naturally, any sacramental symbolism is secondary. The principal idea seems to be that the old has passed away in favor of a new creation; the replacement of the Jewish purifications; and the plenitude of wine as a sign of the messianic days.

[53] *Op. cit.,* 71–74.

[54] *Op. cit. (supra,* n. 11), 347.

Fourth, a baptismal symbolism has been suggested by Niewalda[55] for the walking on the water (6:16–21), the Good Shepherd discourse (10:1–18), and the Lazarus story (11:1–45). All of these meet to some extent his criterion of traditional symbolism. However, they do not meet any criterion of internal evidence. We can see how Lazarus' return to life might be connected in Christian thought with rebirth by baptism, especially in the light of Paul's theology (Col 2:12), but the Evangelist, who knew both ideas, makes no attempt to connect them. Likewise, the connection of baptism and incorporation into the Shepherd's flock is a logical deduction but scarcely an exegetical one.

Fifth, the anointing at Bethany (12:1–11). Fr. Vawter[56] sees here a symbolic reference to the anointing of the dying. In Jn this scene does not serve to prepare for the physical burial of the Lord, as it does in the Synoptics, for there is a real burial described in Jn 19:39–42 which would make such preparation otiose. Rather, the anointing of chap. 12 prepares for the type of burial we hear of in 12:24, the burial of the seed in the ground so that it may bear rich fruit. Thus the anointing has a connection with the glorification and exaltation of the Lord. Then Vawter tells us: "The day of Christ's burial is the day of the Church." This is somehow connected to the suggestion that the anointing in Jn may symbolize the sacrament of final anointing referred to in Jas 5:14–15. We must humbly admit that the logic of this connection escapes us, unless perhaps the author means that the sacrament of anointing predicts our resurrection as the anointing at Bethany predicted Christ's. However, as has been seen more clearly in recent years, the sacrament of anointing was primarily di-

---

[55] *Op. cit.,* 166–167. He thinks this symbolism in the walking on the water is just possible. Also, he sees a possible reference to penance in the Lazarus story (along with Irenaeus): the power of binding and loosing is related to the loosing of Lazarus' feet.

[56] *Art. cit.,* 159–160.

rected against sickness, not against death.[57] This, plus the
fact that the anointing at Bethany was with perfume
(*myron*) and not oil (*elaion*), removes any internal indications of a symbolic reference to extreme unction. As far
as we know, there is no ancient tradition to support such
symbolism.

Sixth, the allegory of the vine (15:1–8). Many[58] have
seen a Eucharistic reference here. Tradition seems to give
good support to this symbolism, beginning with the blessing
over the chalice reported in the *Didache:* "We thank you,
our Father, for the holy vine of David your servant, that
you have revealed to us through Jesus your servant."[59]
Such an early connection of the vine and the Eucharist is
impressive.

There is internal evidence, too, for sacramental symbolism. The figure of the vine is placed in the setting of
the Last Supper; and even if the Evangelist did not mention the Eucharist at the Supper, we can scarcely believe
that he did not know of its place there. The disciples have
just drunk the Eucharistic wine-made-blood, "the fruit of
the vine" (Mk 14:25). The primary stress in the description of the vine and the branches is on unity; this is also
one of the signal effects of the Eucharist in early Christian
theology (1 Cor 10:17).

There are similarities between the vine-and-the-branch
passage and the Eucharistic section in 6:51–58. The
branch must abide in or remain on the vine; in 6:56 we
hear: "The man who feeds on my flesh and drinks my
blood *abides in* me and I in him." Cut off from the vine,
the branch will wither because life comes to the branch

---

[57] Paul Palmer, S.J., "The Purpose of Anointing the Sick,"
Theological Studies, 19 (1958), 309–344; and Kevin Condon,
"The Sacrament of Healing," *Scripture,* 11 (1959), 33–42.

[58] Cullmann, *op. cit.,* 111–113; Barrett, *op. cit.,* 70–71, 394;
Corell, *op. cit.,* 73–74; Niewalda, *op. cit.,* 167.

[59] *Didache,* 9, 2. For other references see Niewalda, *op. cit.,*
76–79.

through the vine; in 6:57 we hear: "The man who feeds on me will have his life through me." The unity represented by the vine demands love (15:9), love so great as to lay down one's life for one's loved ones (15:13). Thus there is a connection between the fruitful vine and the Lord's death.[60] In 6:51 we hear: "The bread that I shall give is my own flesh for the life of the world"; and we note that "give" here is a reference to giving in death. And so it seems that "I am the real vine" (15:1) is very close to "I am the living bread" (6:51). In their primary meaning both metaphors may refer to divine wisdom as the source of life, but both may also have a secondary reference to the Eucharist.[61] Thus, we believe that the proposed Eucharistic symbolism of chap. 15 meets our criteria satisfactorily.

Seventh, the draught of fish and the meal in chap. 21. The catch of 153 fish in 21:6–8, 10–11 is, as Lk 5:1–11 teaches us, probably a symbol of the mission of conversion, i.e., the fish caught symbolize those converted by the disciples as fishers of men. This is reinforced by the emphasis that the net which was the instrument of the catch was not torn (21:11), a symbol which can be interpreted in reference to the Church. Peter's role as the shepherd in 21:15–17 would fit into this general picture.

Now, since this conversion logically implies baptism, are we to think that the Evangelist had baptism specifically in mind? There is evidence for this in antiquity.[62] The internal

---

[60] Barrett, *op. cit.,* 71: "The union, therefore, of the eucharistic cup is the union of love unto death, the love of the cross."

[61] Cullmann, *op. cit.,* 113, draws still another parallel: the branch which is cast off and is to be burned is a reference to Judas, paralleling the reference to Judas in 6:70. This seems farfetched.

[62] E.g., Ephraem the Syrian; see Niewalda, *op. cit.,* 83. In pictorial representations it would be difficult to distinguish which account of the draught of fish was meant, Jn's or Lk's.

case for baptismal symbolism would be strengthened if St.
Jerome's interpretation of the number 153 is correct. In his
commentary on Ez 47:9–12, he sees a connection between
the scene in Jn and that of the fish caught in the miraculous
stream that flows from Ezekiel's Temple. If Jn had the
Ezekiel passage in mind with the number 153,[63] then the
miraculous stream of baptismal water flowing from the
new temple which is Christ (Jn 7:38; 2:21) could have
been meant. However, this type of exegesis is quite complicated and tentative; it would not allow us to characterize
the baptismal interpretation of the scene as more than
possible.

A similar case can be put forward for Eucharistic symbolism in 21:9, 13, with its meal consisting of fish (*op-
sarion*) and a loaf of bread, to which Jesus invited the
seven disciples (21:2). Niewalda[64] points out that the
representation of a meal with seven at table appears in a
Eucharistic context in catacomb art. There are difficulties,
of course: there is no mention of wine at this meal,[65] nor
is the symbolism of the fish (*ichthys*) for Jesus Christ really
applicable here. However, since the symbolism could be
based on the bread alone, these difficulties are probably
not insurmountable.[66]

[63] In Ez, fishermen stand beside the stream from En-gedi to
En-eglaim. Emerton, *Journal of Theological Studies*, 9 (1958),
86 ff., and Ackroyd, *ibid.*, 10 (1959), 94, calculate how the
letters of these names add up to 153 (in Hebrew and in Greek).

[64] *Op. cit.*, 168. He does not seem to find the evidence for
the Eucharistic interpretation of the passage overwhelming.
Again, it is not always easy to distinguish pictorial representation of the meal in Jn 21 from that of other "Eucharistic"
meals recorded in the New Testament.

[65] However, many are willing to see Eucharistic symbolism
in Lk 24:30, where only bread is mentioned.

[66] Perhaps it is well to remind ourselves that we are not asking whether or not the Eucharist was celebrated on the shores
of the lake, but whether or not the account of the meal has
Eucharistic symbolism. Among those who support Eucharistic

Is there a general basis for Eucharistic symbolism in all the postresurrectional meals in the Gospels? If in the reception of the Eucharist the early Christians awaited the return of the Lord (1 Cor 11:26), they may well have read Eucharistic significance into those meals where the resurrected Lord did appear among men. Certainly the vocabulary used of the meal in Jn 21 is significant in the light of the multiplication of the loaves (Jn 6:11) and of the words that the Synoptics record at the Last Supper:

Jn 21:13: *"Jesus took the bread [gave thanks:* D, Syr^s] *and gave it to them, and did the same with the fish."*

Jn 6:11: *"Jesus took the loaves of bread, gave thanks, and distributed them to those seated there, and did the same with the fish."*

Mk 14:22: *"And taking the bread, he blessed, broke, and gave it to them."*

If there are Eucharistic overtones in the multiplication of the loaves (and we believe there are, not only in Jn, but also in the Synoptic accounts), there may well be Eucharistic overtones in the very similar account in Jn 21. And the description of the postresurrectional meal in Jn 21 may have reminded the Christian of the Last Supper as well. But again, we cannot go beyond possibility.

With this we can bring our treatment to a close. Obviously we have not solved all the difficulties, nor have we proposed foolproof criteria which will work in every instance. But we hope that we have made a contribution toward bringing the proposed Johannine sacramentary under workable control.

---

symbolism are Barrett, *op. cit.,* 484: "This meal was probably intended to call to the minds of the readers eucharistic associations"; Cullmann, *op. cit.,* 15; Lightfoot, *op. cit.,* 343.

APPENDIX

The Johannine Sacramentary

The following is a list of passages in which the various authors mentioned throughout the article have seen sacramental symbolism. In the right margin we indicate how these proposed contributions to the sacramentary meet the criteria that we have set up.

Matrimony: Cana   *Remotely possible*
Extreme Unction: Anointing at Bethany   *Rejected*
Penance: Lazarus   *Rejected*
           Jn 20:23   *Council of Trent*[67]
Baptism: Baptism of Jesus—symbolism beyond
   what is found in the Synoptic accounts   *Rejected*
Cana   *Rejected*
Cleansing of the Temple   *Rejected*
Conversation with Nicodemus   *Acceptable*
Conversation with the Samaritan woman   *Acceptable*
Healing at Bethesda   *Rejected*
The walking on the water   *Rejected*
Source of living waters (7:38)   *Acceptable*
Healing of the man born blind   *Acceptable*
The Good Shepherd   *Rejected*
The raising of Lazarus   *Rejected*
The foot washing   *Acceptable*
The miraculous draught of fish (21)   *Possible*
Eucharist:
Cana   *Acceptable*
Cleansing of the Temple   *Rejected*

[67] *DB* 913. Of course, theologians would have to discuss whether Trent is telling us the mind of the Evangelist in reference to Penance, or simply stating that the power of forgiving sins later exercised in the Church in the Sacrament of Penance is an instance of the power of forgiving sins mentioned in Jn 20:22-23. The latter seems more probable.

"My meat is to do the will of my Father" (4:31–34)	*Rejected*
Chapter 6	*Acceptable*
The foot washing	*Rejected*
The vine and the branches	*Acceptable*
Meal of bread and fish (21)	*Possible*
Baptism and Eucharist:	
Blood and water from the spear thrust (19:34)	*Acceptable*
Water and blood as witnesses (1 Jn 5:8)	*Acceptable*

V

The Eucharist and
Baptism in John

We shall confine ourselves here to two scenes in the Fourth
Gospel: the scene in chap. 6 with the multiplication of the
loaves and the bread of life discourse; and the scene in
chap. 3 containing the conversation with Nicodemus. Previously we have considered the whole question of the Johannine sacramentary,[1] but we believe that an understanding of these two chapters is essential if we wish to pursue
our study of the sacramentary. Not only do they provide
the most explicit references in Jn to the Eucharist and
baptism, but also they provide a key to the composition
of the Fourth Gospel and to the role that sacramentalism
played in the mind of the evangelist.

SECTION ONE: THE EUCHARIST IN CHAPTER 6

Our first and longer treatment will concern chap. 6.[2]

[1] *Supra,* chap. IV.
[2] Note that throughout the article we shall cite chap. 6 according to the standard Greek versification, rather than accord-

The problems here center around the bread of life discourse. *First,* the question of the origin of the discourse: (*a*) Was it spoken by Jesus on a historical occasion; or may we regard it as a free construction of the Evangelist, a homily of the later Church, intended to bring out the meaning of the multiplication of the loaves? (*b*) In particular, what about the section 6:51–58? Could its lofty Eucharistic language have been understood by a Galilean audience before the Last Supper? *Second,* the meaning of the discourse: (*a*) Does the whole discourse on bread refer to the teaching given by Jesus Christ, the Word of God, so that "eating the bread of life" is a figurative description of faith in Jesus, God's incarnate revelation? Many of the Fathers believed this, including Clement of Alexandria, Origen, Augustine. Cajetan championed this view,[3] and it is still defended by many modern scholars (Godet, B. Weiss, Bornhäuser, Odeberg, Schlatter, Strathmann). (*b*) Or does the whole discourse refer to the Eucharist (Loisy, Tobac, Buzy, Cullmann, van den Bussche)? (*c*) Or are there two themes: the first half of the discourse referring to Jesus' teaching, the second half to the Eucharist (Lagrange, E. Schweizer, Menoud, Mollat, Mussner)? (*d*) Or, finally, are there two themes running through the whole discourse, as Léon-Dufour maintains?

---

ing to the Vulgate-Confraternity versification which from 6:51 on is one verse ahead of the Greek (e.g., Vulgate 6:60 = Greek 6:59).

[3] The Hussites, accepting a Eucharistic meaning for 6:51–58, interpreted 6:53 as a precept to receive Communion under two species. Cajetan and some of the Tridentine theologians held to a non-Eucharistic interpretation of chap. 6 as a refutation of this heresy. See F. Cavallera, "L'interprétation du chapitre VI de saint Jean. Une controverse exégétique au Concile de Trente," *Revue d'Histoire Ecclésiastique* (1909), 687–709. For patristic opinions see Edmund Siedlecki, *A Patristic Synthesis of John VI,* 54–55 (Mundelein Dissertation, 1956).

1. THE ORIGIN OF THE DISCOURSE

Let us approach the problem step by step. The theory that the discourse is a purely imaginative composition of the Evangelist, without any foundation in the words of Jesus,[4] may be questioned on scientific grounds. Bertil Gärtner[5] has shown that there is a close parallel between the sequence of events in chap. 6 of Jn and the sequence in the narrative of Mk 6:30–54 and 8:11–33. Thus the general framework of Jn 6 is a traditional one witnessed in the Marcan kerygma.

As for the basic phrasing of the theme in Jn 6, namely, the new manna from heaven, we have every reason to believe that this is authentic too. Jesus spoke in a synagogue at Capernaum (6:59); and we may well reason that, according to His custom (Lk 4:16–21), His remarks were based on the scriptural reading. Recent study[6] has established with some plausibility the lectionaries for the synagogue in the time of Jesus, and among the readings in the season of Passover (6:4) were the accounts of the manna in Ex 16 and Nm 11, as well as Is 54 (cited in Jn 6:45).[7] Thus the discourse on the bread of life employing the symbolism of the manna fits perfectly into the historical scene described by John.

Nevertheless, as in other Gospel discourses, we need not

[4] *DB* 2016 lists among the modernist errors the theory that the Johannine discourses are theological meditations lacking historical truth. Also see the decree of the Biblical Commission (*DB* 2112).

[5] *John 6 and the Jewish Passover* (Lund, 1959). See below, pp. 202 and 265.

[6] Aileen Guilding, *The Fourth Gospel and Jewish Worship* (New York, 1960). For precautions see the review in *Catholic Biblical Quarterly,* 22 (1960), 459–461.

[7] Another reading was that of the tree of life in Gn 3; compare Gn 3:3 with Jn 6:50, Gn 3:22 with Jn 6:51, Gn 3:24 with Jn 6:37.

believe that we have a tape recording of Jesus' words. The Evangelists evidence a freedom of *selection* in recording the words of the Master (Jn 21:25). By way of *addition* they often collected various sayings of Jesus on a particular subject to supplement an original discourse (e.g., Mt's Sermon on the Mount). And so we shall see that it is not impossible that the second part of the bread of life discourse (6:51–58) was brought from another and more original setting to be added here.[8]

One formative influence that has been suggested for the discourse of Jn 6 is the liturgical celebration of a Christian Passover.[9] Although the existence of such a feast in the early Church cannot be established with certainty, there are good reasons for believing that there was a Christian Passover feast modeled on the Jewish one, a feast in which the story of the exodus would have been treated as a type of the deliverance wrought by Christ, the Paschal Lamb.[10]

[8] The general principles of Gospel formation enunciated in this paragraph are admitted by the most respected Catholic scholars. F. Prat, S.J., *Life of Christ* (Milwaukee, 1957) I, 28–29, says of the Johannine discourses: ". . . we do not claim that he [John] gives them word for word"; Prat admits that some of the discourses may be composite collections of sayings uttered at different times. G. Ricciotti, *Life of Christ* (Milwaukee, 1947), 388–389, in reference to Jn 6: "Hence the discourse as we have it today is a composite which has collected about a chronologically compact nucleus other sayings of Jesus that do not belong to the same occasion but are related to the same subject. This method of composition, part chronological and part logical, was usual in John's catechesis no less than in that of the other Apostles, and the early Fathers or teachers recognized the fact and acknowledged it far in advance of our modern scholars." Also see above, Postscript to chap. I.

[9] Edward J. Kilmartin, S.J., "Liturgical Influence on John 6," *Catholic Biblical Quarterly,* 22 (1960), 183–191. Also *Scripture,* 12 (1960), 75–78.

[10] We may have an echo of this in 1 Cor 5:7, "Christ, our Passover, has been sacrificed." (This epistle was written around Passover time in A.D. 57.) Also see the typology in 10:1–5.

That the discourse of Jn 6, with its reinterpretation of the manna, would fit well into such a setting is obvious. And, as we shall see, it is quite plausible that the second half of the discourse (6:51–58) with its strong Eucharistic flavor, owes its incorporation into Jn 6 to just such a feast (a Christian Passover feast would have some reference to the Last Supper, the Passover celebrated by Jesus, and to the Eucharist which was the central act of the Last Supper).

Some would go even further and make the Passover liturgy the model for the composition of the whole discourse in Jn 6. In this direction Gärtner, Ziener,[11] and Kilmartin have carefully studied the Jewish Passover ritual as a key to the ritual of the postulated Christian Passover. During the Jewish Passover meal four children ask questions about what is being enacted, and these are compared to the questions of the Jews in Jn 6. First, the wise child asks about the laws of God; so in Jn 6:28 the Jews ask, "How are we to set about this 'working' of God's works?" Second, a child who is too young to ask questions is taught about passages in Scripture; so in 6:32 Jesus interprets the Scripture passages about the manna (after being asked, however). Third, the wicked child asks a question which implies ridicule; so the Jews ridicule Jesus in 6:41–42. Finally, the sincere child asks a practical question about application to daily life; so the Jews ask (6:52), "How can this fellow give us his flesh to eat?"

Personally we find such similarities artificial. Actually the singling out of the first two questions given above is somewhat forced, for in the section 6:25–34 there are more than two questions (e.g., v. 25, v. 34), and the other ques-

---

[11] G. Ziener, "Johannesevangelium und urchristliche Passafeier," *Biblische Zeitschrift*, 2 (1958), 263–274, has a complicated theory of relating Jn to the Jewish Passover. He draws good comparisons between Jn and the Book of Wisdom (part of Wis is a midrash on the exodus) and suggests that the Passover ritual was the source of both. There are possibilities in the theory but it defies proof; the traditions found in Wis could have been known to Jesus Himself.

tions have to be neglected to save the parallel to the Passover meal.[12] To be precise, the question format of chap. 6 is simply an example of the technique of Johannine misunderstanding, and needs no explanation from the Jewish Passover ritual. We may compare chap. 6 and chap. 4 to show how the technique is used:

Jn 4	Jn 6
Ques. [9] "How do you, a Jew, ask me, a Samaritan, for a drink?"	Ques. [25] "Rabbi, when did you come here?"
Ans. [13] "Everyone who drinks water like this will be thirsty again."	Ans. [27] "You should not be working for perishable food."
Ques. [11-12] "Where, then, are you going to get this living water? Surely you don't pretend to be greater than our ancestor Jacob who gave us this well?"	Ques. [30-31] "What sign are you going to perform for us to see? Our ancestors had manna to eat in the desert."
Ans. [14] "The water that I give him will become an internal fountain of water leaping up for eternal life."	Ans. [32-33] "My Father gives you the real bread from heaven. God's bread comes down from heaven and gives life to the world."
Reaction [15] "Sir, give me this water so that I will not get thirsty."	Reaction [34] "Sir, give us this bread all the time."

Since there is no question of an influence of the Passover ritual on the questions of Jn 4, it is not clear why we should see such influence on the questions of Jn 6. The suggested Passover influence breaks down completely when it is applied to the last two of "the four questions," 6:41–42 and 6:52. In the Passover ritual these last two questions are

---

[12] The material of this section of Jn closely parallels Mk 8:1–13; this makes us suspicious of an attempt to base the questions in Jn on an artificial parallel to the Passover ritual.

truly different, one asked by a wicked child, one asked by a sincere child; in Jn these two questions are perfectly parallel, both skeptical and serving identical functions in the narrative.

In short, there may be some influence of the Christian Passover ritual on the preservation and form of Jn 6 (especially on the incorporation of 6:51–58), but we believe that this influence was only secondary. There is no solid evidence that the *whole* pattern of Jn 6 was borrowed from the Passover ritual.

2. THE MEANING OF THE DISCOURSE

Having rooted the basic subject matter of Jn 6 in the deeds and words of Jesus, we come to the question of the meaning of the discourse. Following the obvious indications of the text, we reject from the start the extreme theories which see the whole discourse as referring solely to the teaching of Jesus or as referring solely to the Eucharist. There are statements which indicate quite clearly that Jesus, in speaking about "the bread of life," is referring to doctrine to be believed (6:35, 40, 45, 47). On the other hand, there are statements that just as clearly refer to the Eucharist. One need only compare 6:51[c] to the Lucan Eucharistic formula:

Lk 22:19: "This is my body which is given for you."
Jn 6:51[c]: "The bread that I shall give is my flesh for the life of the world."

The combination of "flesh" and "blood" in 6:53–56, and the use of the realistic verb *trōgō* ("to feed on") are other Eucharistic indications. Thus we must see both doctrinal and Eucharistic themes in Jn 6.

However, it has become increasingly evident that we cannot simply cut the discourse in two so that the first half refers exclusively to the sapiential theme, and the Eucharist does not enter until the second half.[13] The Eucharistic theme runs through the whole discourse, beginning with the multiplication of the loaves itself. In all the Gospels the description of the multiplication(s) of the loaves has Eucharistic overtones since Jesus' action is described in the same terms as His action at the Last Supper:

Multiplication for the 5000 (Mk 6:41): "And taking the five loaves and the two fish, he looked up to heaven, and blessed [*eulogēsen*] and broke up [*kateklasen*] the loaves and gave [*edidou*] them to the disciples to set out for them [the people]."

Multiplication for the 4000 (Mk 8:6): "And taking the seven loaves, he gave thanks [*eucharistēsas*], broke [*eklasen*] and gave [*edidou*] them to his disciples to set out."

Eucharist (Mk 14:22): "And taking bread, he blessed [*eulogēsas*], broke [*eklasen*] and gave [*edōken*] to them."

(Jn 6:11): "Jesus took the loaves and, having given thanks [*eucharistēsas*], distributed [*diedōken*] to those reclining."

While John omits the breaking of the bread, his use of *eucharisteō* in the multiplication of the loaves may be an attempt to underline the Eucharistic signification.[14]

[13] Such a "half and half" theory has been favored by those who regard the second half of the discourse (6:51b–58) as an editorial insertion of sacramental theology. For Bultmann, the real Gospel of John was nonsacramental, and a sacramental passage like 6:51b–58 was the work of an ecclesiastical redactor who tried to make the Gospel conform to common Church theology. For other views of this type see chap. IV.

[14] *Eucharisteō* is the verb found in the Pauline-Lucan accounts of the institution (1 Cor 11:24; Lk 22:19); eventually it became the technical term from which the sacrament took its name. *Eucharisteō* and *eulogeō* both mean "to praise" and represent the Hebrew verb *bārak*. We might note that in Jn 6 *eucharisteō* also appears in v. 23, in that section (vv. 22–24) which is used by the editor to connect the multiplication of the

Also, in Jn, Jesus Himself distributes the bread as He did
at the Last Supper, rather than having His disciples do it
as in the Synoptic multiplication narratives. Only in Jn
(6:12) does Jesus tell the disciples to bring together
(*synagō*—a word with Eucharistic connections[15]) the fragments (*klasmata*).[16] Both these Greek words appear in
the very early Eucharistic formula of the *Didache* (9:4):[17]
"As this fragment of bread [*klasma*] was scattered over the
mountains and brought together [*synachthēsan*] into one, so
may your Church be brought together from the four corners of the earth into your kingdom." These Eucharistic
hints could scarcely have been overlooked by John's Christian audience, especially when 6:4 places the whole chapter
in the same Passover setting as the Last Supper.

There are Eucharistic elements further on in the chapter,
in the introduction to the bread of life discourse. In 6:27
Jesus prepares for the theme of the bread of life by instructing the crowd not to labor for perishable food. This
is obviously a reference to the command in v. 12, "Collect
the fragments [*klasmata*] that are left over so that nothing
will *perish*." The natural, perishable food of everyday life
is thus contrasted to the fragments of the multiplied loaves.

---

loaves and the bread of life discourse. The Eucharistic overtones of the multiplication are intended to last into the discourse.

[15] It is the verb from which we draw the term *synaxis* which
refers to the first part of the Mass.

[16] The word *klasmata* also appears in the Synoptic accounts.
Its use in the *Didache* suggests that it was a common term for
the Eucharistic hosts in the early Church. The cognate noun,
klasis, appears in "the breaking of the bread," a designation of
the Eucharistic meal, and the verb *klaō* appears in the accounts
of the institution.

[17] C. F. D. Moule, "A Note on *Didache* IX, 4," *Journal of
Theological Studies*, 6 (1955), 240–243, presents a strong case
for Jn 6 as the background of the *Didache* passage. Only Jn
(6:3) puts the multiplication and, hence, the scattering of the
fragments on a mountain; only Jn (6:15) connects the scene to
the kingship of Christ.

In 6:31 the Jews bring up the theme of the manna, the bread from heaven,[18] which supplies Jesus with the basic terminology for the bread of life discourse. It is quite likely that the early Church of New Testament times treated manna as a Eucharistic symbol.[19] For instance, 1 Cor 10:3 implicitly contrasts the food (manna) and drink (water from the rock) of the exodus with the Christian food and drink (10:16), the Eucharist.

The fact that there are indications of Eucharistic allusions in the introduction to the first part of the bread of life discourse by no means signifies that 6:35–50 refers primarily to the Eucharist. Rather, as we have mentioned, the primary meaning of the bread of life in 6:35–50 is sapiential. The Jews have misunderstood the multiplication of the loaves and the surplus of fragments; they have thought that Jesus is a second Moses (6:14) come in the last times to repeat the physical miracle of the manna (6:31). The answer given to them is that the new bread from heaven is not physical, but is Jesus' own person, the divine Word descended from heaven to teach men (see Dt 8:3). That this bread is also the Eucharist is only a secondary theme. Yet, if the primary theme is sapiential, the whole concept of divine wisdom as spiritual nourishment is, as Feuillet[20] has pointed out, closely related to the

---

[18] Ex 16:4, 15; Ps 105:40; Ps 78:24; Neh 9:15. Passages of this type are the background for Jn 6:31. The Synoptic counterpart of the Jews' request for manna is in Mk 8:11 ff., where the Pharisees ask for a sign and where Jesus gives His disciples a lecture on taking bread without the leaven of the Pharisees. This theme of unleavened bread could also have Eucharistic overtones.

[19] We are not certain of a Eucharistic reference for the manna in Ap 2:17. There is a good possibility that the "Give us today our future [?] bread" in the Pater Noster is a reference to the manna and the Eucharist. See chap. XII, below, pp. 242–243.

[20] "Les thèmes bibliques majeurs du discours sur le pain de vie (Jn 6)," *Nouvelle Revue Théologique*, 82 (1960), 814–822.

concept of the messianic banquet and the Eucharist. For instance, Jn 6:35 is drawn from the description of wisdom in Sir 24:20:

> "He who eats of me will hunger still;
> he who drinks of me will thirst for more."

It is this same section of Sir (24:17), "I bud forth delights like the vine," which may serve as the background of the vine passage (Jn 15:1) spoken at the Last Supper, a passage which in its context may well be Eucharistic.[21] Again, Jn 6:45 is quoted from Is 54:13; just a few verses later (55:1–3) Is gives a description of the messianic banquet. Thus, to preserve the full meaning of the Old Testament sources for the sapiential theme, we must see in the bread of life a reference to the Eucharist as well as to Jesus' teaching.

In the second part of the discourse (6:51–58), however, the Eucharistic theme comes to the forefront and dominates the stage. Rather than the bread of life which must be received through faith, we now have the *living* bread which must be *eaten* (nay, "fed upon"—*trōgō*), bread identified with the flesh of Jesus. And the theme of drinking, hitherto hinted at only in passing in 6:35, is now placed on an equal level with eating: the blood of the Son of Man must be drunk. Also, the verb "give" in v. 51 and the notion of blood which must be poured forth if it is to be drunk indicate that the factor of sacrifice has entered into the narrative. In all of this, the sapiential theme has receded into the background. Thus we part company from Father Xavier Léon-Dufour[22] who main-

---

This article has now been translated in *Johannine Studies* (Alba House, 1964).

[21] See above, pp. 102–103.

[22] "Le mystère du pain de vie (Jean VI)," *Recherches de Science Religieuse*, 46 (1958), 481–523. Léon-Dufour divides the discourse into vv. 35–47 and 48–58. He finds evidence for the sapiential theme in vv. 48–50, which for him are the second

tains that the whole discourse is to be interpreted on two levels of meaning, sapiential and sacramental. We admit this for the first part of the discourse (6:35–50), but we believe that 6:51–58 is solely sacramental.

Once we admit that the second part of the discourse refers to the Eucharist, we must ask ourselves the question proposed by Lagrange: How could an unprepared Galilean audience, or for that matter the disciples themselves, have understood such a Eucharistic reference?[23] They might have understood the primary sapiential theme of the first half of the discourse,[24] but the second half of the dis-

---

part of the discourse. This we would admit for in our division these verses belong to the first part of the discourse. Part of Léon-Dufour's reason for insisting on a sapiential reading in 51 ff. is that the hearers could not have understood a Eucharistic significance. Again we agree, but we do not believe that 51–58 were spoken on this occasion and hence the problem did not arise. We should note that Léon-Dufour insists that in the second part of the discourse the theme is centered not only on the person of Jesus but also on His sacrifice (thus there is a progress in the two parts of the discourse from the Incarnation to the Redemption). He says (515–516): "Jesus, therefore, invited His contemporaries to find life by faith in His person and His redemptive sacrifice." Personally, we doubt that any Galilean audience could have understood such references to His sacrifice; and if they are present, it is one more reason to remove the second part of the discourse from the scene in Galilee. Feuillet, *art. cit.*, 1055–1056, also finds difficulty with Léon-Dufour's interpretation of the second part of the discourse as primarily sapiential.

[23] Some claim that such a question is meaningless, for John was writing the Gospel for a Christian audience. However, we believe that the Gospel has its roots in the words and deeds of Jesus. True, there may have been a reinterpretation and extension of the meaning of these words and deeds for the Christian audience, but we can also ask what these words and deeds meant in their original milieu in the public life of Jesus.

[24] The secondary sacramental theme of the first half of the discourse would have been understood only by a Christian audience after the Resurrection under the light of the Spirit.

course would seem to be beyond the understanding of those not already familiar with the Eucharist. Feuillet[25] observes: "It is quite improbable that Jesus would have ever spoken to His audience [of the Eucharist] in such precise terms during His public ministry." These considerations lead us to believe that 6:51–58 was not originally part of the discourse on the bread of life.

Are we not, then, forced to the position that we rejected at the beginning of the paper, namely, that this section is a non-Johannine interpolation? Not at all, for we maintain that it is a *Johannine* interpolation.[26] Recently, Eugen Ruckstuhl[27] has refuted all attempts to show that the lan-

---

[25] *Art. cit.*, 1056. Another Catholic supporter of the theory that 6:51–58 belongs to another occasion is A. Wikenhauser, *Das Evangelium nach Johannes*, 2 ed. (Regensburg, 1957), 135–136. For a general statement of principle see n. 8 above.

[26] This statement implies a modern, scientific approach to the problem of the composition of the Fourth Gospel. Tradition makes John son of Zebedee the author of this Gospel, but "author" should be understood in the broad biblical applicability of the term and not necessarily in the restricted sense of writer. A workable *hypothesis* of the origins of the Gospel implies the existence of a Johannine school of disciples. One may posit the following steps in the composition of the Gospel: (1) A body of traditional material about Jesus which had come down from John—this material would be similar to source material underlying the Synoptic Gospels in terms of antiquity and historical value. (2) This material was preached, developed, and formed over a number of years by John and disciples under his guidance. (3) A disciple of John organized the developed material from stage 2 into a written Gospel, a Gospel which subsequently may have undergone several editions. (4) After John's death another disciple gave the Gospel a final editing or redaction in which new Johannine material from stage 2 was incorporated and, consequently, some Gospel material was rearranged. It is the work of this last stage that is referred to as Johannine interpolation.

[27] *Die literarische Einheit des Johannesevangeliums* (Freiburg, 1951), 220–271.

guage of 6:51–58 is not Johannine, and he thinks that there is enough evidence to characterize the section as genuinely Johannine.[28] And, as we have pointed out, the sacramental import of this section is not contrary to the rest of the chapter; 6:51–58 simply specifies and clarifies a theme which underlies the whole scene.

Naturally, we can only surmise about the origins of this interpolation. Nevertheless, we see a great deal of truth in the oft-made observation that the specific Eucharistic language of 6:51–58 fits in better with the setting of the Last Supper than with any other scene in Jesus' life. The absence of an account of the Eucharistic institution in the Johannine account of the Last Supper has always been an embarrassment. May not the answer be that in the editing of the Gospel the Johannine account of the Eucharist has been transplanted to chap. 6[29] and made a part of the bread of life discourse in order to bring out more clearly the truth that Jesus is the food of man, not only as divine wisdom, but also in the sacrament? We have seen above how closely 6:51ᶜ resembles the Eucharistic institution for-

---

[28] Eduard Schweizer, "Das johanneische Zeugnis vom Herrenmahl," *Evangelische Theologie,* 12 (1952–1953), 353–354, another expert on Johannine characteristics, thinks that no decision on the authenticity of 6:51ᵇ–58 is possible on linguistic grounds. Nevertheless, Ruckstuhl's arguments have convinced J. Jeremias that the section is Johannine, see "Joh 6:51ᶜ–58— redacktionell?" *Zeitschrift für die neutestamentliche Wissenschaft,* 44 (1952–1953), 256–257.

[29] This would not be the only example in Jn of such transplanting of Holy Week scenes for interpretative reasons. The best solution of the problem about the cleansing of the Temple seems to be that it occurred during the last days of Jesus' life as reported in the Synoptics. Jn's placing of the scene at the beginning of the ministry serves to highlight two themes: (*a*) Jesus as the replacement of Jewish institutions, a theme developed throughout the Gospel; (*b*) the fulfillment of Mal 3:1: first the messenger is sent, i.e., John the Baptist as reported in Jn 1; then the Lord comes to the Temple in the cleansing scene of Jn 2.

mula found in the Pauline-Lucan tradition; this verse could
well be called the Johannine institution formula.[30]

If our theory is correct, the Eucharistic words of Jesus
spoken at the Last Supper were introduced into chap. 6
by blending these words with phrases from the original
bread of life discourse. Thus the final product was a second
bread of life discourse (6:51–58) centered on the Eucharist but carefully paralleling the first discourse (6:35–50).
We have indicated the parallels in an accompanying chart
which places the two discourses side by side. We do not
claim that the composition of the second discourse was a
purely literary process. It could well have been the product
of liturgical preaching in which the Lord's words on the
bread of life were combined with His Eucharistic words.
Nevertheless, there is surely some literary artistry in the
final construction of chap. 6 with the two carefully balanced discourses.[31] Both discourses begin with the theme

[30] The word "flesh" in the Johannine formula ("The bread
that I shall give is my own flesh for the life of the world") is
probably closer to the original Aramaic expression of Jesus
than is the word "body" which occurs in the other Eucharistic
formulae. Jn and Lk both have the idea of the flesh or body
being *given*. In considering the Pauline-Lucan formula J.
Jeremias has called into doubt the originality of this phrase
"which is [given] for you," because of the difficulty of retrovert-
ing it into Aramaic. Yet the fact that a similar expression is
preserved in the Johannine tradition which is often independent
and often archaic is an argument against Jeremias. The use of
didōmi by Jn in 6:51c is unusual (*tithēmi* is the normal expression for the laying down of life, as in 10:11, 15; 13:37;
15:13); the use of the verb may have been influenced by 6:11.

[31] In this process of construction perhaps we can allow some
weight to P. Borgen's suggestion, "The Unity of the Discourse
in John 6," *Zeitschrift für die neutestamentliche Wissenschaft*,
50 (1959), 277–278, that in vv. 51–58 we have a commentary
on the "eat" of v. 31: "He gave them bread from heaven *to
eat*." For Borgen this proves that there is a unity in the discourse
as it now stands since the other terms of the Old Testament
citation in v. 31 are explained in vv. 35–50. He expressly states

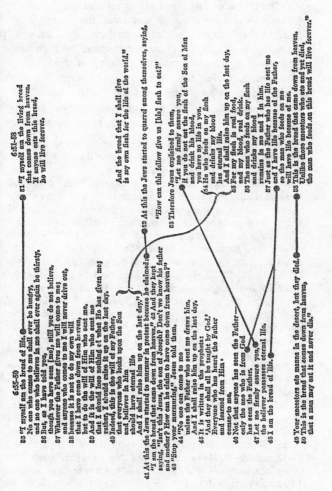

6:35-50

35 "I myself am the bread of life.
No one who comes to me shall ever be hungry,
and no one who believes in me shall ever again be thirsty.
36 But, as I have told you,
though you have seen [me], still you do not believe.
37 Whatever the Father gives me will come to me;
and anyone who comes to me I will never drive out,
38 because it is not to do my own will
that I have come down from heaven,
but to do the will of Him who sent me.
39 And it is the will of Him who sent me
that I should lose nothing of what He has given me;
rather, I should raise it up on the last day.
40 Indeed, this is the will of my Father,
that everyone who looks upon the Son
and believes in him
should have eternal life
And I shall raise him up on the last day."
41 At this the Jews started to murmur in protest because he claimed,
"I am the bread that came down from heaven," 42 And they kept
saying, "Isn't this Jesus, the son of Joseph? Don't we know his father
and mother? How can he claim to have come down from heaven?"
43 "Stop your murmuring," Jesus told them.
44 "No one can come to me
unless the Father who sent me draws him.
And I shall raise him up on the last day.
45 It is written in the prophets:
'And they shall all be taught by God.'
Everyone who has heard the Father
and learned from Him,
comes to me.
46 Not that anyone has seen the Father—
only the one who is from God
has seen the Father.
47 Let me firmly assure you,
the believer possesses eternal life.
48 I am the bread of life.
49 Your ancestors ate manna in the desert, but they died.
50 This is the bread that comes down from heaven,
that a man may eat it and never die."

6:51-58

51 "I myself am the living bread
that comes down from heaven.
If anyone eats this bread,
he will live forever."

And the bread that I shall give
is my own flesh for the life of the world."

52 At this the Jews started to quarrel among themselves, saying,

"How can this fellow give us [his] flesh to eat?"

53 Therefore Jesus explained to them,

"Let me firmly assure you,
if you do not eat the flesh of the Son of Man
and drink his blood,
you have no life in you.
54 He who feeds on my flesh
and drinks my blood
has eternal life.
And I shall raise him up on the last day.
55 For my flesh is real food,
and my blood, real drink.
56 The man who feeds on my flesh
and drinks my blood
remains in me and I in him.
57 Just as the Father who has life sent me
and I have life because of the Father,
so the man who feeds on me
will have life because of me.
58 This is the bread that came down from heaven.
Unlike those ancestors who ate and yet died,
the man who feeds on this bread will live forever."

of Jesus as the bread of life or living bread; both end
with the theme of this bread giving immortality, something
denied to the Israelites who had eaten the manna in the
desert. Both discourses are interrupted by a question which
shows the basic Jewish misunderstanding. In both cases
the answer clarifies the primary meaning of the bread: v.
45 mentions divine teaching; vv. 53–54 stress the flesh
and blood of Jesus. Notice also the double "amen" formula (translated as "Let me firmly assure you") in vv.
47 and 53; and the resurrection theme in vv. 40 and 54.[32]

---

that this does not prove the historical unity of the discourse,
for he admits that various sources supplied the material which
has now been woven into a literary unity.

[32] It will be noted that some of these parallels (especially
those of similar beginnings and similar endings) hinge on making the division of the two discourses between vv. 50 and 51.
This is not a division that all would accept. Johannes Schneider,
"Zur Frage der Komposition von Joh 6, 27–58(59)," *In Memoriam Ernst Lohmeyer,* ed. by W. Schmauch (Stuttgart, 1951),
132–142, prefers a division based on the questions of the Jews:
27–40, 41–51, 52–58. This destroys the obvious parallelism between 35 and 51 (Schneider actually makes 51 serve a double
role, ending the second section and introducing the third). H.
Schürmann, "Joh 6, 51c—ein Schlussel zur johanneischen
Brotrede," *Biblische Zeitschrift,* 2 (1958), 244–262, divides the
discourse into 26–52 and 53–58. He believes the primary reference in v. 51c is to the death on Calvary rather than to the
Eucharist, and so this verse belongs to the first section. However,
as we have insisted, v. 51 contains what is virtually an institu-
tional formula with a Eucharistic emphasis that cannot be
denied. There is present in v. 51 a reference to the sacrificial
death, as there is also in the Pauline-Lucan formula of institution, but this does not make v. 51 less Eucharistic. Finally,
Léon-Dufour, *art. cit.,* has argued strongly for a division into
35–47 and 48–58. He points out that then both parts begin with
"I am the bread of life" (vv. 35, 48). Our division achieves
the same result as far as the beginnings of the two discourses
are concerned, and, in addition, has the same endings for each
discourse, which Léon-Dufour's division does not. In fact, v.
48 is not the beginning of a new section, but achieves an inclu-

What prompted this juxtaposing of the two discourses? As we have mentioned, the second discourse with its clear Eucharistic theme serves to bring out the Eucharistic meaning which is latent and secondary in the first discourse. Such a clarification may have had its *Sitz-im-leben* in the Christian Passover service referred to above. The fact that the original bread of life discourse (35–50) had its Johannine setting near Passover time and that it mentioned the manna and the Israelites in the desert would make it a reading admirably suited for a Christian Passover. Naturally, the Christian feast would also re-present the Lord's action on the Passover eve before He died. Thus the bread of life discourse and the Eucharistic action may have been placed in close juxtaposition by the liturgy itself. This, of course, is only an hypothesis, but it is not implausible. In the Mass itself we have a juxtaposition like that of chap. 6. Just as the first discourse in chap. 6 primarily treats of Jesus' divine teaching, so the first part of the Mass contains the teaching word of God as presented to us in Scripture (Lesson and Gospel—Old Testament and New Testament) and by the Church (homily). In each case this first part prepares us for the Word of God who is to come to us sacramentally in the Eucharist; and the second discourse in chap. 6, just as the second part of the Mass (the Offertory and Canon) is centered on the Eucharist. It is this same twofold sapiential-sacramental approach that St. Thomas gives us in the antiphons of Lauds on the feast of Corpus Christi:[33]

---

sion with v. 35, and this inclusion marked the end of the original bread of life discourse (35–50). One of Léon-Dufour's main arguments for his division is that the theme of the second part of the discourse (for him, 48–58) is "give . . . eat," verbs that are not used of the bread of life with any frequency in the first half of the discourse. Actually, however, the verb "give" begins to appear only in v. 51 ff.

[33] Feuillet, *art. cit.* (*supra,* n. 20), 1059–1060.

Ant. 1:   *Wisdom* has built herself a house;
          she has mixed her wine and set her table (Prv
          9:1–2).
Ant. 2:   You have nourished your people with the bread
          of angels, and you have supplied them with
          bread from heaven.

In concluding our remarks on chap. 6, we would point
out that it is only a theory such as the one we have suggested[34] that meets all the complexities of the chapter: (*a*)
there are Eucharistic overtones throughout the chapter;
(*b*) vv. 35–50 have primarily a sapiential theme; (*c*) the
Eucharistic reference in vv. 51–58 is much clearer than
that of the rest of the chapter, and is the primary sense of
the passage; (*d*) there is a certain abrupt shift of emphasis
between the two sections of chap. 6 (35–50 and 51–58);
(*e*) vv. 60 ff. refer more directly to 35–50 than to 51–58;[35]

[34] Elements of this theory can be found in the articles of J.
Jeremias (*supra*, n. 28) and of A. Feuillet.

[35] G. Bornkamm, "Die eucharistiche Rede im Johannes-
Evangelium," *Zeitschrift für die neutestamentliche Wissenschaft*,
47 (1956), 161–169. He points out that there is no reference to
the Eucharist in vv. 60 ff., no reference to "eating . . . drinking." Rather, the topics are belief (64), coming to Jesus (65),
and the *words* of life (68)—all topics which match the
sapiential theme of 35–50. In particular, the elliptic sentence of
v. 62, "If then you behold the Son of Man ascending [*ana-
bainō*] to where he was before," makes better sense if the Jews
have just been complaining about His coming down (*kata-
bainō*), as reported in vv. 41–43. Also we might note that the
theme of "murmuring" is shared by vv. 61 and 41; and the
theme of selection by the Father in vv. 65 and 37. Not all agree,
however, with Bornkamm's argument for a connection between
35–50 and 60 ff. Among the dissenters are Wilhelm Wilkens,
"Das Abendmahlszeugnis im vierten Evangelium," *Evangelische
Theologie*, 18 (1958), 362 ff.; and H. Schürmann, as summarized
in *New Testament Abstracts*, 4 (1959), #116. One argument
advanced is that the "flesh" of 6:63 refers to the flesh mentioned
in 6:51–58. We doubt this, for 6:63 fits more into the sapien-

(*f*) there is no account of the institution of the Eucharist in the Johannine narrative of the Last Supper; (*g*) there may be a strong liturgical influence of a Christian Passover ritual on Jn 6.

SECTION TWO: BAPTISM IN CHAPTER 3

In chap. 3 we are faced with a situation very similar to that of chap. 6. The burden of Jesus' remarks to Nicodemus is that to see or enter God's kingdom man must be begotten from above (3:3), begotten of Spirit (3:5).[36] The reason advanced is that flesh can beget only flesh, while only Spirit can beget spirit. Man, who is on the natural level, the level of flesh, cannot reach the divine level unless God raises him up or, more exactly, unless God causes him to be begotten over again, this time in the supernatural world. Just as at creation God brought man into being by breathing into the dust the breath of life, so is this new gift of life communicated through the divine Spirit or breath.[37] It is the heavenly Son of Man who has descended from heaven (3:13) who communicates this Spirit that is the agent of begetting from above. To the man who believes, Jesus will communicate the Spirit once He has been

---

tial theme than it does into the Eucharistic theme. "It is the Spirit that is the life-giving factor; the flesh is of no value" is a direct parallel to Jn 3:6, "Flesh begets flesh, and Spirit begets spirit." The contrast is between the materialistic and spiritual orders of knowledge (see 6:27), a contrast found many times in the New Testament without the slightest Eucharistic connotation (Rom 2:28–29; 8:4; Gal 5:16; 6:8).

[36] The Evangelist is speaking of the personal Spirit of God, but Nicodemus could have understood spirit only in the Old Testament sense of God's life-giving power. On Jn 3 see the excellent article of F. M. Braun, O.P., "La vie d'en haut (Jn III, 1–15)," *Revue des Sciences Philosophiques et Théologiques*, 40 (1956), 3–24.

[37] Gn 2:7. Also see Jb 34:14; Ez 36:25–26.

lifted up (3:14–15—on the cross and in return to the Father).

In all of this there is no emphasis on the sacrament of baptism: the theme is one of eschatological begetting through the pouring out of God's Spirit by the agency of Jesus. The picture of God's spirit being poured out in the final times, which is a frequent one in the Old Testament,[38] lay in the possible range of Nicodemus' understanding, whereas he could scarcely have been expected to understand the theme of Christian baptism. However, there is one verse in the whole passage which does seem to refer directly to baptism and the sacramental communication of the Spirit (3:5): "Let me solemnly assure you, no one can enter the kingdom of God without being begotten of *water* and Spirit." This is the only reference in the Nicodemus discourse to water as the agency of begetting. It can be contrasted with 3:3, "Let me solemnly assure you, no one can see the kingdom of God without being begotten from above." This almost perfectly parallel verse omits any mention of water, as does also v. 8 which mentions simply a begetting of the Spirit.

Faced with the clear sacramental import of 3:5, Bultmann[39] is forced once again to resort to his ecclesiastical redactor who has inserted the reference to water to bring the chapter in line with ecclesiastical sacramental theology. This suggestion must be rejected here for the same reason that we rejected a similar suggestion in chap. 6, namely, there is present a secondary baptismal reference throughout the *whole* Nicodemus episode.[40] The notion of the new begetting which is at the heart of Jn 3 had baptismal significance for the early Church even without the mention of water. 1 Pt, which many scholars consider as a baptis-

---

[38] Is 4:4; Zech 12:10; 13:1; 1QS 4:20–21.

[39] *Das Evangelium des Johannes,* 16 ed. (Göttingen, 1959), 98, n. 2.

[40] This sacramental reference would have been understood by the Christian after the Resurrection.

mal homily drawn from a primitive liturgy, says, "You have been *born anew*."[41] Ti 3:5 speaks of the "washing of regeneration."[42] Again, if in Jn 3 the begetting is accomplished through Spirit, we should note that elsewhere in Jn[43] the Spirit is connected with water (and thus with baptism). For instance, in 7:38–39 we are told that the living water that is to flow from within Jesus is the Spirit. Once more, if in 3:14 begetting from above depends on the Son of Man's being lifted up, we must remember that it was blood and *water* that flowed from Christ's side when He was lifted up (19:34). Finally, the very context of chap. 3 points to a baptismal reference, for the Nicodemus episode is immediately followed by the reentrance of John the Baptist and the remark that Jesus was baptizing in Judea (3:22).

With all of these indications, it is difficult not to believe that along with the principal nonsacramental meaning of the Nicodemus scene, the Evangelist intended a secondary sacramental meaning, much as in 6:35–50. Against this background 3:5, with its specific mention of being begotten of water, no longer stands out as an extraneous interpolation lacking harmony with the rest of the account. However, it remains more precisely and primarily sacramental than the other verses, and we must still answer the question of whether or not it is a Johannine interpolation designed

---

[41] I Pt 1:23, *anagennaomai*, to be compared with Jn's *gennaomai anōthen*. There is a play in John on both Greek words. *Gennaomai* in this passage means primarily "be begotten," but it can also mean "be born" (which is the way the early versions understood it). *Anōthen* means primarily "from above" (as in 3:31), but it can also mean "again." The secondary meaning of "born again" or "rebirth" fits in even more closely with a baptismal motif.

[42] *Loutron palingenesias.*

[43] And not only in Jn. John the Baptist's prediction that the one to come would baptize with a Holy Spirit is found in all the Gospels. See chap. VIII, below, pp. 176–179.

to clarify the underlying sacramentality of the story.[44] Here, with only one verse (or, perhaps, part of a verse if just the words "of water" are brought into question), we are hard-pressed for evidence.[45] On the one hand, the verse does seem to form a doublet with v. 3. On the other hand, the Old Testament consistently connects a washing with the outpouring of the spirit in eschatological times,[46] and so v. 5 could be fitted into the primary nonsacramental theme of the passage and could have been spoken by Jesus on this occasion.

The evidence is not strong enough to warrant a judgment at this time.[47]

In summation, then, our study of these two passages shows us that there is a very real Johannine interest in the sacraments of the Eucharist and of baptism. This interest stems from the earlier stages of the Gospel, not as the primary meaning of the narrative (for the Evangelist respects the original circumstances in which Jesus taught),

[44] Braun, *art. cit.*, believes that it is. M.-J. Lagrange, O.P., *evangile selon Saint Jean*, 8 ed. (Paris, 1948), 72: "The one real difficulty is that this treatment [3:1–21] would appear more natural on the lips of a Christian catechist quite a while after the Church had been founded, rather than as the first speech of Jesus himself." And so Lagrange makes a distinction between the fundamental thought of the passage and some of the expressions. For what we mean by "Johannine interpolation" see n. 26 above.

[45] We should note that the Council of Trent has used Jn 3:5 in a definition of faith (*DB* 858): "If anyone should say that true and natural water is not of necessity for Baptism and should distort those words of our Lord Jesus Christ, 'Unless a man be reborn of water and Holy Spirit,' to some metaphor, let him be anathema."

[46] See n. 38 above.

[47] We remember that in the interpolated passage 6:51–58 we found what might be the Johannine formula for the institution of the Eucharist. It is interesting to note that some theologians, including Estius, connect the institution of baptism to 3:5.

but as a deeper secondary meaning intelligible to the Christian after the Resurrection. This type of sacramental reference pervades many of the Johannine narratives;[48] and, on this level of secondary reference, John may be called the most sacramental of all the Gospels.

At a later stage in the development of the Gospel,[49] probably through the use of pericopes in the liturgy of circles influenced by John, a more specific sacramental emphasis was introduced (e.g., 6:51–58, and perhaps 3:5, and a few other passages). The examples where this specific sacramentalism is spelled out for the reader are rather rare, a fact that has been responsible for the charge that Jn is not a sacramental Gospel. However, since these specifically sacramental passages are not intrusions, but only serve to point up a sacramental theme that is already present, albeit on a secondary level, this charge is false.

This solution, we believe, takes into account both the historical and theological interests of the author.

[48] For a list of these passages see the end of chap. IV, above.
[49] See n. 26 above.

VI

The Theology of the
Incarnation in John

Since "incarnation" means literally "entering or becoming flesh," when we think of the Incarnation in St. John, we naturally think of Jn 1:14: "The Word became flesh." This verse, however, has often been studied; hence in this essay we have elected to go into the wider implications of the Word's becoming flesh.

THE FACT OF THE INCARNATION

The fact of the Incarnation is very important in the Johannine writings (for our present purposes we use this term to refer to the Gospel and Epistles; unless otherwise indicated, all references are to the Gospel). Particularly in 1 Jn we find a determined insistence on the fact that Jesus Christ came in the flesh. Early heresies may account for such stress. The Docetists were teaching that the humanity of Christ was but an appearance, a phantasm through which God dealt with man. Cerinthus held that Christ, a spiritual being, descended upon Jesus, a normal man, at the baptism in the Jordan and remained with Jesus until just before the passion. Thus he divided Jesus and the Christ and denied that the Christ had ever suffered or shed blood.

Against such denials of the Incarnation, 1 Jn 4:2–3 stresses: "Every spirit that acknowledges Jesus Christ *come in the flesh* belongs to God." And 1 Jn 5:6 emphasizes that Jesus Christ came in water and in blood, not in water alone—a poetic way of stating that Jesus was the Christ not only at the baptism (water), but all through His life and at His death (blood). This same interest in assuring us of the reality of the Incarnation possibly governs some parts of the Gospel too, for instance 6:51 ff, where there is such insistence on the flesh and blood of the Son of Man. In particular, 19:34–35, which solemnly testifies that blood, as well as water, came from the side of the pierced corpse, may have been directed against Docetist theories.

Thus while the Johannine writings emphasize the divinity of Jesus Christ (perhaps with greater precision than the rest of the New Testament), they are also very insistent on the true humanity of Jesus.

THE IMPLICATIONS OF THE INCARNATION

But the Evangelist was too profound to stop at proclaiming the fact of the Incarnation; his main purpose was not apologetics. Rather, he wished primarily to spell out for his Christian readers what this fact meant for them. If we read a present Greek tense in Jn 20:31, he was writing to those who already believed in Jesus Christ ("that you may continue to have faith"). And if we accept the usual date for the final *writing* of the Gospel (the last years of the first century A.D.), the work was addressed to a community that had believed for many years.

In many ways the problems of these Christians would not be unfamiliar to us. They had baptism and the Eucharist, the chief sacramental sources of grace. But what did this have to do with Jesus who walked in Galilee? True, the most ancient preaching of the Church, enshrined in the Synoptic Gospels, tells us that Jesus had ordered the disciples to baptize in the divine name and to commemorate His death through the Eucharist. But why? It is in John's Gospel that we come closest to an answer, even though Jn tells us neither of the command to baptize nor of the institution of the Eucharist at the Last Supper. It takes the existence of these two sacraments for granted and seeks to show how they are rooted in Jesus' ministry and in the Incarnation.

The fact that Word became flesh means more than the taking on of a human nature. It means that in His whole method of dealing with men the Son of God will act as Son of Man and work through the things of the flesh. Today, in some circles, it has become fashionable to deprecate as hopelessly abstruse the strenuous debates of the early Christian centuries about the person and natures of Jesus Christ. But these debates show that instinctively Christians realized how important it was that nothing be allowed to obscure the true divinity and true humanity of Jesus. In recent times, in the face of liberal onslaught, orthodox Christians have been so busy insisting that Jesus was nothing less than God that there has been a danger of obscuring the fact that He was truly man in every way except sin. Even today, as the current theological debate about the limitations of the human knowledge of Christ shows, theologians have not worked out all the implications of the humanity of Christ.

Jn brings that humanity clearly before its early Christian audience by showing that Christ, by continuing to operate in His Church through baptism and the Eucharist, is only continuing what He did on earth during His ministry. If the Son came down from heaven to lift men up (3:13–16), He does so through the things of this earth. While Jesus spoke to the Samaritan woman (4:13–14), He insisted that water would be the source of life for men. God had creatively begotten man in the beginning by breathing on him and giving man His spirit or breath (Gn 2:7). Now, through Jesus, God was breathing His Holy Spirit upon men (Jn 20:22) and begetting them from above (3:3).

But He would not do so in a purely invisible, intangible way. Jesus the Man would use the water of this world to cleanse men and communicate the Spirit. As 3:5 states, this begetting from above is of water, as well as of Spirit. Indeed, the Spirit would not be given (or if we stick close to the best Greek text of 7:39, the Spirit would not even be a reality for man) until Jesus was raised up on the cross, and *water* and blood flowed from His side. It was then (19:30) that He handed over the Spirit.

Again, it was through such material things as bread and wine that Jesus would give to men the food of eternal life. Jesus insists that His flesh and blood are really food and drink (6:55) and that man cannot have life without them (6:53). They are a food more real than the barley bread and fishes He had multiplied.

Thus, when Jn tells us that the Word became flesh, it means more than the fact of the Incarnation. The whole of God's message, in the full sense of "Word," inextricably bound itself to the sphere of the flesh. Jn shows this by stressing that Jesus communicated His greatest gift, *life*, through the things of this world. Baptism and Eucharist, which are the lifeblood of Christian existence in the Church, are merely the explication of the implications of the Incarnation.

APPLICATION OF THIS THEOLOGY

As the Lutheran theologian Dietrich Bonhoeffer has pointed out, one of the greatest defeats religion has suffered in modern times is its acceptance of a role which allots to it only the fringes of human existence. "There are no atheists in foxholes" is an axiom symptomatic of a world view that only danger, suffering, need, and death evoke the presence of God. And, to some extent, religion has tacitly acquiesced by publicly proclaiming its purpose as the salvation of souls, as if that were its only goal. But does not the catechism teach us that the reason for human existence is twofold: to know, love, and serve God *in this world*, and to be happy with Him forever in the next?

Yes, *in this world!* Religion has to be worldly, in the best sense of the word. "God *loved the world* so much that he actually gave his only Son" (3:16; also 1 Jn 4:9). And Jesus never forgot that He came as the light *of the world* (8:12). Whether we phrase the purpose of His mission in terms of the coming of the kingdom into time (Synoptic Gospels) or of the gift of life to men (Jn), it is a mission to this world. He speaks of heaven and hell, but rarely and without detail. His concern is the knowing and loving and serving God in this life—the things we can do. He leaves to His Father the mysterious allotment of gifts in the next life. The Son became incarnate to teach men how to live a life in this world and not primarily to unveil the secrets of the next.

It is true that Jesus had some harsh things to say about the world that refused to believe in Him (7:7), but He kept trying to penetrate it with His love (14:31). His purpose was to save the world (3:17; 12:47)—a purpose so characteristic that He was called the Savior of the world (4:42; 1 Jn 4:14). That is why He sought to overthrow the prince of this world (12:31; 14:30), that He might claim it as His own. The disciples whom Jesus sent forth did not belong to this world as if they were its possession (17:14, 16), but their task was to continue Jesus' mission to the world (17:23). Their faith would overcome the world (1 Jn 5:4).

The Incarnation, then, means that the Church, which is the Body of Christ, is just as inextricably bound to this world as was its Master. Once the Word became flesh, a purely spiritual religion, or one with its vision too farsightedly fixed on the next world, became impossible. No one can find Christ outside the world; nor can one find the real world outside Christ, because the Incarnation has changed the nature of the world. The reality of the world, as Bonhoeffer insists, involves the God who has become manifest in Jesus Christ. And today perhaps more than at any time since the Incarnation, the Church must fight to prove the place of Christ in this world. The Church must open the eyes of the world to see that it is the world of Christ. If the Church is where Jesus reigns over the world, the Church cannot turn its back on this world. And indeed the only way the Church can defend its place in the world is not by settling for an existence on the fringes of life, but by assuring Christ's place in all of life and in the whole world.

Hence we cannot settle for the salvation of souls. This life is too important a part of human existence to be written off as merely a trial. If this were not true, the Word would not have become flesh and God would not have loved the world. The salvation of the soul is a transition from a *rich life* based on acceptance of God through Jesus and service in His name. The next world does not constitute a refuge from this world, but involves a continuation of the Christian life begun here below. That is why John assures us that he who believes already possesses eternal life and has passed from death to life (5:24). The salvation of the soul cannot in any sense be looked upon as a consolation prize dangled before those neurotically incapable of facing the demands of this life. It is because this life and the next life constitute a continuum that John can emphasize the here and now aspect of judgment (3:18–19). Men must be brought to praise God in this world as in the next. God's will must come about on this earth as well as in heaven.

The Johannine theology of the Incarnation contains in nucleus a very important lesson for the Church of all time: a docetic spirituality or a docetic conception of the apostolate is not true to a Jesus Christ who came in water and blood (1 Jn 5:6).

VII

The Qumran Scrolls and
the Johannine Gospel
and Epistles[1]

The Qumran Scrolls are part of a large number of scrolls and fragments of manuscripts found since 1947 in the hills along the western shore of the Dead Sea. Found near the ruins of an ancient settlement called today Khirbet Qumrân, the Qumran literary material is what remains of the library of a community or sect of Jews who occupied the settlement between 130 B.C. and A.D. 68. While many of the

[1] This article is the outgrowth of a seminar paper presented in February of 1955 at Johns Hopkins University. The writer is indebted to Professor William F. Albright for his kindness in reading the manuscript and for his helpful suggestions. Since 1955 an enormous literature on the Scrolls has appeared but nothing to affect materially our conclusions here. The reader who desires accurate general information about the Scrolls is fortunate to have now in paperback J. T. Milik's *Ten Years of Discovery in the Wilderness of Judea* (London: SCM, 1959) and Frank M. Cross, Jr.'s *The Ancient Library of Qumran* (New York: Doubleday, 1961). The best translation is G. Vermès' *The Dead Sea Scrolls in English* (Penguin, 1962). The abbreviations used for the Qumran literature in this article are standard.

scrolls and fragments are from copies of biblical books, others represent writings composed in the community. Since such literature comes from a period just before the New Testament, naturally much interest has been focused on comparing the Scrolls and the New Testament.[2] We shall be particularly concerned with the relations between the Qumran literature and the Johannine writings.[3]

Such a discussion can follow varied lines. The method of "historical" identifications within the Scrolls has already been employed, but not with much success. Dupont-Sommer's first book[4] on the Scrolls painted a very provocative portrait of the Teacher of Righteousness (the great hero of Qumran)—a just man, nay "divine," who, having been persecuted and put to death by the wicked priest, came back to life and founded a church. The volatile

---

[2] Already in the notes he supplied for his translation of 1QS (A.S.O.R. Supp. Studies, #10–12, 1951) W. H. Brownlee pointed out New Testament parallels, as Bo Reicke had already done for CD in "The Jewish 'Damascus Documents' and the New Testament," *Symbolae Biblicae Upsalienses,* 6 (1946). See also *The Scrolls and the New Testament,* ed. by Krister Stendahl (New York: Harper, 1957).

[3] We do not intend to treat the Apocalypse, not primarily because of the authorship problem but because this literary genre has so many stereotyped qualities that it offers great difficulties for establishing interrelationship. F. M. Braun, O.P., "L'arrière-fond judaïque du quatrième évangile et la Communauté de l'Alliance," *Revue Biblique,* 62 (1955), 27–31, considers similarities to the Apocalypse without discovering anything decisive. Braun's article appeared when ours was virtually finished (the topics treated and the conclusions are, by coincidence, quite similar), but we have been able to take advantage of his observations in notes. The name Braun used in the notes, then, refers to F. M. Braun. The most complete treatment since 1955 of the relations between Qumran and the Johannine writings is that of Herbert Braun, *Theologische Rundschau,* 28 (1962), 193–234, an article with a very complete bibliography.

[4] *The Dead Sea Scrolls* (Eng. transl., 1952), 33–44 and 98 f.

French press immediately interpreted this as a proof that there was a Christ before our Jesus, and that the latter was nothing but a pale image of the former.[5] While recognizing the value of the many original observations of Dupont-Sommer, a good number of scholars[6] have rejected the theory of the Teacher's death and resurrection (which are dependent on his interpretation of a very obscure text, 1 QpHab xi, 4–7); and under closer examination, many of the similarities between the Qumran Teacher and Jesus Christ have been found wanting.

Another example of "historical" identification is that of J. Teicher,[7] who claims that the community described in the Qumran Scrolls is that of the Ebionites, the second-century Jewish-Christian group, who were destroyed by Diocletian. For Teicher the wicked priest and the Teacher are Paul and Christ. Despite interesting similarities between the Scrolls and Ebionite literature (which may well indicate that some of the Qumran ideas were adopted by the Ebionites), the excavations at Khirbet Qumran eliminate Teicher's hypothesis by showing that the Qumran commu-

---

[5] H. H. Rowley, *The Zadokite Fragments and the Dead Sea Scrolls* (1952), 20, n. 3, lists some of the wilder statements. Dupont-Sommer, *op. cit.*, 99, says that Jesus Christ appears in many respects "as an astonishing reincarnation of the Master of Justice [Teacher of Righteousness]." Then he goes on to list the similarities.

[6] The list is indeed long, and the complete references can be found in Rowley, *op. cit.*, 20, n. 4. It includes Lambert, Vermès, de Vaux, Goossens, Bonsirven, Delcor. We found of particular value J. Coppens, "Les Documents du Désert de Juda et les Origines du Christianisme," *Cahiers du Libre Examen* (1953), 23–39. An exhaustive treatment rejecting such parallels can now be found in Jean Carmignac, *Christ and the Teacher of Righteousness* (Baltimore: Helicon, 1962).

[7] Teicher's articles constitute a long series, chiefly in the *Journal of Jewish Studies* from 1951 on. For a complete treatment see J. A. Fitzmyer, "The Qumran Scrolls, the Ebionites and Their Literature," *Theological Studies,* 16 (1955), 335–372, and reprinted in the Stendahl volume (n. 2 above).

nity was destroyed in A.D. 70. Today the majority of writers recognize the Qumran community to be Essene,[8] although perhaps not in exactly the same stage of development as the Essenes described by Josephus and Philo. At any rate, in view of our very incomplete knowledge of the history of the Qumran community, an attempt to build a theory of Qumran-Christian relationship on identifications of characters within the Scrolls seems unwise.

However, if we establish relationships on the basis of terminology and ideology, which this article hopes to do, we are on much more solid ground. There is enough of Qumran literature to determine certain aspects of the sectarians' thought and its phrasing, aspects which we may compare to similar points in the Johannine literature. Even here we should note the wise cautions that Msgr. Coppens offers.[9] Similarities in thought and terminology between two such groups of documents could be expected because they are mutually dependent on the Old Testament and the Pseudepigrapha, and because they are dealing with roughly the same religious subject matter. Therefore, to establish interdependence, we must concentrate on similarities which are *peculiar* to the two.

MODIFIED DUALISM

The outstanding resemblance between the Scrolls and the New Testament seems to be the modified dualism which is prevalent in both. By dualism we mean the doctrine that the universe is under the dominion of two opposing principles, one good and the other evil. Modified dualism adds the corrective that these principles are not uncreated, but are both dependent on God the Creator.

[8] Some still opt for another group. S. Lieberman, *Journal of Biblical Literature* 71 (1952), 199–206, shows similarities to the rabbinic *Haberim* (members of a society which observed ritual cleanliness more strictly).

[9] *Op. cit.*, 26–27.

In the Old Testament there is really no predominant dualism.[10] True, there are evil spirits, such as the tempter of Gn 3, and evil men whose ways are opposed to those of good man (Ps 1). But it does not emphasize any theory that the world is divided into two great camps locked in eternal struggle. In their very practical outlook, the Hebrew Scriptures are more interested in the individual man's struggle to follow the Law and live righteously. In the Qumran literature we find a new outlook. All men are aligned in two opposing forces, the one of light and truth, the other of darkness and perversion, with each faction ruled by a spirit or prince. While much of their ideology is phrased in a quasi-biblical language, the guiding inspiration of the dualism is clearly extrabiblical.

In a series of brilliant articles, K. G. Kuhn of Heidelberg seems to have successfully identified this source as Iranian Zoroastrianism.[11] In its primitive form, the Zoroastrian religion[12] taught a dualism where the forces of good

---

[10] K. G. Kuhn, "Die Sektenschrift und die iranische Religion," *Zeitschrift für Theologie und Kirche,* 49 (1952), 303: "This dualistic ideology is totally alien to Old Testament thought, nor can it be explained as an outgrowth of the Old Testament." There is dualism in the Pseudepigrapha, especially in the *Test. XII Patr.* (cf. Judah 20, Asher 5). Yet here one must beware of interpolations, both sectarian and Christian. Fragments of the Pseudepigrapha (*Jubilees, Enoch,* and *Test. XII Patr.*) have been found at Qumran; these indicate use of the Pseudepigrapha by the sectarians, but not necessarily authorship.

[11] The first article, "Die in Palästina gefundenen hebraïschen Texte und das Neue Testament," *Zeitschrift für Theologie und Kirche,* 47 (1950), 192–211, was written before the most important Qumran texts were available. It should be modified by the later article mentioned in note 10. Also see Kuhn's article in the Stendahl volume, 98 ff.

[12] This religion has undergone many important changes in its long existence (cf. J. Finegan, *The Archaeology of World Religions* [1952], chap. II). In the period of Sassanian restoration, beginning of the third century A.D., it became strongly mythological. The reference here is to the much purer teachings

and evil, led by Ahura Mazda and Angra Mainyu, respectively, are in combat. As Kuhn stresses, this dualism is not physical (i.e., an opposition between matter and spirit); it is an *ethical* struggle between truth and deceit, light and darkness. And it is *eschatological,* for the ultimate triumph of Ahura Mazda is definitely envisaged.[13] In comparing the dualism of Qumran with early Zoroastrianism, Kuhn has found a great deal of similarity; for in the former the ethical, eschatological trend predominates too. In fact, there are interesting points of resemblance between passages of the Gathas and the Scrolls.[14] One great difference separates them: in Zoroastrianism the good and evil spirits are coexistent, independent, uncreated forces; in Qumran thought, as will be seen, they are both created by God. The imported dualism of Qumran has come into contact with the Old Testament theology of God the Creator, and is subservient to that great truth.

Zoroastrian influence on Qumran is not at all difficult to postulate if we realize that many Jews remained in Mesopotamia after the Captivity, and lived side by side with Iranians. Such proximity may well have influenced Jewish thought, especially in those elements which were compatible with the Hebrew religion.[15] From time to time Babylonian Jews returned to Palestine (witness Ezra in the late fifth century); and undoubtedly the formation of the Maccabean free state in the second century drew many more. It seems to have been just at the end of the Maccabean wars that the Qumran community came into existence. If the founders of the community were of Babylonian

---

of Zoroaster himself (tenth or sixth century B.C.) as represented in the Gathas. See below, n. 22, on Zervanite form of dualism.

[13] Kuhn, "Die Sektenschrift," 307. Finegan, *op. cit.,* 90.

[14] Kuhn, *ibid.,* 304: "As for the terminology, and, even more, the whole pattern of thought, there is an obvious parallelism between the Manual of Discipline and this Iranian ideology."

[15] *Ibid.,* p. 310.

Jewry, or in contact with it, the strain of Zoroastrian influence need not astound us.

When we turn to the Johannine writings, we find there
also a modified dualism. Once again there is talk of forces
of light and truth struggling with forces of darkness and
perversion. There are hints of this elsewhere in the New
Testament, especially in St. Paul; but nowhere does it
reach the intensity of St. John's works. To account for this,
many suggestions have been made. The fact that the Fourth
Gospel was so popular with the Gnostics gave rise among
the critics to the hypothesis of a Gnostic background. However, the discovery of the Gnostic codices at Chenoboskion
in Upper Egypt in 1945[16] has considerably enlightened
us on the true nature of this heresy. As W. F. Albright
remarks, "We now know that the Church Fathers did not
appreciably exaggerate their accounts of Gnosticism, and
that the gap between Christianity and any form of second-
century Gnosticism was tremendous. The efforts of recent
historians of religion to picture a Gnosticism which resembled the Gospel of John more closely than anything
known from Patristic tradition have been nullified. . . ."[17]
And besides, as Kuhn points out, the dualism of Gnosticism
is a physical one; the dualism of John is ethical and eschatological, like that of Qumran.[18] Both streams may have

[16] There are about forty treatises in Coptic from about the
third or fourth century. They reflect Greek manuscripts of the
second or third century. For an accurate but popular account,
cf. Victor Gold, *Biblical Archaeologist,* 15 (1952), 70–88.

[17] W. F. Albright, "The Bible After Twenty Years of
Archaeology," reprint from *Religion and Life* (1954), 548. I
enjoyed the privilege of reading in manuscript Professor Al-
bright's article on "Recent Discoveries in Palestine and the
Gospel of St. John," now published in *The Background of the
New Testament and its Eschatology* (Studies in Honor of C. H.
Dodd, ed. by W. D. Davies and D. Daube, 1956), 153–171.

[18] Kuhn, "Die Sektenschrift," 303: "This dualism is, however, not of a physical nature, as was later that of Gnosticism."
Again, 315, of the Qumran dualism: ". . . that it actually is

had their very ancient sources in Zoroastrian dualism, but into Gnosticism have poured the muddy tributaries of pagan Greek philosophy and Judeo-Christian heresy; and in the end Gnosticism flows far away indeed from the Evangelist's "living waters."[19]

Now a new attempt has been made to identify the source of the modified dualism of St. John. Kuhn, Albright, Reicke, Brownlee, Braun, and Mowry see in the ideology and terminology of Qumran the Jewish background of Johannine thought and phrasing. A careful comparison of the two literatures on various points connected with this modified dualism will enable the reader to review some of the evidence for such a theory.

---

not of a physical and substantial, but of an ethical nature. This links the texts of the sect with primitive Iranian ideology and distinguishes it clearly from Gnosticism." Bo Reicke, "Traces of Gnosticism in the Dead Sea Scrolls?" *New Testament Studies,* 1 (1954–1955), 137–141, also clearly distinguishes between later Gnosticism and Qumran thought. It is at the most pre-Gnostic. For the nature of St. John's dualism, independently of the Qumran question, cf. E. K. Lee, *The Religious Thought of St. John* (1950), 109: ". . . it has no point of contact with metaphysical dualism"; 112: "The dualism is . . . ethical . . . and is neither absolute nor final."

[19] For an interesting schema of all this, cf. Lucetta Mowry, "The Dead Sea Scrolls and the Background for the Gospel of John," *Biblical Archaeologist,* 17 (1954), 86. We might add a note on one special aspect of the Gnostic thesis, i.e., that the background of the Johannine Gospel was Mandean Gnosticism. In 1930 there were found some Manichean codices (published by Polotsky) which establish that Mandeanism is secondary in relation to Manicheanism. Thus W. F. Albright says that a fifth-century date for the Mandean sect (although its sources may be earlier) is probable, and its influence on John's Gospel is out of the question; cf. *The Bible After Twenty Years,* 540–541 and 548. Nevertheless, it seems that the later Mandeans had their roots in an early Palestinian group of followers of John the Baptist, and therefore the problem of the Proto-Mandeans and the Fourth Gospel cannot be summarily dismissed.

a) Creation. Qumran states unequivocally the biblical doctrine of creation: "From the God of knowledge exists all that is and will be" (1 QS iii, 15). "And by his knowledge everything has been brought into being. And everything that is, he established by his purpose; and apart from him, nothing is done" (xi, 11).[20] We get a very similar statement in the Prologue of St. John, "All things were made through him, and apart from him nothing came to be."[21]

The Qumran literature goes on to state specifically that the two spirits, or leaders, of the forces of good and evil were created: "He created the spirits of light and darkness . . ." (1 QS iii, 25). For John, as we shall see, the problem does not arise; and so there is no similar statement. If the Zoroastrian background of Qumran dualism is correct, the specific statement of the creation of the two spirits may have been intended as a corrective. Miss Mowry suggests the possibility of a similar apologetic motive in John.[22] Perhaps the position of his universal statement of creation at the very beginning of his Gospel was directed against the idea of an uncreated evil spirit. Yet John is never specific on the creation of such a spirit, and he

[20] This statement seems to have been an important axiom; cf 1 QH x, 9, and also i, 20.

[21] We might note that Qumran says things were made through "His knowledge" and John says through the Logos. To this, see Reicke, *op. cit.,* 140: "It is evident that what the Qumran text calls 'the knowledge' and 'the thought' of God is actually his creative intellect, or very much the same as what the Fourth Gospel calls the Logos of God."

[22] Mowry, *op. cit.,* 83. St. Irenaeus, *Adv. Haer.,* 3, 11, states that the Prologue was against Cerinthus and his dualism. The above-given suggestions of correction of Zoroastrian thought would now have to be modified by what H. Michaud has pointed out in *Vetus Testamentum,* 5 (1955), 137–147: namely, that in the Zervanite branch of the Persian religion the two Spirits or principles are not uncreated, but are subject to the God Zervan.

never returns with emphasis to the theme of the universality of creation.[23]

b) *The Two Spirits.* The world, according to Qumran, is divided under two created leaders, one of whom God hates, while loving the other. The good spirit is called variously "the spirit of truth, the prince of lights, the angel of His truth, the holy spirit."[24] The evil spirit is called "the spirit of perversion, the angel of darkness, the angel of destruction."[25] Most often the name "Belial" is applied to him. This evil spirit seems to have subordinate spirits in his forces too, for the spirits of Belial are mentioned (CD 14:5).

In any case the names applied to the two principal spirits are clearly of a personal nature. As personal entities outside of man, they help or hinder man: "the God of Israel and his angel of truth have helped all the sons of light" (1 QS iii, 24–25; 1 QM xiii, 10). "And it is because of the angel of darkness that all the sons of righteousness go astray" (1 QS iii, 21–22). Yet they also conduct their struggle within man: "Until now the spirits of truth and perversion strive within man's heart" (iv, 23–24).[26] Consequently, in many instances, one gets the definite impression that the spirits are being spoken of impersonally as

[23] For other New Testament texts, cf. Col 1:16; 1 Cor 8:6; Heb 1:2.

[24] 1 QS iii, 18, 20, 24; CD 7:19.

[25] 1 QS iii, 19, 21; iv, 12; CD 2:4. The name "Mastema" comes up too—1 QS iii, 23; CD 20:3—and it seems to refer to the evil spirit. In 1 QM xiii, 11, a difficult text, Gaster (*The Dead Sea Scriptures*, 1956, 298) reads: "But for corruption thou hast made Belial, an angel of hostility [i.e., Mastema]."

[26] Kuhn, "Die Sektenschrift," 301, n. 4: "Here (1 QS iv, 23), however, it is a dualism within and not between individuals: the two spirits, that of truth and that of perversion, join battle within man, and the pious attains ultimate salvation when God frees man from the spirit of perversion within him. . . ."

ways of acting.[27] The two aspects are not necessarily contradictory: it is natural to shift from speaking of two personal spirits exercising a dominion over man to speaking of two spirits of acting by which man shows his respective adherence to their dominion.

In St. John we have both pairs of terms which Qumran uses interchangeably: light and darkness, truth and perversion. However, in his theology there is a difference between the leader of the forces of light and the Spirit of Truth; and so for the present we shall concentrate on only the light and darkness antinomy. For St. John, "God is light, and in him is no darkness" (1 Jn 1:5). With the Son of God, Jesus Christ, light has come into the world,[28] so that Christ can call Himself "the light of the world" (Jn 9:5). Thus in the Fourth Gospel there is no created spirit of light such as we find in the Qumran literature—the leader of the forces of light is the uncreated Word Himself.

John often speaks of the darkness, and he mentions an evil spirit—the devil or Satan.[29] Yet nowhere does he characterize Satan in the exact terminology of Qumran as the leader, spirit, or angel of the forces of darkness. (St. Luke with his mention of the "power of darkness" and St. Paul's Belial are terminologically closer to Qumran on this point than John is.)[30] Perhaps we may see a similarity to the Qumran literature in the struggle which John paints between Christ and "the prince of this world."[31]

[27] So also Braun, *op. cit.*, 13.

[28] Jn 12:46: "I have come a light into the world." Also 1:4 and 9.

[29] As Fr. Braun points out, *op. cit.*, 13–17, Satan and Mastema are variations of the same root (*śṭm*).

[30] Lk 22:53: "But this is your hour, and the power of darkness." Also 2 Cor 6:14–15. "Or what fellowship has light with darkness? What harmony is there between Christ and Belial?" Notice the parallelism: Christ-light versus Belial-darkness. On this point cf. also 2 Cor 11:14: ". . . for Satan disguises himself as an angel of light."

[31] Jn 12:31, 14:30, 16:11. (In the Prologue notice that the world is almost equated with the darkness.) The "prince of this

In summary we may say that there is a similar general outlook in John and in the Qumran literature on the forces of light and darkness, each with its personal leader. Yet in John, Christ as the light of the world is a significant development over Qumran's created angel of light. There is difference too in the terminology for the leader of darkness.

c) The Struggle. In the Qumran literature we are told that between the two spirits there is undying enmity and bitter conflict—a struggle which, until the last age, is waged on equal terms.[32] Clearly, however, the evil spirit is equal only by the sufferance of God,[33] and at the end God will intervene and crush him: "Now God through the mysteries of his understanding and through his glorious wisdom has appointed a period for the existence of wrongdoing; but at the season of visitation, he will destroy it forever; and then the truth of the world will appear forever" (1 QS iv, 18–19). Apparently, this divine intervention will be seen in a great battle where, thanks to God and His angels, the sons of light will be victorious. 1 QM gives a detailed plan for the organization of the forces, for standards, signals, and weapons of battle. The punishment of the wicked, after their defeat, will be severe, and their sufferings are graphically described in apocalyptic language: multitude of plagues, eternal ruin, everlasting terror, destruction in the fire of the dark regions, calamities of darkness.[34] The end result will be that "wickedness will disappear before justice as darkness before light."[35]

---

world" has no power over Christ, is judged by Christ, and will be cast out by Him. St. Paul in 2 Cor 4:4 speaks of the "god of this world."

[32] 1 QS iv, 17 and 25: "For God has set them in equal parts until the final period. . . ."

[33] CD 6:9: "And during all these years Belial shall be let loose against Israel. . . ."

[34] CD 9a:2; 1 QS iv, 12; 1 QH iii, 28 ff.

[35] 1 Q27 frag. 1, 1:5. English trans. in Vermès, 209.

In this whole picture of the struggle it is noteworthy that the writers always seem to be living in the period of trial, when Belial is still loose and waging war on equal terms. 1 QM, with all its minute details, is still a description of a future battle.

When we turn to St. John, we find there also a struggle between light and darkness, but a struggle which is passing through its climax and where victory is already decided. Christ has brought light into the world; darkness has tried to overcome this light, but "the light shines on in the darkness, for the darkness did not overcome it" (Jn 1:5). As a result, "the darkness is passing away and indeed the true light is now shining" (1 Jn 2:8).[36] John also phrases the victorious aspect of the conflict in terms of Christ's casting out the prince of this world (Jn 12:31), so that the Savior can cry out, "But take courage, I have overcome the world" (16:33). The victory, as we know, has not reached its culmination; only the second coming of Christ can establish the conclusive triumph of light. The Apocalypse presents the ultimate battle between the forces of good and evil. However, it must be admitted that even in this work we have no real parallel to the detailed accounts of 1 QM.

Once again, in summary, we see a similarity of thought between the two groups of writings on the conflict, and both are sure of the ultimate success of light. Yet here, as before, Christ makes a tremendous difference in John's outlook. For Qumran victory is still in the future; for John light is already triumphant.[37]

[36] This victory theme is echoed in Col 1:13: "He has rescued us from the power of darkness and transferred us into the kingdom of his beloved Son, in whom we have our redemption, the remission of our sins."

[37] Cf. Coppens, *op. cit.*, 35: "To the men at Qumran the end of time has not come; they await it. They live in expectation of the Judgment Day. For the Christians, especially St. John, 'the world is already judged.'"

d) Man's Role. Msgr. Coppens has said that the Qumran community gives no evidence of deep abstract religious speculations.[38] This seems particularly true in the problem of predestination and free will—a problem at the root of the domination of man by the spirits of light and darkness. As is inevitable when two trends of thought meet and are harmonized, difficulties occur which did not exist before the union. From the Old Testament there came to Qumran the basically simple Hebrew notions of morality, involving the obviously free behavior of man and his consequent reward or punishment. From outside, presumably from Zoroastrianism, came the idea of two spirits dominating the human race, so that man acts according to one or the other: this is a concept which, when developed logically, would lead to a deterministic predestination. The sectarians never seem to have defined the conflict between these two notions, or to have attempted a speculative solution of it. Throughout their works are statements which favor one or the other view; but to me it does not seem accurate to classify them definitely on either side as if they had passed a reflex judgment on the problem. It was only later, when Jewish thought came into closer and closer contact with Hellenic and Hellenistic philosophies, that the full depth of the problem was realized and discussed; twenty centuries afterward it is still a mystery.

Grossouw says of man's role according to Qumran theology: "The so-baffling difference in the conduct of good people and bad people is reduced here to the influence of 'the spirit of truth' and 'the spirit of perversion or deceit.' "[39] And of these spirits he says: "On the other hand, their mastery over man's moral actions seems to be absolute, the consequence of which would be that these actions are determined and no longer free."[40] Certainly

[38] *Ibid.,* 33.

[39] "The Dead Sea Scrolls and the New Testament," *Studia Catholica,* 26 (1951), 289–299, and 27 (1952), 1–9. Cf. 293.

[40] *Ibid.,* 297. Also Braun, *op. cit.,* 13. Kuhn, "Die Sektenschrift," 312: "For each individual, God has determined before-

there are many statements in the Qumran literature which can be so interpreted. 1 QS iii, 15 ff., states: "From the God of knowledge exists all that is and will be. Before they existed, he established all the design of them. And after they exist, according to their ordinances (in accordance with his glorious purpose), they fulfill their task; and nothing can be changed. . . . Now, he created man for dominion over the world and assigned him two spirits by which to walk until the season of his visitation." Again in iv, 15, we find, "In these (two spirits) are the families of all mankind; and in their divisions do all their hosts receive an inheritance according to their societies and in their ways do they walk." And finally iv, 24, adds: "Until now the spirits of truth and perversion strive within man's heart; they walk in wisdom and folly; and according as man's inheritance is in truth and righteousness, so he hates evil; but in so far as his heritage is in the portion of perversity and wickedness in him, so he abominates truth."

Thus man would seem to be placed under one or the other spirit and to behave accordingly. In fact, the two spirits are so in control that they can be said to raise up men for their work: "For aforetime rose Moses and Aaron through the prince of the Lights. But Belial raised Jochanneh and his brother with his evil device . . ." (CD 7:19).[41]

---

hand to which side he shall belong, and once he is in existence his acts and destiny are unchangeable." Of interest is the comment of Josephus, *Ant.* 13, 5: "But the sect of the Essenes affirm that fate governs all things, and that nothing befalls man but what is according to its determination."

[41] These are the Jannes and the Jambres of 2 Tm 3:8. In relation to the sinful generation of the desert, CD has some strong phrases—2:6–8: "For God chose them not from the beginning of the world, and ere they were *formed* he knew their works. And he abhorred *their* generations *from of old* and hid his face from *their* land until they were consumed" (italicized words emended by Charles). 2:10: "But them he hated he made to go astray." However, this language reflects a certain Hebrew idiom of thought. Compare the Johannine quote of Is 6:10 (Jn 12:

In the case of the sons of light, there seems to be a special divine predilection whereby they are chosen by God almost independently of their works. "For God has chosen them for an eternal covenant" (1 QS iv, 22). In fact they may be called "the ones chosen according to God's good pleasure."[42]

Such texts certainly seem to favor determinism. When we peruse some other statements, however, we find observations which appear to demand freedom of will. Throughout 1 QS the importance of virtuous works is emphasized, and even the men of the community are blamed for succumbing to temptation and committing bad deeds. In general, the evil are punished precisely because they have rejected the will of God and have done *their own will.* "Because they did their own will and kept not the commandment of their Maker" (CD 3:7 and 4:9–10). A heinous sin is the refusal to accept the sectarians' interpretation of the Torah, and this refusal is spoken of as deliberate.[43] A very clear passage is 1 QS v, 11, where the wicked are said to have committed both "unknown sins" and "deliberate sins."[44] And finally we might note the strong emphasis of the Qumran texts on repentance, and

---

40): "He has blinded their eyes, and hardened their hearts, lest they see."

[42] I QS viii, 6. Brownlee translates this "the chosen of grace"; but this seems a little too Christian, influenced by Rom 11:5, "A remnant, chosen by grace." We might also quote 1 QS xi, 7, "To those whom God chose he has given them as an eternal possession," and CD 9a:23: "Moses said, 'Not for your righteousness or for the uprightness of your heart do you go in to inherit these nations, but because He loved your fathers and because He would keep the oath.'" The whole of 1 QH i stresses man's dependence on God. These texts seem deterministic; yet they can have perfectly orthodox meanings. What they actually meant to their sectarian authors is difficult to say.

[43] 1 QS iii, 1: "For his soul has refused instruction and knowledge of righteous laws."

[44] The words are "hidden" and "with a high hand." Brownlee translates them as unconscious and conscious sins.

the possibilities of reform offered to recalcitrant sectarians. All these ideas can scarcely be harmonized with a hopeless determinism.[45]

In St. John no such conflict of ideas exists. Of course there is a very orthodox statement of God's predilection: "You have not chosen me, but I have chosen you" (Jn 15: 16).[46] There is no hint, however, of anyone's being determined to evil without choice. Rather the culpable deliberateness of man's adherence to darkness is emphasized: "The light has come into the world, yet men have loved the darkness rather than the light, for their works were evil. For everyone who does evil hates the light, and does not come to the light, that his deeds may not be exposed" (Jn 3:19–20). In view of this obstinate refusal, Christ tries to persuade men to come to the light before it is too late. "Yet a little while the light is among you. Walk while you have the light, that darkness may not overtake you. He who walks in darkness does not know where he goes" (Jn 12:35).[47] We might note that this idea of walking in light and darkness is very similar to the two ways in which men are to walk according to the Qumran texts.[48]

Yet in spite of all Christ's pleading and that of His apostles, some will always continue to walk in darkness. "If we say that we have fellowship with him, and walk in darkness, we lie, and are not practicing the truth" (1 Jn

[45] Kuhn, "Die Sektenschrift," 300, n. 4, sees these two trends in Qumran thought.

[46] Cf. Mk 13:20; 1 Pt 2:9; and esp. Eph 1:4: "Even as he chose us in him before the foundation of the world."

[47] The leading of men from light to darkness is also the mission of St. Paul, Acts 26:18: "I am now sending you, to open their eyes that they may turn from darkness to light and from the dominion of Satan to God." Note the parallelism: darkness-dominion of Satan *versus* light-dominion of God. Grossouw, *op. cit.*, 6, sees this as one of the strongest New Testament similarities to Qumran.

[48] Of course we must remember Is 50:10: ". . . his servant who walks in darkness and has no light."

1:6). The free and deliberate choice of darkness is the basis for God's ultimate judgment of man: "Now this is the judgment: The light has come into the world, yet men have loved the darkness rather than the light" (Jn 3:19).

In summary, we find that in the Qumran texts, men are aligned under the banners of light and darkness, and this seemingly without much choice on man's part. Yet other passages suppose that man deliberately walks in either of the two ways. In John's terminology, too, man walks in the ranks of either light or darkness, but he does so freely inasmuch as he accepts or does not accept Christ, the light of the world.

e) The Sons of Light. What ultimately constitutes a man one of the sons of light (1 QS i, 9; iii, 24; and *passim*)? It is clear from the above that, for Qumran, refusal to do God's will makes one a son of darkness. Yet if we are to say that doing God's will makes one a son of light, we must understand "God's will" in a very restricted sense. Apparently the sectarians felt that no one could do what God wanted unless he was acquainted with the Torah as explained in the Qumran community. Nowhere is the question broached of those who do good works and are not members of the community. Thus, for all practical purposes, the sons of light are equated with the sectarians. Some citations from the Qumran literature make this quite clear.

In 1 QM we have a description of the forces of the sons of light in their ultimate struggle with the sons of darkness; the former consist of the sectarians. 1 QS i, 7–8 and 11, tells us: "All who dedicate themselves to do God's ordinances shall be brought into the covenant of friendship, to be united (or, to become a community) in God's counsel. . . . All who dedicate themselves to his truth shall bring all their mind and their strength and their property into the Community of God." The short poetical citation of 1 QS viii, 5–8, describes the community as the "witnesses of truth" and "those chosen according to God's pleasure." They are the ones who have been set apart as a house of holiness in Israel (ix, 6). And so we see that the Qumran sons of light are marked by the exclusiveness typical of small sectarian movements whether in Israel or in Christianity.[49]

The precise factor in the community which sanctifies its members is their acceptance of, and obedience to, the teaching of the sect. The early chapters of 1 QS give the Covenant of the community. They are told that they have "to walk before him perfectly (in) all things that are revealed according to their appointed seasons . . ." (i, 8–9).[50] The idea of submissiveness to revealed teaching comes up again in the instruction of iii, 13: "For the wise man, that he may instruct and teach all the sons of light in the generations of all mankind with regard to all the varieties of their spirits. . . ." The hearts of the sectarians are illumined with the "wisdom of life"; and they can look upon the "light of life."[51]

Historically, God seems to have raised up the Teacher of Righteousness to instruct men in this marvelous wis-

---

[49] This Qumran exclusiveness is seen in their consideration of themselves as princes. CD 8:6: ". . . the penitents of Israel who went forth out of the land of Judah and sojourned in the land of Damascus, all of whom God called princes." And again in the *pesher*-commentary on Ps 37, published by J. M. Allegro in the *Pal. Expl. Quart.* 86 (1954), 72 (ii, 4a): ". . . The Congregation of His Elect will be the Chieftains and Princes." Reicke, *op. cit.* in note 2, sees in this a similarity to St. Peter's "chosen race, a royal priesthood" (1 Pt 2:9).

[50] There are numerous citations in the Qumran literature about a special revelation. CD 2:1: "And now, hearken unto me all you who have entered into the covenant, and I will disclose to you the ways of the wicked." Again CD 5:1–2: "God confirmed the covenant of Israel forever, revealing unto them the hidden things wherein all Israel had erred: his holy Sabbaths and his glorious festivals." Charles and others see a possible reference to the calendar of the *Book of Jubilees* which the sectarians followed.

[51] The passages are 1 QS ii, 3, and iii, 7; Brownlee translates: "life-giving wisdom" and "life-giving light."

dom. CD 1:7 says: "And he raised them up a Teacher of Righteousness to lead them in the way of his heart."[52] Since this revealed wisdom is a special interpretation of the Torah, throughout the history of the sect there has been a strong emphasis on studying the Law. The enigmatic figure called "the Star" is described in CD 9ᵃ:8 as one who studied the Law. In the present circumstances the communication of such teaching is the function of the overseer (*mebaqqer*)* of the camp; it is he who "shall instruct the many in the works of God, and shall make them understand his wondrous mighty acts, and shall narrate before them the things of the world . . ." (CD 16:1).

Acceptance of such teaching is not conceived of as purely passive; it implies that sectarians do good works in conformity with this instruction. 1 QS iv, 2, gives a list of the desirable virtues which are the way of the good spirit: truth, humility, patience, compassion, understanding, wisdom, zeal, purity—an interesting parallel to St. Paul's fruits of the Spirit (Gal 5:22 ff.). Periodically the neophyte is to be examined "with respect to his understanding and his deeds in Torah, in accordance with the views of the sons of Aaron."[53] CD 10 ff gives a detailed series of laws for the community to follow. And, as we see from 1 QS vi, 24 ff., backsliding or misbehavior was seriously punished. And so in general the sons of light, the Qumran Community, can truly be said to be "the doers of the law in the house of Judah whom God will deliver from the house of

---

[52] In 1 QpHab ii, 8, those are condemned who will not accept what they hear from the mouth of the priest whom God has sent "to give the meaning of all the words of his servants the prophets."

* See the discussion of *mebaqqer* above, chap. II, pp. 49–52.

[53] 1 QS v, 21. The idea of examination is found also in 1 QS v, 24, and vi, 17. We may say that ix, 13 sets the ideal of the community: ". . . to do God's will according to all that has been revealed for any time at that time, and to learn all the wisdom found with reference to the times."

judgment for the sake of their labor and their 'faith' in the Teacher of Righteousness."[54]

When we turn to the "sons of light" in St. John we find ourselves at a distance from Qumran. As we would expect, good men are attracted to the light of Christ. "But he who does the truth comes to the light that his deeds may be made manifest, for they have been performed in God" (Jn 3:21). Yet it is not good deeds that constitute one a son of light—it is *faith in Christ, the light of the world!* ". . . believe in the light, that you may become sons of light."—"I have come a light into the world, that whoever believes in me may not remain in the darkness" (Jn 12: 36, 46). This same idea is expressed in Jn 8:12: "I am the light of the world. He who follows me does not walk in the darkness, but will have the light of life."[55]

Nevertheless, if by faith in Christ we are constituted sons of light, our obligations to perform good works have

[54] 1 QpHab viii, 1—a commentary on Hab 2:4; the famous verse quoted in Rom 1:17; cf. Gal 3:11 and Heb 10:38 f. Brownlee remarks (*op. cit.*, note 57): "Interestingly enough this commentator agrees with Paul in interpreting *aemunato* as a personal faith which brings salvation." Undoubtedly the *pesher* offers an interpretation of Habakkuk which is intermediary between the literal Old Testament sense and that of Paul, but does the Qumran document mean any more than fidelity to the Teacher's exposition of the Law? CD 9:50–51 says that God will reward all those "who hold fast by these judgments in going out and coming in according to the Law, and listen to the voice of the Teacher and confess before God (saying), 'We have done wickedly. . . .'"

[55] Note the parallelism of the term "the light of life" here and at Qumran. For "sons of light," cf. 1 Thes 5:5: "For you are all children of the light and children of the day. We are not of night, nor of darkness." Eph 5:8: "For you once were darkness, but now you are light in the Lord." Also there is the difficult Lk 16:8: ". . . for the children of this world are in relation to their own generation more prudent than are the children of the light." Could "children of the light" have a definite sectarian meaning here?

not ceased. Rather we are now expected to walk as sons of light, and to conduct ourselves virtuously.[56] Naturally, this includes all the virtues, but John stresses charity. "He who says that he is in the light, and hates his brother, is in the darkness still. He who loves his brother abides in the light, and for him there is no stumbling" (1 Jn 2:9–10). And in this way, just as those who walk in the darkness are judged, so those sons of light who believe in Christ and keep His commandments are saved from their sins: "But if we walk in the light as he also is in the light, we have fellowship with one another, and the blood of Jesus Christ, his Son, cleanses us from all sin" (1 Jn 1:7).

Summing up this point, we say that, while Qumran and St. John characterize good men in much the same way, they differ greatly in their notion of what brings one into the domain of light. For Qumran it is acceptance of the community's interpretation of the Law; for John it is faith in Jesus Christ. Both insist that sons of light live up to their name in virtuous behavior.

These five points of comparison should enable us to form an idea of the similarities and differences that exist between the modified dualistic concept of light and darkness in the Qumran and in the Johannine literature. In retrospect, it should be evident that *the basic difference between the two theologies is Christ*. Both believe in the creation of all things by God. Both conceive of the world as divided into the two camps of light and darkness, and see these camps arranged under personal leadership. For Qumran the leaders are the two created spirits or angels of light and

---

[56] Eph 5:9 continues, "Walk, then, as children of the light for the fruit of the light is in all goodness and justice and truth), testing what is well pleasing to God; and have no fellowship with the unfruitful works of darkness." The RSV translates the Greek (*dokimazontes*) as "try to learn what is pleasing to the Lord." Compare this to the Qumran quote in n. 53. Also Rom 13:12: "The day is at hand. Let us therefore lay aside the works of darkness, and put on the armor of light. Let us walk becomingly as in the day."

darkness (truth and perversion); for St. John, however, the leader of light is the uncreated Word, while the leader of evil is the prince of this world. For Qumran the struggle between the forces is still on an equal plane, although light will shine victoriously at the end; for John light is already conquering darkness. Both the literatures maintain that all men are to be assigned to either of the two camps. Yet throughout the Qumran literature there is a curious mixture of determinism and free will, while John is quite clear that men remain in darkness because they obstinately turn away from light. And, finally, Christ is also the point of difference between John and Qumran with respect to the ultimate constituent of the sons of light. If the terminology and ideology are often the same, St. John's whole outlook has been radically reoriented by the revelation that is Christ.

Granting this all-important difference, we may ask if the similarities are sufficient to posit dependence of St. John's outlook upon Qumran ideology. We have considered only one point: modified dualism; in succeeding pages we shall take up others, e.g., the spirits of truth and perversion, the emphasis on charity, the fountain of living waters. With this added evidence the reader will be in a better position to make a judgment. Yet this much may be said of the dualism already discussed: in no other literature do we have so close a terminological and ideological parallel to Johannine usage.[57] Can such peculiar similarities between the two trains of thought (which were in existence in the same small region of the world at the same period of time) be coincidental?

OTHER SIMILARITIES

a) Truth and Perversity. For Qumran the terms "truth" and "perversity" are interchangeable with "light and darkness" as expression of modified dualism. In 1 QS iii, 19 the leaders of the forces of light and darkness are called

[57] Cf. Braun, *op. cit.,* 31.

the spirits of truth and perversion.[58] The way of the spirit of truth (iv, 2 ff.) is contrasted in detail with the way of the spirit of perversion (iv, 9 ff.); and in one or the other way all men walk.

In the New Testament "the spirit of truth" is a term peculiar to St. John.[59] In his theology we notice a difference between the leader of the forces of light (Christ) and the Spirit of truth (the Paraclete or the Holy Spirit). There are three places where the latter term is used with a personal meaning. In Jn 14:16–17, Christ says: "And I will ask the Father and he will give you another Paraclete to dwell with you forever, the Spirit of truth whom the world cannot receive, because it neither sees him nor knows him." This is continued in 15:26: "But when the Paraclete has come, whom I will send you from the Father, the Spirit of truth who proceeds from the Father, he will bear witness concerning me." And finally 16:13 says: "But when he, the Spirit of truth, has come, he will teach you all the truth." Thus, if St. John found "light" an ideal term for the revelation that is Jesus Christ,[60] he seems to have discovered in the "Spirit of truth" an apt description for the Holy Spirit, the true witness of Christ.[61]

Yet in 1 Jn 4:1–6 one finds a different use of "the spirit of truth" in opposition to "the spirit of error": "Beloved,

[58] In CD 2:12, we hear of men who are anointed with God's holy spirit and thus made seers of the truth.

[59] Cf. Jas 1:18: "He has begotten us by the word of truth."

[60] The term "truth" is also applied to Christ: "I am the way, and the truth and the life" (Jn 14:6); "And the Word was made flesh, and dwelt among us. And we saw his glory . . . full of grace and truth" (1:14). It is interesting to take a concordance and see the number of times "truth" is used in Jn in a sense obviously more meaningful than "veracity."

[61] John never uses the term "spirit of perversion." However, he clearly regards the devil as diametrically opposed to truth: "He was a murderer from the beginning and has not stood in the truth because there is no truth in him. When he tells a lie, he speaks from his very nature, for he is a liar and the father of lies" (8:44).

do not believe every spirit, but test the spirits to see whether
they are of God; because many false prophets have gone
forth into the world. . . . We are of God. He who knows
God listens to us; he who is not of God does not listen to
us. By this we know the spirit of truth and the spirit of
error."[62] Here we certainly find a remarkable similarity to
the two spirits of 1 QS.[63]

The similarity grows even more striking when we compare sections of Qumran and Johannine phraseology. In
1 QS i, 5; v, 3; and viii, 2, the sectarians are urged "to
practice" or "to do the truth." Jn 3:21 says: "But he who
does the truth[64] comes to the light that his deeds may be
made manifest, for they have been performed in God." The
same expression occurs in 1 Jn 1:6: "If we say that we
have fellowship with him, and walk in darkness, we lie, and
are not *practicing the truth.*"

The Qumran texts also share with John the idea of walking in truth.[65] "I rejoiced greatly that I found some of your
children walking in truth . . ." (2 Jn 4). An almost identical statement occurs in 3 Jn 3: "I rejoiced greatly when
some brethren came and bore witness to your truth, even

[62] Notice in this passage the peculiar phrase "test the spirit."
A similar expression occurs in 1 QS v, 20–21: "Now, when
he [the neophyte] enters into the covenant to do according to
all these ordinances, to be united to a holy congregation, they
shall examine his spirit in the community . . ." (also v, 24,
and vi, 17). The term is roughly the same; but John seems to
refer to *charismata*, the gifts of the Spirit, while Qumran is
talking about a way of behavior.

[63] Another interesting combination of spirit and truth occurs
in Jn 4:23: "But the hour is coming, and is now here, when the
true worshipers will worship the Father in spirit and in truth.
. . . God is spirit, and they who worship him must worship in
spirit and truth."

[64] This expression is peculiar to St. John. Ap 22:15 speaks of
"everyone who loves and practices falsehood."

[65] 1 QS iv, 6 and 15, speaks of walking in the ways of two
spirits.

as you walk in the truth. I have no greater joy than to hear
that my children are walking in the truth."

Because of their devotion to truth, the sectarians are
called "witnesses of truth" (1 QS viii, 6).[66] Only in the
Fourth Gospel, where it is used both of John the Baptist
and of Christ, does this phrase occur in the New Testament: "You have sent to John, and he has borne witness to
the truth" (5:33); and "I am a king. This is why I was
born, and why I have come into the world, to bear witness
to the truth" (18:37).[67]

In both the Qumran texts and St. John, truth is seen as a
medium of purification and sanctification. 1 QS iv, 20–21,
states: "And then God will purge by his truth all the deeds
of man . . . to cleanse him through a holy spirit from all
wicked practices, sprinkling upon him a spirit of truth
[Brownlee capitalizes "spirit"] as purifying water." This
may be compared with Jn 17:17–19: "Sanctify them in
truth. Your word is truth. Even as you have sent me into
the world, so I also have sent them into the world. And
for them I sanctify myself, that they also may be sanctified
in truth."

Finally, we may compare two sentences which we have
quoted in part before, but which are most effective when
seen together: "According as man's inheritance is in truth
and righteousness, so he hates evil; but in so far as his
heritage is in the portion of perversity and wickedness in
him, so he abominates truth" (1 QS iv, 24).—"For every
one who does evil hates the light, and does not come to
the light, so that his deeds may not be exposed. But he who
does the truth comes to the light, that his deeds may be
made manifest, for they have been performed in God" (Jn
3:20–21).

b) Brotherly Love. The Qumran literature (and, of
course, the Bible itself) maintains the principle that one

[66] Brownlee suggests a cross reference to Is 43:10–12: "You
are my witnesses and my servant whom I have chosen."
[67] Also cf. 3 Jn 3 in the preceding paragraph.

must hate evil and love good. 1 QS i, 3–4, urges those who
seek God "to love everything that he has chosen, and to
hate everything that he has rejected; to keep far from every
evil and to cling to every good deed." (Also CD 3:1:
". . . to choose what he approves, and to reject what he
hates.") As might be expected, however, we encounter
difficulty when we pass from evil and good to persons
who do evil and good.[68]

The Qumran texts inculcate a hatred of those who are
not sons of light, i.e., are not members of the community.[69]
1 QS i, 10, requires one "to hate all the sons of darkness
each according to his guilt in provoking God's vengeance!"
The Levites of Qumran curse the sons of Belial: "May you
be cursed without compassion, according to the darkness
of your deeds, and damned in the gloom of eternal fire!
May God not favor you when you call; and may he not be
forgiving to pardon your iniquities" (ii, 7–8). The sectarian
is admonished to separate himself from perverse men, and
to conceal from them the community's special interpretation
of the Law (v, 11, and ix, 17–18).[70]

Yet within the Qumran texts, as Grossouw remarks, "several passages struggle as it were to break through their
narrow boundaries (of hatred)."[71] The hymn of 1 QS x,
18, is magnificent in its spirituality: "I will repay no man
with evil's due; (only) with good will I pursue a man; for

[68] The Old Testament is quite clear about love for one who
has offended: Lv 19:18 commands, "Take no revenge and cher-
ish no grudge against your fellow countrymen. You shall love
your neighbor as yourself." Yet, in practice, love of enemy does
not seem to have received great emphasis in Old Testament
morality.

[69] Kuhn, "Die Sektenschrift," 306, sees close parallels to this
in the Zoroastrian *Yasna*. These Qumran passages may well
be adopted formulae which had lost some of their original
venom.

[70] Grossouw, *op. cit.*, 292, sees in this a resemblance to the
Christian *disciplina arcani*.

[71] *Ibid.*

with God is the judgment of every living thing." Continuing in xi, 1, the author speaks of the duty "to teach the
straying of spirit understanding, and to make murmurers
wise through instruction; and to respond humbly before the
haughty of spirit, and with broken spirit to men of injustice."

These two trends are puzzling. Certainly Qumran never
reached the heights of Mt 5:44: "But I say to you, love
your enemies, do good to those who hate you, and pray
for those who persecute and calumniate you, so that you
may be children of your Father in heaven, who makes his
sun to rise on the good and the evil."[72] Christianity represents both a doctrinal and a moral development over all
that went before. Yet, and we shall see this especially in
the question of brotherly love, "One gets a strong impression that in these [Qumran] writings man's mind is preparing for the Christian precept of love."[73] The formulae
of hate are found in the initiation ceremonies and for-
malized instructions of 1 QS: they may be ancient, stylized
enunciations of evil as personified in the sons of Belial.[74]

---

[72] Also Mt 19:19 and parallels. Coppens, *op. cit.,* 32, points
out that, even at its height, Qumran never attained to the
paternity of God: "We seek in vain a text recalling the one
where St. Paul asserts the presence of the Spirit in the heart
of the believers, inviting and urging them to speak to God as
their Father with a note of the intimacy of family relations."

[73] Grossouw, *op. cit.,* 292.

[74] Braun, *op. cit.,* 17–18, suggests that this opposition to the
sons of Belial may be echoed in John's opposition to the world:
"Do not love the world, or the things that are in the world. If
anyone loves the world, the love of the Father is not in him"
(1 Jn 2:15). This distrust of the world demands that the Christian, to a certain extent, separate himself from the world: "They
are not of the world, even as I am not of the world" (Jn
17:16). If Braun is correct in seeing a parallel to Qumran in
this, St. John's theology still presents a great clarification: our
hatred is for evil as represented in the world, and not for the
people who do evil. However, even John speaks of "the children

The hymns are, perhaps, more representative of the ideal of personal piety at Qumran.

Whatever may be the moral defects in the sectarians' dealing with outsiders, the fraternal affection is truly edifying. Over and over again 1 QS insists that there be a spirit of loving devotion in the community.[75] The instruction of i, 10, says that all who join the group have "to love all the sons of light, each according to his lot in God's counsel." This is made more practical in v, 26: "One shall not speak to his brother in anger, or in complaint, or with a (stiff) neck or a callous heart, or a wicked spirit; nor shall he hate him. . . ." If there are to be rebukes, they must be administered in the manner least calculated to offend.[76] Punishments for sins against one's brother are quite severe (vii, 4–8).

In the New Testament, while the Synoptics transmit Christ's command of universal charity, it is John who stresses love of one's brother within the Christian community.[77] Christ's great commandment for John is that of mutual love within the Church: "A new commandment I give you, that you love one another: that as I have loved you, you also love one another. By this will all men know that you are my disciples, if you have love for one another"

---

of the devil" (1 Jn 3:10), which is not too far from "the sons of Belial."

[75] ii, 24; v, 4 and 25; viii, 2; x, 26. Braun, *op. cit.*, 19, sees in this communal spirit an approach to the *agape* of John.

[76] CD 10:10 ff. outlines a process of rebuking before witnesses, and states that a sinner on the testimony of reliable witnesses can be excluded from "the Purity of the Community." As many have noticed, the process bears a resemblance to Mt 18: 15–17 on fraternal correction. Josephus, *Bell.*, 2, 8, says of the Essenes: "They dispense their anger after a just manner and restrain their passion."

[77] Grossouw, *op. cit.*, 298: "It is St. John who in the New Testament speaks exclusively, and very often, of the love of one's brothers or the love of each other, but never of the love of one's neighbor (in the Christian sense of the word neighbor)."

(13:34–35; also 15:12). This theme runs all through the Johannine epistles, e.g., "He who loves his brother abides in the light, and for him there is no stumbling" (1 Jn 2:10).[78] It reaches breathtaking heights in 1 Jn 4:7–8: "Beloved, let us love one another, for love is from God. . . . He who does not love does not know God, for God is love."

The prevalence of the theme of brotherly love in both the Qumran and the Johannine literature is not a conclusive proof of interrelationship. But it is certainly remarkable that the New Testament writer who shares so many other ideological and terminological peculiarities with Qumran should also stress the particular aspect of charity which is emphasized more at Qumran than anywhere else in Jewish literature before Christ.

c) *Fountain of Living Waters.* The metaphorical use of this term occurs several times in the Old Testament. In Jer 2:13 it refers to God: "For my people have committed two evils: they have forsaken me, the fountain of living waters, and hewed out cisterns for themselves, broken cisterns, that can hold no water." And again, in Ps 36:9: "For with you is the fountain of life; in your light do we see light." Prv 13:14 gives another application: "The teaching of the wise is a fountain of life."[79]

CD has its own use for the metaphor: the community's interpretation of the Law is the well of living waters. 9ᵇ:28 warns: "So are all the men who entered into the New Covenant in the land of Damascus and yet turned backward and acted treacherously and departed from the spring

[78] Cf. also 1 Jn 3:11, 18, 23; 2 Jn 5. And, of course, there is the *koinōnia* ("fellowship") of 1 Jn 1:3 and 6–7.

[79] For similar usage, cf. Jer 17:13; Prv 14:27; 16:22; Sir 21: 16 (13). Ct 4:15 compares the beloved to "a well of living waters." In this connection, C. H. Dodd, *The Interpretation of the Fourth Gospel* (1954), 312, tells us: "In rabbinic tradition water was a frequent symbol of the Torah, as cleansing, as satisfying thirst, and as promoting life."

of living waters." On the other hand, of those who stay in the community it may be said: "They dug a well of many waters: and he that despises them shall not live" (5:3). The most specific identification occurs in a commentary on Nm 21:18 (CD 8:6): "The well is the Law, and they who dug it are the penitents of Israel who went forth out of the land of Judah and sojourned in the land of Damascus."

In the New Testament this terminology occurs in only two books, the Fourth Gospel and Apocalypse. In his conversation with the Samaritan woman, Christ says, "He, however, who drinks of the water that I will give him shall never thirst; but the water that I will give him shall become in him a fountain of water, springing up unto eternal life" (Jn 4:14). And again in 7:38 he cries out, "As the Scripture says, 'From within him [Jesus or the believer?] there shall flow rivers of living water.' "[80] Ap 7:17 speaks of the Lamb guiding those who have suffered for Christ "to the fountain of the water of life." And toward the end of Ap (21:6), Christ, the Alpha and Omega, promises, "To him who thirsts I will give of the fountain of the water of life freely."[81]

Because of the occurrence of the term in the Old Testament, this usage is not a conclusive proof of interrelationship between the Qumran and the Johannine literature. But it is interesting to notice that the metaphor betrays the characteristic interests of Qumran and of St. John. For Qumran the water of life comes from the community's discipline and lore; for John it is given by Christ to those who believe in him—the same difference we found in the discussion of "the sons of light."

[80] The precise OT passage intended by Jn is not certain: perhaps Ps 78:15–16 and Zech 14:8. Braun, *op. cit.*, 25, has noticed this similarity of the "fountains of living water," and he mentions the use of the Well of the Oath and the Well of the Vision in *Jubil.* 16:11 and 24:1.

[81] Ap 21:6; also 22:1 and 17.

CONCLUSIONS

Our primary purpose was to present enough evidence to enable the reader to draw his own conclusions. It would seem somewhat abrupt, however, to close without evaluating the parallels.

First, and of this there should be no question, there remains a tremendous chasm between Qumran thought and Christianity. No matter how impressive the terminological and ideological similarities are, the difference that Jesus Christ makes between the two cannot be minimized. Therefore, we would do well to avoid any policy of hunting for Christian parallels to every line of the Qumran texts. The Essene sectarians were not Christians, and the recognition of this will prevent many misinterpretations. On the other hand, it is even more incorrect to turn the early Christians into Essenes. In his second volume on the Scrolls, Dupont-Sommer rejects some of the wild conclusions that were based on his first work.[82] Yet he still states, "Christianity, I repeat, is not Essenism, it is '*an* Essenism' as Renan said." We do not think that the adaptation of Essene terminology and ideology to Christianity in the New Testament makes Christianity *an* Essenism any more than the use of Platonic terminology and ideology by the Fathers makes it a Platonism. Christianity is too unique to be classified as any earlier "ism."

Having made these very important reservations, we can turn to evaluate the evidence. If we add the similarities we have just discussed to what we saw about the modified dualism, the argument for interrelation between the Johannine writings and the Qumran literature is indeed strong. The resemblances do not seem to indicate immediate relationship, however, as if St. John were himself a sectarian or were personally familiar with the Qumran literature.

---

[82] *Op. cit.*, chap. 9. For the effects of his first work, see notes 4, 5, and 6. In our opinion, Dupont-Sommer himself offered sufficient basis for some of these exaggerations.

Rather they indicate a more general acquaintance with the thought and style of expression which we have found at Qumran. The ideas of Qumran must have been fairly widespread in certain Jewish circles in the early first century A.D.[83] Probably it is only through such sources that Qumran had its indirect effect on the Johannine literature.

W. F. Albright has pointed out how important this interrelationship is for dating the Fourth Gospel.[84] We now realize that John's peculiar terminology (which was often the reason for a late dating of the Gospel) has parallels in a Palestinian tradition which flourished before the Christian Era. Therefore, even if we allow time for the oral transmission of the Gospel in the Diaspora, we may still date its final writing within the first century A.D.—a far cry from the very late dating of some critics. As for authorship, the knowledge that the tradition of the Fourth Gospel is local Palestinian weakens the position of those who deny that it contains tradition from John the Apostle.

The reader may wonder how the Qumran parallels in John compare with those of other books of the New Testament. After the Johannine literature, the Pauline corpus shows the greatest affinities to Qumran. In the notes of the section on dualism, we mentioned Pauline passages which betray sectarian terminology; but a thorough study of all similarities would require another article just as long as the present one. (The importance of these similarities should not be neglected, Albright observes, for they show a closeness between Paul and John which has been too often denied.[85]) Certainly the parallels throw an interesting light on St. Paul's "mysteries" and on his theology of faith.[86]

[83] Josephus, *Bell.*, 2, 8, speaks of the Essenes: "They have no certain city, but many of them dwell in every city."

[84] "Recent Discoveries . . ." (note 17), 170–171.

[85] *Op. cit.*, 167.

[86] Grossouw, *op. cit.*, 1–4, and Braun, *op. cit.*, 32–34, give examples. For the Qumran parallels and the Pauline "mystery" passages see R. E. Brown, *Catholic Biblical Quarterly* 20 (1958), 436–443.

The Epistle to the Hebrews has also some interesting points of contact with the Qumran literature.[87] The remaining New Testament books show scattered Qumran affinities,[88] but less frequently than the Johannine or Pauline works.

These facts may cause us to wonder why similarities to Qumran thought are more frequent in some portions of the New Testament than in others.[89] At the present there are only indications toward a solution. For St. John the answer may lie in a verse of the Fourth Gospel: "Again the next day John (the Baptist) was standing there and two of his disciples" (1:35). One of these disciples was Andrew; his anonymous confrère has traditionally been identified as John, son of Zebedee. Now virtually everyone who has studied the Qumran texts in the light of the New Testament has recognized the startling Qumran parallels in the

---

[87] Braun, *op. cit.*, 37: "Among the New Testament writings, Hebrews is the one which gives the fullest answer to the basic tendencies of the Sect." C. Spicq. *L'Épitre aux Hébreux*, I, 109–138, points out the proximity of Hebrews to the Johannine literature; consequently, Qumran similarities should not be surprising. May not the principal argument of the Epistle, i.e., that Christ is a priest although He is from Judah, be directed against the expectation of the two Messiahs, from Aaron and from Israel? For more complete treatments see Spicq, *Revue de Qumran* 1 (1959), 365–390, and Herbert Braun, *Theologische Rundschau* 30 (1964), 1–38.

[88] We have given some in footnotes; Grossouw, 5–8, and Braun, 39–40, give others. Sherman E. Johnson, "The Dead Sea Manual of Discipline and the Jerusalem Church of Acts," *Zeitschr, f. d. alttest. Wissensch.*, 66 (1954), 106–120, mentions these parallels between Qumran and the early Church as described in Acts: baptism, communal sharing, poverty, communal meals, organization. These suggestions need to be critically evaluated. See above, chap. II, B.

[89] In "Recent Discoveries . . ." Albright suggests that it is not a question of a fundamental difference between the Synoptics and John; the latter has simply emphasized certain aspects of Christ's teaching, including certain aspects that resembled the teaching of the Essenes most closely.

narratives concerning John the Baptist;[90] almost every detail of his life and preaching has a *possible* Qumran affinity. From this it would seem likely that the Baptist, before his contact with Christ, was in relationship with Qumran or other Essenes (perhaps he was raised by the community,[91] or in contact with the community, or the head of a quasi-Essene group). If this is true, and if John, son of Zebedee, was his disciple, we can explain very well the Qumran impact on the Fourth Gospel.

External evidence adds an interesting note. Tradition is almost unanimous that this Gospel was written at Ephesus.[92] Acts 18:24 ff. speaks of the presence at Ephesus of disciples of John the Baptist who were not yet fully Christian.[93] An hypothesis might be constructed that John the Baptist was familiar with the Qumran Essenes and their thought, and that through him certain of these ideas passed on to his disciples, including John, son of Zebedee. The latter formed his ideas of Jesus in the light of this

[90] Cf. especially two articles by Brownlee: "John the Baptist in the New Light of Ancient Scrolls," *Interpretation* 9 (1955), 71–90; and "A Comparison of the Covenanters of the Dead Sea Scrolls with pre-Christian Jewish Sects," *Biblical Archaeologist,* 13 (1950), 69–72. Also Grossouw, *op. cit.,* 5, on the Benedictus. See below, chap. VIII, n. 8.

[91] Suggested by Brownlee, "John the Baptist," 73.

[92] St. Irenaeus, *Adv. Haer.,* 3, 11, 1 (PG 7, 879–880), tells us that it was directed against Cerinthus. St. Jerome, *In Evang. Matt. Prol.* (PL 26, 18–19), adds the name of Ebion to John's adversaries. Victorinus Petaviensis, *In Apocalypsin,* 11, 1 (PL 5, 333D), mentions Valentinus, Cerinthus, and Ebion. This is significant because, as we mentioned, there are similarities between Ebionite doctrines and those of Qumran.

[93] We should note that some of the Pauline Epistles which have affinities to the Qumran literature are centered around Ephesus (Eph, 1 and 2 Corinthians, written at Ephesus or shortly after his departure; Timothy to his disciple at Ephesus). Spicq, *op. cit.,* I, chap. 7, attributes the authorship of Hebrews, which has Qumran influences too, to Apollos (the disciple of John the Baptist), who was at Ephesus.

background, and, of course, remembered and stressed those *logia* of Jesus which were in close harmony with his own feelings. Later at Ephesus, disciples of the Baptist who had not accepted Christ became part of the audience[94] to whom the Johannine preaching was directed, and Christ was interpreted to them in familiar terms. Christ is the light they speak of; true sons of the light are those who believe in him; the "spirit of truth" is the Holy Spirit, etc. Yet such an hypothesis,[95] while it fulfills the tradition of the origin of the Gospel, is based on so many surmises that it can remain only an interesting possibility for the present.

[94] There were, most likely, other causes too—whence our hesitancy to interpret all details of the Gospel in anti-Essene terms.

[95] Braun, *op. cit.*, 42–44, proposes a theory similar to ours.

VIII

John the Baptist in the Gospel of John

Jn 1:26:   I baptize in water . . . (1:33) he . . . baptizes in a Holy Spirit.

Jn 1:29:   Behold the lamb of God who takes away the world's sin.

Jn 1:30:   After me is coming one who ranks ahead of me because he existed before me.

These three verses represent the Johannine picture of John the Baptist's (JBap) witness to Jesus. Only the first is found in the Synoptics. The meaning of these verses in the whole complex of Jn (i.e., their Gospel sense; the *Sitz im Evangelium*) is relatively clear. They refer respectively to the coming of the Holy Spirit, the value of Jesus' death as a propitiation for sin,[1] and the preexistence of the Word:

[1] Here there is some doubt. The propitiatory value of Christ's death is clearer in 1 Jn (2:2; 3:5) than in Jn. Some maintain that the "lamb of God" is a reference to Jesus as the paschal lamb of the New Testament. Jn's word *amnos* appears in 1 Pt 1:19 in what may be a reference to Jesus the paschal lamb. Also there are many paschal lamb features in Jn's description of the crucifixion (condemned at the time the lambs were being

all themes found in Johannine theology. Thus the author of Jn sees in the opening witness of JBap to Jesus a sketch of the great revelation that would come to men through Jesus' ministry. This does not mean that this rather complete theological insight was all understood at the Jordan; for, as Jn makes clear (14:26; 16:13–15), it was only after the coming of the Spirit that the disciples understood the fullness of the truth about Jesus.[2] Let us emphasize, however, that the final meaning that the statements of JBap came to bear *in the Gospel* is their literal scriptural sense and their inspired sense.

Our purpose here is to investigate what these three sayings meant to JBap, i.e., what they meant when they were first uttered (historical sense).[3] We see three general ways to approach this question:

a) We might claim that the historical sense is exactly the same as the Gospel sense, i.e., JBap intended to refer to the Holy Spirit, the salvific death of Christ, and the preexistence of the Word. *A priori,* this is not impossible. Wearing the mantle of the prophets, JBap certainly was the recipient of a divine call; and it is not impossible that God could have revealed to him all these truths. Yet we find this extremely unlikely. The Synoptic account of JBap's expectation of one to come after him implies a primitive picture of violent judgment. During Jesus' ministry, JBap sent his disciples to ask of Him a question which implies that JBap did not understand the essential nature of that

---

sacrificed; no bone broken; the hyssop; the body not left on the cross until the next day). Others see in the "lamb of God" a reference to the Suffering Servant of Is 53:7 led to slaughter like an *amnos* before its shearers, who *bears* [but not "takes away"] the sins of others. There is no real difficulty in seeing a double reference in Jn's thought.

[2] Also 2:22; 12:16; 14:9; Lk 24:25–27.

[3] This could be called the *Sitz im Leben,* but not with the connotation given to that term by the form critics, where *Leben* is the life of the primitive Church. Rather it is a *Sitz im Leben Jesu.*

ministry.[4] And, at least for the question of the Holy Spirit, we discover that the disciples of JBap had never even heard that there was such a Holy Spirit (Acts 19:2).

b) If, *salvo meliore judicio,* we find this first solution unacceptable, neither do we favor the other extreme solution that would assume without serious discussion that these sayings, because they are harmonious with Johannine theology, were invented by the Evangelist and placed on the lips of JBap.[5] As the Pontifical Biblical Commission has insisted in its 1964 instruction, in handling the reminiscences of Jesus' ministry, the Evangelists exercised considerable freedom by way of selecting, synthesizing, and "explicating." Although this instruction, particularly in the verb "explicating," opens up the (limited) possibility of creativity on the Evangelist's part, from the viewpoint of scientific method we should first see if a disputed passage can be explained as stemming from Jesus' ministry. Only as a last resort do we fall back on the "explicating" of the Evangelist; otherwise we are in danger of neglecting the full picture of Jesus' ministry by excising too quickly the difficult passages. In the instance we are discussing here, for one of the three sayings Jn attributes to JBap, the one on baptizing in a Holy Spirit, we have a similar saying in the Synoptic Gospels.

c) We shall attempt a middle solution, i.e., that the statements were actually made by JBap, but that he intended by them a meaning perfectly consonant with the Synoptic

[4] Mt 11:3 (Lk 7:19): "Are you he who is to come, or do we look for someone else?" There is nothing whatsoever in the context to indicate that JBap understood who Jesus was, and was only using the occasion to bring the truth to his disciples who did not understand.

[5] This theory might spring from the idea that the picture of JBap in Jn and that of the Synoptics are not able to be reconciled, a point made in Carl Kraeling, *John the Baptist* (New York: Scribner's, 1951), 127. More important is Baldensperger's hypothesis that Jn is waging a polemic against JBap's disciples in citing passages which show the superiority of Jesus.

picture of his expectations of the one to come. With slight adaptation these statements were incorporated into the Fourth Gospel because in the light of Christian faith they were seen to be even more applicable to Jesus than JBap had realized. The presence of peculiar tradition about JBap in this Gospel *may* stem from the fact that John, son of Zebedee, the traditional source of the Gospel material, was a disciple of JBap (if John was the unnamed disciple of Jn 1:35–40).

BAPTISM IN THE HOLY SPIRIT (1:33)

The three Synoptics have the promise that the one to come after JBap would baptize in a holy spirit. Mt 3:11 and Lk 3:16: "He will baptize you in a holy spirit and fire"; Mk 1:8 and Jn just mention "in a holy spirit." Long before the discoveries at Qumran, Van Imschoot pointed out the real meaning of this passage.[6] JBap preached in an expectant atmosphere of apocalyptic judgment: "Repent for the kingdom of heaven is at hand" (Mt 3:2); "You brood of vipers! Who warned you to flee from the coming wrath?" (Lk 3:7); "Even now the axe is laid to the root of the trees; every tree that does not bear good fruit is cut down and thrown into the fire" (Lk 3:9). The statement about baptism is to be understood in this light. Indeed, in Mt and Lk it is immediately followed by a graphic picture of such judgment: "His winnowing fork is in his hand to clean out his threshing floor. And he will gather the wheat into his barn, but the chaff he will burn up with unquenchable fire" (Mt 3:12; Lk 3:17).

There are many Old Testament references to judgment by fire which can illustrate JBap's prediction of a baptism by fire.[7] But there are also references that promise that God will cleanse man by His spirit in the last days. Is 4:4:

---

[6] "Baptême d'eau et baptême d'esprit saint," *Ephemerides Theologiae Lovanienses*, 13 (1936), 653–666.

[7] Am 7:4; Is 31:9; 66:15–16; Zech 13:9; Mal 3:2.

"[In that day] when the Lord shall have *washed away* the filth of the daughters of Zion, and *cleansed* the bloodstains of Jerusalem from its midst by a spirit of judgment and by a *spirit of burning*." Here we have a cleansing with a spirit of burning: all the elements of a baptism in fire and spirit. In this case, the spirit is a destructive force and synonymous with fire. There are other cases where the cleansing with the spirit seems to be beneficial. Ez 36:25–26: "I will sprinkle *clean water* upon you, and you will be clean from all your uncleannesses. . . . A new heart will I give you, and a new *spirit* will I put within you."

These texts can now be superbly augmented from the Dead Sea Scrolls. 1 QS 4:13 speaks of the destruction of iniquity by fire. But for the just, in the time of divine visitation (4:19), "God will purge by His truth every deed of man, refining for Himself the body of man by abolishing from the midst of his flesh every evil spirit, and *by cleansing him through a holy spirit* from all wicked practices, and He will sprinkle on him *a spirit of truth as purifying water*" (4:20–21). If we remember that Qumran both practiced in the present a type of baptism with water for those who were penitent,[8] and then expected at the divine visitation a destruction of evil by fire and a cleansing of the good by a holy spirit, we have an excellent parallel for

[8] John A. T. Robinson, "The Baptism of John and the Qumran Community," *Harvard Theological Review*, 50 (1957), 175–191, points out some similarities between the Qumran washing and JBap's baptism: (*a*) the external ablution is useless without repentance; (*b*) it is given to Jews and not to pagan converts; (*c*) it is designed to set up a penitent nucleus in Israel for the coming of God; (*d*) it is preliminary to a dispensation of God's spirit. Of course, there are differences too: JBap's baptism is offered on a more universal scale; and it is not designed to set up a monastic community withdrawn from life, but can be received by those willing to reform their daily lives (Lk 3:10–14). Nevertheless, the Dead Sea Scrolls give us the best parallel we have yet had to JBap's baptism of repentance.

JBap's statement: "I baptize you in water, but he will baptize you in a holy spirit and fire."

This interpretation of the passage on baptism in a holy spirit admirably suits JBap's apocalyptic outlook: he expected the one to come to cleanse the evil with a judgment of fire and to cleanse the good with a purifying spirit, i.e., a new breath of life. That a destroying spirit is not meant (that "holy spirit" is not a synonym for "fire") is seen in the interpretative passage that follows JBap's statement in Mt and Lk: "he will baptize in a holy spirit" is parallel to "he will gather the wheat into his barn"; "he will baptize in fire" is parallel to "the chaff he will burn up with unquenchable fire." While Jesus did provoke a certain crisis or judgment among men, He did not visibly introduce a judgment of fire as JBap anticipated; so there was a tendency for the words "and fire" to disappear from the accounts of JBap's words. The part about the holy spirit, however, was treated by the Evangelists as a prophecy of the distribution of the Holy Spirit both at Pentecost and through baptism (Jn 7:38–9; Acts 1:5; 19:1–6).

THE LAMB OF GOD WHO TAKES AWAY
THE WORLD'S SIN (1:29)

This passage, too, we would interpret in the light of JBap's expectations of apocalyptic judgment.[9] In the context of final judgment, we find in Jewish apocalyptic writings the picture of a conquering lamb who destroys evil in the world. *The Testament of Joseph* 19:8 speaks of a lamb (*amnos*) who overcomes the evil beasts and crushes them

---

[9] We shall use here suggestions of C. H. Dodd, *The Interpretation of the Fourth Gospel* (Cambridge University, 1954), 230–237. Dodd would make the apocalyptic lamb the literal sense of the text. We suggest that it is the historical sense of the text; but the literal or Gospel sense of the text, while not excluding the apocalyptic lamb, concerns chiefly the paschal lamb and/or the Suffering Servant. See C. K. Barrett, "The Lamb of God," *New Testament Studies*, 1 (1955), 210–218.

underfoot.[10] In *Enoch* 90:38, in the great animal allegory
of history, there comes at the end a horned bull who turns
into a lamb[11] with black horns. In the context of the Last
Judgment, we are told that the Lord of the sheep rejoiced
over the lamb who is the leader of all the animals. This
picture of the conquering lamb of the last times appears in
the New Testament Ap too.[12] In Ap the lamb was slain
and by his blood redeemed men from every nation (5:9—
notice in Jn that the lamb of God takes away *the world's
sin*). This feature is, of course, a Christian adaptation of
the conquering lamb motif. Yet some of the older features
of the apocalyptic lamb are still present: in 7:17 the lamb
is the leader of peoples; in 17:14 the lamb conquers and
crushes the evil of the earth.

We suggest that when JBap called the one to come after
him "the lamb of God who takes away the world's sin,"
he was speaking in the framework of this Jewish apocalyptic expectation: the lamb to be raised up by God to destroy
evil in the world.[13] Of course, it may be objected that the

[10] There are Christian interpolations in this passage, e.g., the
lamb is born of a virgin of Judah. Charles, however, does not
think the main picture is an interpolation (text in *Apocrypha
and Pseudepigrapha*, II, 353). It appears in the Armenian version which is said to have less Christian interpolation.

[11] The Ethiopic of *Enoch* actually has "word" not "lamb."
Charles (II, 260) suggests that in the process of translation
Hebrew *mlh*, "word," and *ṭlh*, "lamb," were confused. Certainly
the context virtually demands some change, for "word" makes
no sense at all.

[12] The word *arnion* is used in Ap, but we do not think the
vocabulary difference is significant. As Dodd, *op. cit.*, 236, points
out, *arnion* is actually a diminutive, an inconsistency for the
mighty lamb it is describing. This might not bother the scribe of
Ap, but may have persuaded the better Grecian of Jn to use
amnos.

[13] However, we cannot rule out the possibility that JBap
meant the statement in a Suffering Servant sense, for this idea
could lie within his range of thought. He certainly knew Is; and,
in addition, the Synoptic description of the baptism of Jesus at

text actually speaks of taking away[14] sin and not of destroying it. But perhaps we have here a slight adaptation
of the original statement by Jn to fit Jesus who took away
sin not by violent destruction of evil but by voluntarily
laying down His life. However, on this point of "takes
away" and "destroys," we should notice the parallel passages in 1 Jn which may betray the original meaning of our
text in Jn:

1 Jn 3:5: ephanerōthē 'ina tas 'amartias *arē*
            "He appeared to take away sins."
1 Jn 3:8: ephanerōthē 'ina *lusē* ta erga tou diabolou
            "He appeared to destroy the works of the
            devil."
Here "take away" is parallel to "destroy."

THE ONE WHO RANKS AHEAD OF ME BECAUSE HE EXISTED BEFORE ME (1:30)

Here we deal with the most difficult passage of all. To
explain it we must go into the relation of JBap to Elijah.
John A. T. Robinson[15] has brilliantly shown that JBap
gives no indication of ever having thought of himself as

the Jordan is in a Suffering Servant context: Is 42:1: "Behold
my servant [*pais*] in whom my soul is pleased. I have put my
spirit on him"; Mk 1:10–11: "The Spirit descended upon him.
. . . You are my beloved son [*'uios*]; in you I am well pleased."
(Is *'uios* preferred to *pais* to bring out better Jesus' nature?)

[14] *airō*. Since *airō* means "to take away" and not "to take on,"
some authors deny that the text, in its Gospel sense, can refer
to the Suffering Servant of Is 53:4 who bears (*pherō*) our sins.
This may be a little too precise. In selecting Greek words, the
author of Jn is trying to get a good expression for what Jesus
actually did; a reference to the Suffering Servant is by way of
allusion, and we need not expect Jn to choose the exact LXX
vocabulary of Is. Would Jn draw any great distinction between
Christ having borne our sins and having taken them away?

[15] "Elijah, John and Jesus, an Essay in Detection," *New Testament Studies*, 4 (1957–1958), 263–281.

playing the role of Elijah. Jesus identified him as Elijah
(Mt 11:3–14),[16] and this identification has naturally become traditional; but there is no reason to believe that JBap
was aware of it. In Jn 1:21 JBap specifically denies that
he is Elijah. In both Mk 6:14–15 and 8:28, there is a distinction made between JBap and Elijah. In Mt 17:10–13,
the disciples of Jesus (among whom were former disciples
of JBap, like Peter and John) ask, "Why do the scribes
say that first Elijah must come?" They do not understand
that JBap came in the role of Elijah until Jesus explains
it to them.

Rather JBap seems to have conceived of his role only in
terms of the Isaian voice in the desert (a text associated
with him in all four Gospels).[17] If he pictured anyone in
terms of Elijah it was the one to come after him. Indeed,
"the one who is to come" may be a title for Elijah. Mal
3:1 has the words: "Behold he is coming," seemingly applied to the messenger sent to prepare the way. When in
Mt 11:3–14 the disciples of JBap ask Jesus if He is the one
who is to come (*erchomenos*), He answers that JBap is
"Elijah, *who is to come* (*mellōn erchesthai*)." And the
characteristics JBap attributes to the one who is to come
are amazingly Elijahlike. Mal 3:2; 4:1; Sir 48:1 all compare Elijah and his work to a refining, burning fire; JBap

[16] By citing the text of Mal 3, 1: "Behold I send my messenger to prepare the way before me." Mk does not narrate this
scene; but, not wanting to omit this identification, joins the
quote from Mal to the Isaian citation about a voice crying in
the desert. This accounts for the strange combinations in Mk
1:2–3.

[17] It is true that JBap wore the dress of Elijah (Mk 1:6 and
2 Kgs 1:8). Yet the hairy mantle was really the standard
prophetic uniform (Zech 13:4), and may simply have indicated
that JBap came as a prophet. Vaganay makes an interesting
suggestion in *La question synoptique* (Tournai: Desclée, 1954),
356: Lk, stressing that Christ is the prophet, deliberately does
not reproduce passages in Mk or the other sources where JBap
is identified with Elijah. This could be a sign of early difficulties
on who was playing the role of Elijah.

says that the one who is to come will burn the chaff with unquenchable fire, and baptize with fire.

If JBap actually did expect an Elijahlike figure, we have at last the explanation of why he sent his disciples to see if Jesus really was the one to come—Jesus was not acting in the way JBap expected! And Jesus answered him in terms of Is: His was not the role of a destroying judge;[18] but that of the gentle healer and preacher predicted by Is 35:5–6 and 61:1. Again this theory would explain Lk 9:52–56 where James and John (probably a disciple of JBap at one time) wonder if they are to act as Elijah did in bidding fire to come down from heaven (1 Kgs 18:38) to consume the Samaritan villagers. Jesus emphatically rebukes them for the Son of Man is not come to destroy but to save.

This preparatory material concerning JBap's outlook on the one to come as an Elijahlike figure[19] has been given to clarify the text: "After me is coming one who ranks ahead of me because he existed before me." Of no other figure in the Old Testament could JBap have said that as truly as of Elijah, who had existed nine hundred years before him, and yet was expected to come as a messenger

[18] However, some of the incidents reported in Lk show that there were Elijahlike features in Jesus' ministry. Jesus raised the widow's son (Lk 7:11–17) as Elijah raised the son of the widow of Zarephath (Sarepta—1 Kgs 17:18–24). Jesus did not perform miracles at Nazareth, and justified Himself by recalling Elijah (Lk 4:24–26). Also we might compare the Greek *analēmpseōs* ("When the days were fulfilled for his *going up*") in Lk 9:51 with roughly the same expression for Elijah going up into heaven in 2 Kgs 2:11 (*analambanō* and derivatives are not too commonly used in this sense in the Greek Bible). Finally there is the enigmatic statement of Lk 12:49: "I came to cast fire upon the earth; and would that it were already kindled."

[19] In *Enoch* 89:52 Elijah is spoken of as a sheep kept in God's presence. JBap speaks of Jesus as the "Lamb of God." Is this another instance of JBap's identifying Jesus with Elijah?

before God's final judgment.[20] We emphasize the tentative
nature of this explanation; however, it does bring this third
statement within the purview of JBap's primitive eschatological outlook. Jn retained this statement because it was
true of Jesus who, though not Elijah, had existed in the
person of the Word from all eternity.

[20] In JBap's expectation of an Elijahlike figure, we might possibly find a connection with Qumran's expectations. A. S. van
der Woude, "Le Maitre de Justice et les deux Messies," *La
Secte de Qumran* (Desclée de Brouwer, 1959), 131–134, maintains that the awaited messiah of Aaron represents Elijah. He
cites Jewish tradition that Elijah was a priest (and indeed, the
reference to Elijah in Mal 3:1 follows a discussion of the
priestly ideal). We remain skeptical, however, because Elijah
was not a Zadokite priest; and we doubt that Qumran would
have expected an ideal priestly messiah who was not a Zadokite.

Part Two

Section 2

*The Relation Between the Fourth Gospel
and the Synoptic Gospels*

IX

The Problem of
Historicity in John

In using the word "problem" in the title of this paper, we
are not merely being verbose; for we intend to stress that
the historicity of Jn is a problem with both a positive and
a negative side. In the first part of this paper we shall stress
the positive side: the really historical characteristics of the
Johannine tradition which have often been neglected. But
then, in the second part of the paper, we shall point out
the historical limits inherent in Jn which forbid its being
interpreted *simply* as a history.

I. THE REAL HISTORICITY OF JN

It is well known that the categorical rejection of the
historicity of Jn, so familiar in earlier critical exegesis, can
no longer be maintained.[1] We may still find writers stating

[1] See A. J. B. Higgins, *The Historicity of the Fourth Gospel*
(London: Lutterworth, 1960); A. M. Hunter, "Recent Trends
in Johannine Studies," *Expository Times,* 71 (1960), 164–167
and 219–222; John A. T. Robinson, "The New Look on the
Fourth Gospel," *Studia Evangelica* (The Oxford Congress Papers of 1957; Berlin: Akademie, 1959), 338–350.

that the Fourth Gospel cannot be seriously considered as a witness to the historical Jesus, but these represent a type of uncritical traditionalism which arises with age, even in heterodoxy. Let us review briefly the grounds for the change in view.

First of all, there are fewer and fewer supporters of the view that Jn is a late second-century document which lies closer to the Gnosticism of the Hellenistic world than to the Palestinian milieu of Jesus. The Rylands and Bodmer papyri make virtually impossible a date much later than A.D. 100 for the final writing of the complete Gospel. Besides this, the discovery of the Gnostic writings of the late second century, like the *Evangelium Veritatis,* has shown that this Gnosticism is basically quite different from the thought pattern of Jn and is, as the Fathers said it was, a real heresy. While the Gnostics did favor Jn, there is evidence as well for strong orthodox use of Jn in the second century.[2]

While the more radical theories on the origin of Jn have been losing support, the basic Palestinian aspects of the Johannine tradition have been better verified. It was, of course, realized long ago that the author of Jn had Palestinian pretensions. No other Gospel gives such a wealth of place names, exact locations, and such a varied list of active *dramatis personae.* But it was often felt that such "name-dropping" was a part of the fictional trappings of the pseudonymous author. Now, however, a better knowledge of Palestinian geography gained through archaeology has confirmed a host of Johannine localities[3] (e.g., the pool

[2] F.-M. Braun, O.P., *Jean le Théologien et son évangile dans l'église ancienne* (Paris: Gabalda, 1959)—summarized in our review in *Catholic Biblical Quarterly,* 22 (1960), 219–222.

[3] W. F. Albright, *The Archeology of Palestine* (Penguin, 1960 ed.), 243–248. Also R. D. Potter, O.P., "Topography and Archeology in the Fourth Gospel," *Studia Evangelica,* 329–337. Some of Potter's confirmations, however, are really assumptions.

of Bethesda,[4] Bethany near Jerusalem,[5] the Lithostrotos). Some others may still escape identification (e.g., Bethany beyond Jordan, Ephraim[6]), but at least the theory of the invention of names for purely allegorical purposes is now *passé*.[7] This vindication covers personal names and titles as well.[8] And careful analysis has virtually ruled out the idea that Jn, like the apocrypha, interlards stories with personal names just to give them a ring of authenticity.[9]

The authentic Palestinian milieu of the Johannine tradition has been further clarified by the Qumran discoveries.[10] The abstract language, the dualism of light and darkness, and other features which once seemed to rule out Palestinian origin now help to confirm it. For much of the very same vocabulary, mentality, and theological outlook found in Jn is found also at Qumran both before and during

[4] A report on the well-known excavations of the pool is that of B. Bagatti, O.F.M., in *Bibbia e Oriente*, 1 (1959), 12–14. We now have the evidence of the name in the Qumran copper scroll (XI, 12), *byt 'šdtyn;* see J. Milik, *Revue Biblique*, 66 (1959), 347–348; and J. Jeremias, *Expository Times*, 71 (1959–1960), 228.

[5] W. F. Albright, "Bethany in the Old Testament," *Bulletin of the American Schools of Oriental Research*, 4 (1922–1923), 158–160.

[6] However, see *ibid.*, "Ophrah and Ephraim," 124–133.

[7] D. Mollat, S.J., "Remarques sur le vocabulaire spatial du quatrième évangile," *Studia Evangelica*, 321–328, points out that while Jn does often draw a theological message from a place name, his genius is in seeing deeper meaning in what is really part of the story, not in creation.

[8] Albright, *Archeology of Palestine*, 244.

[9] Higgins, *op. cit.*, 53–60, submits this theory to a penetrating criticism. There is really no consistent pattern to the use of the names; and no theory explains them except that of their having originally been part of the story.

[10] Cf. above, chap. VII. W. F. Albright, "Recent Discoveries in Palestine and the Gospel of John," *The Background of the New Testament and its Eschatalogy* (Dodd Anniversary Volume; Cambridge University Press, 1956), 153–171.

Christ's time. A real Palestinian background has been discovered against which the Jesus of Jn can be plausibly pictured.

Thus we may well say that many of the internal obstacles to a belief in the historicity of Jn have been removed.

Second, we may turn to the relation of Jn to the Synoptics. How can the external problem of differences from the Synoptic tradition be resolved? Can two such diverse traditions both claim historicity?

The assumption behind this question is often false: namely that the Synoptic Gospels are themselves histories, and therefore, if Jn is historical, it has to agree with them. Today, however, we have come to a realization that none of the Gospels are histories or biographies in the modern sense.[11] Rather, the tradition behind the Synoptic Gospels is that of the preaching and teaching of the primitive Church. This preaching and teaching stems from eyewitnesses—therefore it is historical (a historicity, however, to be judged according to the standards of preaching and teaching, not those of the camera or tape recorder). Nevertheless, most Catholic writers agree that the ultimate recorders of this preaching and teaching, the Synoptic Evangelists, were not themselves eyewitnesses. They had to accept the schematic outline of the ministry of Jesus which

---

[11] This does *not* mean that the Gospels are not historical. They *do* give us the words and deeds of Jesus. Something can be historical without being a history—it is a question of the principle of organization. The recent monitum of the Holy Office wisely insists on the historicity of the Gospels. This is something quite different from stating that the Gospels were intended as scientific histories. The Instruction of the Biblical Commission of April 21, 1964, is a very careful delineation of the development that has taken place in the three stages of (*a*) what Jesus said and did, (*b*) what the Apostles preached, (*c*) and what the Evangelists wrote.

was passed on to them,[12] and then fit the isolated sayings of Jesus into it as best they could, often without real chronological guidance. Their principle of organizing the Gospel material was theological, rather than primarily biographical. Each one of the three Synoptists (or perhaps their forerunners[13]) selected and organized the deeds and sayings of Jesus according to the message he was trying to convey to his readers. Thus, in a very real sense, each one was a theologian. In their company as theologians, John the Theologian seems not at all out of place even though John still remains *the* Theologian in a unique way. And so, with this clearer view of the literary form of the Gospels, differences in the two traditions are not so difficult to accept.

Nevertheless, it has become clearer, as we probe beneath the surface, that the differences (at least, as they relate to historicity) are not as acute as might first seem. To give a few examples, the Johannine picture of the Baptist is far more exalted than that of the Synoptics. But, if we get behind the Gospel sense to the historical details of the Baptist's actual ministry,[14] the two traditions present the Baptist in the same light of primitive eschatological

[12] This outline, seen at its clearest in Mk, is basically that of the Petrine preaching: baptism, ministry in Galilee, journey to Jerusalem, passion, death, and resurrection (see esp. Acts 10: 37–41). It was probably the official kerygma of the early Church, for Paul uses it too (Acts 13:23–30).

[13] We are giving, of course, a simplified picture. Much of the organization and selection must have been already present in the sources used by the Evangelists. The Evangelists are really recording the kerygma and didache as it was known to different churches.

[14] We presume here a distinction between *Gospel sense* (the meaning that an event or saying has in its present place in the Gospel) and *historical meaning* (the meaning that it had when it first occurred or was first uttered). Both the increased insight of the primitive Church and the role of the Evangelist as theologian require such a distinction.

expectation.[15] Again, the long discourses in Jn, often centered around the "I am" statements of Jesus, seem quite different from the parables through which Jesus of the Synoptics preached the Kingdom of God. Yet Msgr. Cerfaux[16] has shown that for Jn the kingdom of God is present in Jesus, and that the metaphors used in Jn (e.g., "I am the shepherd . . . the vine . . . the gate") employ the same figures of speech found in the Synoptic parables. Even such a peculiarly Johannine feature as realized eschatology is not as different as one might guess. For, while the Synoptics seem to emphasize a parousia eschatology, careful studies like those of Feuillet[17] show that in the Synoptic tradition there has been a certain reinterpretation of Jesus' own eschatology which, in some aspects, was truly a realized eschatology.

If, then, some of the differences between the two traditions are not so sharp as might first seem, the chronology of the two traditions still seems to separate them. The frequent trips to Jerusalem in Jn, and the three Passovers of Jn, implying at least a two-year ministry, seem difficult to reconcile with the one trip to Jerusalem in the Synoptic ministry, a ministry that seems to endure at most one year. It is here that a knowledge of the literary form of the Synoptics comes to our aid: they are giving us the simplified chronological and topological outline of the ministry as presented in the early kerygma (note 12 above), and not a detailed history. Therefore it is perfectly possible that Jn's more detailed indications are historical. The idea that Jn

[15] For detail, see above, chap. VIII.

[16] "Le thème littéraire parabolique dans l'Évangile de saint Jean," *Recueil Lucien Cerfaux* (Louvain, 1954), II, 17–26. See also John A. T. Robinson, "The Parable of John 10, 1–5," *Zeitschrift für neutestamentliche Wissenschaft*, 46 (1955), 233–240.

[17] For a modified statement of his views see: "Les origines et la signification de Mt 10, 23b," *Catholic Biblical Quarterly*, 23 (1961), 182–198. Also "Parousie," in Vigouroux, *Dictionnaire de la Bible, Supplément*, VI, 1331–1419.

invented feasts as occasions for the discourses connected to them is still encountered.[18] That this is not a totally workable hypothesis is clear. For instance, the mention of the first Passover in 2:13, of the unnamed feast in 5:1, and of Dedication in 10:22 can scarcely be explained in this way, for the connection with what happens on those occasions is not clearly enough marked. A more serious possibility is the Passover feast of 6:4 which provides occasion for the multiplication of the loaves and for the discourse on that bread of life which replaces the manna. But even here the Synoptic accounts of the multiplication seem to indicate springtime (Mk 6:39; Mt 14:19), which would agree with Jn's statement that Passover was near. And Bertil Gärtner's[19] close analysis of the discourse on the bread of life shows that it reflects themes which were being read to the Galilean Jews in their synagogues at Passover time. Thus all indications point to Jn's Passover as being historical. As for the other great feast in Jn, the Tabernacles feast of 7:2, it seems less plausible to maintain that Jn invented the feast to match the discourse than to imagine that Jesus actually did speak to the Jews on their feast, and centered His remarks on the theme of the feast[20] (although the speeches as we have them now show the hand of an editor).

The chronological difference on the date of the Last Supper (Jn on 14th Nisan; Synoptics on 15th Nisan) has still not been solved. Many now accept Jn's chronology as the official one. In that case either the Synoptics reflect a different calendar, or (and more probably in our opinion)

---

[18] E.g., Lucetta Mowry, "The DSS and the Background for the Gospel of John," *Biblical Archeologist,* 17 (#4, 1954), 88–89. See our review of Aileen Guilding, *The Fourth Gospel and Jewish Worship* (New York: Oxford, 1960), in *Catholic Biblical Quarterly* 22 (1960), 459–461.

[19] *John 6 and the Jewish Passover* (Lund: Gleerup, 1959).

[20] For this, see our pamphlet commentary on Jn in the *New Testament Reading Guide* (Collegeville: Liturgical Press, 1960), 43 ff.

there has been a simplification in the Synoptic tradition whereby a meal with Passover characteristics has become a Passover meal.[21]

In any case, from the overall picture, we may say with confidence that even on the score of differences from the Synoptics, the case against Johannine historicity has been greatly weakened.

Third and finally, we must look at the other side of the coin. In some circles it has not been the differences from the Synoptics which raised the difficulties, but the similarities to the Synoptics. Because in some stories Jn runs close to the Synoptic version, it has been suggested that the Johannine tradition is not original, but simply an imaginative reshuffling of Synoptic details according to some theological motif. A good example would be the story of the raising of Lazarus.[22] This would have been put together from the Synoptic raising narratives (son of widow of Nain in Lk 7; Jairus' daughter in Mk 5), the story of Martha and Mary (Lk 10:38–42), and the parable of Lazarus and the rich man (Lk 16:19–31).[23]

In answering this objection we must draw some careful distinctions. It seems plausible to us that the *final writer* of Jn knew at least part of the Synoptic tradition, and, in

[21] Cf. below, p. 207 ff.

[22] For instance, see Alan Richardson's explanation in his Torch Bible commentary on Jn (London: SCM, 1959), 139.

[23] Note all the Lucan parallels. Many scholars are now coming to the view that in some cases it was the Lucan tradition which borrowed from the Johannine (oral) tradition, e.g., E. Osty, "Les points de contact entre le récit de la Passion dans saint Luc et saint Jean," *Recherches de Science Religieuse,* 39 (1951), 146–154. In reference to the Lazarus story, there is a strong possibility that the second half of the Lucan parable, which introduces a new theme of returning from the dead, has been influenced by the Johannine story—R. Dunkerley, "Lazarus," *New Testament Studies* 5 (1958–1959), 321–327.

particular, some written form of Mk.[24] For instance, Jn and Mk share not only details (the 200 denarii in the multiplication scene; the 300 denarii in the anointing scene), but even a really peculiar expression, i.e., the adjective *pistikos* modifying the nard of Jn 12:3 and Mk 14:3.

Familiarity with the Synoptic tradition probably goes back beyond the written form of Jn to the oral stage of the Johannine tradition. It is not unlikely that sometimes the Johannine Gospel was preached to groups already familiar with the Synoptic tradition, and that in stories that were similar there may have been a certain crisscross transferal of details.[25] This need not lead us to the view of S. Mendner[26] or of Bultmann whereby a limited conformity to the Synoptic tradition was artificially introduced into the Johannine Gospel to make it acceptable. There may have been a few deliberate borrowings, particularly of phrases, but most of it was probably fusion by a type of osmosis.[27]

Now, having allowed a moderate familiarity with the Synoptics, we would stress, however, that the Johannine tradition is basically not dependent on the Synoptics. Most Catholic scholars today no longer regard Jn as a supple-

[24] E. K. Lee, "St. Mark and the Fourth Gospel," *New Testament Studies,* 3 (1956–1957), 50–58, gives many parallels, some of them not probative. A connection with Mt is proposed by H. F. D. Sparks, "St. John's Knowledge of Matthew," *Journal of Theological Studies,* 3 (1952), 58–61.

[25] In reference to n. 23 above, we should point out that all the influence was not from Jn to Lk, e.g., the Johannine account of the anointing in 12:1–8 was influenced by Lk's story of the penitent woman (7:37–38), especially as to the anointing of the feet—André Legault, "An Application of the Form-Critique Method," *Catholic Biblical Quarterly* 16 (1954), 145.

[26] "Zum Problem 'Johannes und die Synoptiker,'" *New Testament Studies,* 4 (1957–1958), 282–307. He holds that the multiplication of the loaves in Jn 6 was simply taken over from the Synoptics.

[27] See instances in P. Borgen, "John and the Synoptics in the Passion Narrative," *New Testament Studies,* 5 (1958–1959), 246–259.

ment to the Synoptics, but as an independent kerygma and didache. We might add parenthetically that the fact that an independent kerygma and didache could survive alongside the official kerygma and didache as represented in the Synoptics (see note 12 above) is the best sign that the source of this independent tradition was a figure greatly respected in the Church. No better candidate for authorship has been found than John, son of Zebedee, one of the Twelve.[28] While we doubt that he *wrote* the Gospel in its *final* form, we believe that he remains the most logical choice for identification as the Beloved Disciple mentioned in the Gospel as the source of its tradition (Jn 21:24; 19:35).

The independence of the Johannine tradition means not only that Jn's stories are not quilt creations from Synoptic patches, but also that where they narrate the same stories, Jn has as much claim to be studied as have the Synoptics. Thus, if the story of the ruler's son in Jn 4:46–54 reflects the same event as the two variant forms of the story of the centurion's servant in Mt 8:5–13 and Lk 7:1–10,[29] any reconstruction of the historical event must take into account all three narratives. While this view naturally opposes that of the critics and their minimal estimate of Johannine historicity, it also opposes a view common to many Catholics who, in treating the Synoptic Gospels as histories, have assumed that the only way to explain (away) Jn was to assume that the author theologized events. But if, as we have insisted, each Evangelist is a theologian, we must take the author of Jn just as seriously as the rest, even in the narratives common to all; and we must make due allowance for the theological purpose of *each* Gospel. For in-

[28] Personally, we regard as unsuccessful the constant search for another author. For instance, see the work of P. Parker, "John and John Mark," *Journal of Biblical Literature*, 79 (1960), 97–110, who suggests that Mark was the author. For our theory of the composition of the Gospel see above, chap. V, n. 26.

[29] Higgins' treatment (*op. cit.*, 22–26) is interesting, although we do not necessarily agree with all his conclusions.

stance, in another essay,[30] we have compared Jn and the Synoptics in their very different treatments of common materials (e.g., agony in the garden, trial before Sanhedrin, temptations) and have suggested that sometimes the Johannine tradition may reflect less theological organization. In the same line of thought, Dodd[31] has studied logia that are similar in Jn and the Synoptics, and concluded that the Johannine form of the words is independent of that of the Synoptics.

We believe that this approach has wide implications. It has been fashionable to admit that the Johannine discourses are, in good part, the theological reflections of John himself, since they do not resemble Jesus' way of speaking in the Synoptics.[32] The new emphasis on the independence and originality of the Johannine tradition should cause a rethinking of this position. The Qumran discoveries have shown us that the vocabulary of the Johannine Christ is not as strange as might first seem.[33] Then, too, we realize

[30] Cf. chap. XI, below.

[31] "Some Johannine *'Herrnworte'* with Parallels in the Synoptic Gospels," *New Testament Studies*, 2 (1955–1956), 75–86. Also *Historical Tradition in the Fourth Gospel* (Cambridge, 1963).

[32] The argument that in Jn Jesus speaks the same way the author does is based on the theory that a section like 3:31–36 is the Evangelist's reflections. We believe that they are a Johannine fragment of Jesus' own words, placed here by the disciple-editor. See our pamphlet commentary, 29. For authoritative statements about Johannine theologizing, see *DB* 2016, 2112.

[33] P. Benoit, "Qumrân et le Nouveau Testament," *New Testament Studies*, 7 (1961), 287–288, although he recognizes the Palestinian aspect of Jn, thinks that the Qumran layer in the Gospel may, at least in part, be more recent and have been influenced by the situation at Ephesus. We would agree that the presence at Ephesus of disciples of John the Baptist and perhaps of others who shared Qumran thought patterns may have supplied the occasion of the composition of Jn (see chap. VII). But we suggest that this Ephesus background caused John to select material from Jesus' ministry which would appeal to a

that many of the Synoptic sermons are themselves composed of isolated sayings united around a theme. We might
allow more of this in the Johannine discourses. If John,
son of Zebedee, is the source of the Johannine tradition, we
might expect that his closeness as an eyewitness would mark
his personal tradition with characteristics different from
those of the official tradition (which would have lost some
of its intimate eyewitness details in being preached by many
different individuals). Each eyewitness sees according to his
own interests and predispositions. If John was a disciple of
the Baptist (the bridge between Qumran and the New Testament?), he may have had a background which peculiarly
disposed him to appreciate and preserve certain aspects of
Jesus' teaching that did not survive, save in echoes (Mt
11:25–30), in the official tradition. In neglecting such possibilities, some of the older treatments of the Johannine
discourses, no matter how well meaning, do not respect the
independence of the Johannine tradition. Jn has its own
right to be heard, not only where it confirms the Synoptic
tradition, but also where it goes its own way.

Yet, and this we would emphasize lest we be misunderstood, we are not proposing any complete solution to the
problem of the Johannine discourse. In the whole question
of the relation of Jn to the Synoptics, no amount of explanation can disguise the fact that the author of the Fourth
Gospel has made his personal contributions of a formative
nature. There is a symbolic insight in Jn which expands the
significance of the materials used. There is a dramatic
adeptness which, partly by selection, perhaps, and partly
by organization, produces scenes that are nearly perfect
drama (e.g., the blind man scene in chap. 9; the trial of
Jesus). In these features and many others (use of numeric
patterns; inclusion; etc.) this Gospel differs significantly
from the others. The fact that we do not simply write off
the best part of the Gospel as Johannine creation does not

Qumranlike mentality; we doubt that it caused him simply to
rephrase the message of Jesus in a Qumran garb.

mean that in any way we would deny the distinctively Johannine method of handling basic materials, a method which has implications in any treatment of the historicity of Jn.

II. THE HISTORICAL LIMITS OF JN

These last remarks lead us very nicely into the second part of our paper, which will question some of the usage that has been made of Jn, usage that distorts the real historicity of Jn. The limitations of which we speak are twofold.

First, while Jn deals with historical materials—the deeds and sayings of Jesus—the Gospel makes no pretension of being a history. Jn 20:30-31 specifically enunciates a theological intent: "Many other signs also Jesus worked . . . which are not written in this book. But these are written that you may continue to believe that Jesus is the Christ, the Son of God." We must evaluate what Jn narrates according to this standard. He does give us a series of feasts that imply a two- or three-year public ministry. These feasts were not narrated, however, to supply a chronological outline of Jesus' ministry, but for the sake of leading the readers to increased faith. There is no assurance that there were only three Passovers in Jesus' ministry, nor that the trips to Jerusalem narrated in Jn were the only ones made by Jesus. Rather we are specifically told that much has been omitted.

We might exemplify the implications that flow from recognizing that Jn is not a history in the strict sense. As is well known, Jn tells of a cleansing of the Temple near the first Passover of 2:13; Mt (21:10-17) describes a cleansing of the Temple on the day Jesus entered Jerusalem shortly before His death; Mk (11:15-19) puts the cleansing on the day *after* Jesus entered Jerusalem. Let us accept the common opinion that the three accounts refer to the same cleansing. It is often pointed out that in the simplified

Synoptic outline Jesus came to Jerusalem only once in His
public ministry (at the time of His passion), and that therefore Mt and Mk had to place the Temple incident where
they did. Jn, on the other hand, with many trips to Jerusalem had greater liberty. This is true, and the Johannine
placing of the incident *may* be historical. We say "may"
for, since Jn is not primarily a history, some theological
purpose, rather than chronological one, may have guided
the placing of the event.[34] The author may have placed it
shortly after the introduction of the Baptist to show the
fulfillment of Mal 3:1: the Baptist is the messenger who
was to have prepared the way (1[a]); now suddenly the Lord
has come to the Temple (1[b]). Or in a Gospel where the
rejection of official Judaism plays such a role, the author
may have wanted to set the theme of the destruction of
the Temple and its replacement by Jesus right at the head
of the book. Or, finally, the disciple-editor may not have
known where to place such an isolated incident, and simply
have put it here. In any case, the Johannine position cannot be taken as the historical one without careful examination.

There is a *second* limitation on the historical use of Jn.
As we have suggested above, John, son of Zebedee, is the
source of the Johannine tradition. But there are many indications that he was not the final writer of the tradition.
In fact, 21:24 seems to refer to him in the third person,
and he may even have been dead when the final chapter was
added to the Gospel.[35] This leads us to the theory of a
disciple-editor as the final writer. This editor seems to have
worked with a basic tradition stemming from John himself,
and to have added other Johannine pericopes wherever they
seemed to match the context.[36] Whence, probably, we have

[34] If Jn's sequence is historical, then we have to say that the
Synoptic tradition was guided by theological intent.

[35] See our pamphlet commentary, 97–100. Also see above,
chap. V, n. 26.

[36] *Ibid.*, 13, #7, and references there.

the composite nature of the Last Discourse, the bread of life discourse, and other sections in Jn. Thus, once again we find ourselves deprived of a completely chronological approach to Christ's ministry.

• These two considerations affect the usability of Jn in writing a life of Christ. A frequent practice is to take the Johannine feasts as an outline of Jesus' ministry, and to divide up the Synoptic material to fit into this outline. Consequently authors are able to tell us in what year the Sermon on the Mount was given, etc. Whatever validity this procedure may have for limited sections such as the passion accounts, on a more general scale it does not recognize the Johannine limitations of which we have just spoken, nor does it recognize that the Synoptic material itself has only a very elementary chronological arrangement.

By way of example, is the journey to Jerusalem in the Synoptics to be identified with Jn's account of Jesus' going up to Jerusalem at the feast of Tabernacles in chap. 7?[37] It is true that Jn never mentions His returning to Galilee, but then Jn does not tell us much of what happened between Tabernacles and Dedication (chap. 10), or between Dedication and Passover (11:55)—a total period of some eight months. (And is this a really consecutive sequence of feasts? That another annual cycle of feasts has been omitted because it did not fit Jn's theological purpose is a possibility that cannot *a priori* be discounted.) But granting Jn's sequence as chronological, what are we to consider the real historical contents of the Synoptic journey to Jerusalem? Lk's journey (chaps. 9–19) can scarcely be taken as a description of all that happened on the trip, since most Lucan scholars now recognize that in this journey Lk groups much of his non-Marcan material without any real sequence (material which Mt puts elsewhere). In synchronizing this

[37] There are some indications of this. Before the trip to Jerusalem, Mk 9:30 has Jesus passing through Galilee secretly; this might match the information in Jn 7:1 and 7:10. The theme of death seems to hover over the beginning of the journey in Lk 9:51, as it does over Jn 7:6–8.

with Jn, we are left with a case of *ignotum per ignotius*

Again we might take the multiplication of the loaves in
the two traditions as a possible point of chronological agreement. The multiplication in Jn occurs near the second Passover of which he speaks. Can we say that whatever follows
the multiplication in the Synoptics should be placed in the
second year of the Johannine ministry? But Jn (as well as
Lk) mentions only one multiplication, while Mk-Mt mention two. And if the Marcan narrative units following each
multiplication are studied carefully, we find ourselves with
two very similar sequences:

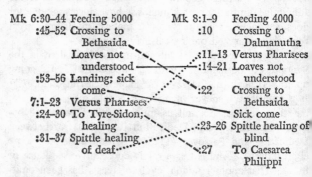

Mk 6:30–44	Feeding 5000	Mk 8:1–9	Feeding 4000
:45–52	Crossing to Bethsaida	:10	Crossing to Dalmanutha
	Loaves not understood	:11–13	Versus Pharisees
		:14–21	Loaves not understood
:53–56	Landing; sick come	:22	Crossing to Bethsaida
7:1–23	Versus Pharisees		Sick come
:24–30	To Tyre-Sidon; healing	:23–26	Spittle healing of blind
:31–37	Spittle healing of deaf	:27	To Caesarea Philippi

These units undoubtedly deal with real events, but the similarity of sequence would suggest that we are dealing with
two preaching units, rather than with two really chronological sequences. Elsewhere[38] we have shown how Jn's sequence in chap. 6 resembles that of Mk 6:30–54 and 8:11–
33, leaving out all of what is in between. The difficulties of
writing a truly scientific biography from such materials are
obvious.

We shall close our paper with a more detailed study of
some passages in which the two traditions might be thought
to dovetail. First, we shall treat two passages early in the
Johannine account of the ministry (2:12 and 4:44); then
we shall discuss the date of the Last Supper.

[38] Pamphlet commentary, 37. Also see below, p. 265.

The Synoptic tradition follows the baptism with a Galilean ministry, a ministry that takes place after the Baptist's arrest according to Mk 1:14 and Mt 4:12. Again according to Mk-Mt, the ministry begins around Capernaum, while according to Lk (4:16) Jesus first comes to Nazareth, and then, having been rejected, goes to Capernaum (4:31). The Johannine picture is different. Jesus returns after the baptism to Cana, then goes to Jerusalem and has a ministry in Judea (3:22–4:3) before John the Baptist's arrest. Are there any indications how the two pictures can be harmonized?

Following the Cana incident, we hear in Jn 2:12:

"After this he went down to Capernaum with his mother and [his] brothers [and his disciples], and there they [he] stayed for a few days."

Does this represent the ministry at Capernaum mentioned in the Synoptics? In particular, is it to be harmonized with Lk's account of the transferal to Capernaum after an earlier ministry around Nazareth? Or does this rather echo the scene in Mk 3:31 when His mother and His brothers come to where He is ("at home" according to 3:20—presumably Capernaum)?

To get any sort of chronological help, we would first have to ask if the passage in Jn constitutes a real sequence. The value of "after this" as a time indication is disputed.[39] As the many textual variants show, the verse offers difficulties when we try to fit it into its context. The brothers of Jesus are mentioned—were they at Cana too? Why do they follow Him to Capernaum since they were unbelievers (7:5)? Or did "brothers" perhaps originally refer to His

[39] (From here on we shall refer to the standard commentaries on Jn by using simply their authors' names.) Bernard (I, 83) and Lagrange (63) take *meta touto* in Jn to refer to close chronological sequence, as opposed to the vague *meta tauta*. Bultmann (85[6]) and Barrett (162) maintain that there is no difference between the two phrases, and that each is vague.

disciples, and was it only later that some manuscripts, for-
getting the original meaning, added "and his disciples"?[40]
At any rate, there is a difficulty in even the mention of the
mother of Jesus and His brothers, for they are of little
importance to what follows (the brothers do not reappear
until chap. 7; Mary, not until the foot of the cross). Did
the original text say *"they* stayed for a few days," and was
it changed to *"he* stayed" in some manuscripts[41] to make
the sentence fit in with the next pericope where He goes
up to Jerusalem?[42] Or is it the phrase "for a few days"
that is the harmonization with the next pericope?[43] And
what is the purpose of the short visit to Capernaum which
is so far off the direct road from Cana to Jerusalem?[44]

All of these difficulties suggest that we are not dealing
with a real sequence.[45] This could be one of those vague
echoes of the Synoptic traditions (drawn from passages
such as those mentioned above) which have come over
into the Johannine tradition.[46] Or it could be an isolated
morsel of independent Johannine tradition that resembles
some elements in the Synoptics. This particular passage may
have been inserted by the disciple-editor into the narrative

[40] A phrase omitted by Sin, it, ar, eth, copt.

[41] P66c, F, G, 565, 1241, it, boh.

[42] Hoskyns, 192, supports "he stayed" as the original reading,
for he thinks that Jesus' mother and brethren may have remained at Capernaum. Mk 3:31 does not necessarily imply that
they had been at Nazareth; and 6:3 mentions specifically
only His sisters as dwelling at Nazareth.

[43] So Bultmann, 85[5].

[44] Lagrange, 63, suggests He came this way to avoid going
through Samaria.

[45] The verse could be omitted and the narrative would actually
go along very well.

[46] Loisy, 147, recognized this in principle, but phrased it with
cynicism: "He is conducted to Capernaum only to do justice
to the Synoptic tradition." Lightfoot, 111, suggests that the purpose of v. 12 is "to remind the reader of the earlier tradition
according to which the first and greater part of the Lord's work
was laid in Galilee."

of the beginning of the ministry in Galilee simply because that seemed the most logical place.[47] If this is so, 2:12 would be of little real use in writing a chronological history of the ministry of the Lord.

Another problem concerns 4:44. Notice its strange relation to its context:

> [43]Now after two days he departed to Galilee. [44]For Jesus himself [had] testified that a prophet has no honor in his own country. [45]So [*oun*] when he came to Galilee, the Galileans welcomed him, having seen all that he had done in Jerusalem at the feast; for they too had gone to the feast.

V. 43 is clearly connected to what precedes, for in the Samaritan story (4:40) we hear that He stayed there two days. And v. 45 connects to what follows (the scene at Cana with the royal official), as well as recalls the signs done in Jerusalem (2:23). But v. 44 offers great difficulty: the reference to the lack of honor in His own country seems to contradict the joyful reception of v. 45 (notice the *oun* which begins v. 45).

Many have tried to resolve the difficulty by suggesting that "his own country" refers to Judea. This explanation is strange on three accounts: (*a*) In Jn Jesus clearly hails from Nazareth and Galilee (1:46; 2:1; 7:42; 7:52; 19:19); in fact, there seems more emphasis on Jesus' Galilean origins in Jn than in the other Gospels. (*b*) If this were a reference to Judea, it should have come when Jesus was leaving Judea (4:3), not when He is leaving Samaria. (*c*) If this refers to Judea, it would appear that He is coming into Galilee to receive the human honor denied to Him in Judea. This would be abhorrent in the thought pattern of Jn (2:24–25; 5:41–44).

[47] We cannot *a priori* exclude all intention of harmonizing on the part of the final editor. The tendency to harmonize appears already in the second century, e.g., Tatian, and Papyrus Egerton 2.

Once we reject the Judean explanation, however, and take "his own country" to refer to Galilee, we are left with the context problem. As Lagrange[48] has put it: "There is no apparent means of explaining the whole passage according to the rules of strict logic." Many have noticed the parenthetical character of v. 44.[49] And the verse does recall a saying in the Synoptic tradition on the occasion of the rejection of Jesus at Nazareth:

Jn 4:44:   *prophētēs en tȩ̄ idią patridi timēn ouk echei*
Mk 6:4:   *ouk estin prophētēs atimos ei mē en tȩ̄ patridi
                autou*
Lk 4:24:   *oudeis prophētēs dektos estin en tȩ̄ patridi autou*

The verse in Jn has some Johannine characteristics, e.g., "Jesus had testified [*martyreō*]" and "his *own* [*idia*] country"; but *timē* for "honor" is a *hapax* in Jn (*doxa* is the usual word).[50] Could this verse, then, be another Johannine reminiscence of the Synoptic tradition?[51] Note that other fragments of this scene in Mk 6:1–6 appear in Jn, e.g., Mk 6:1 = Jn 4:43; Mk 6:2 = Jn 7:15; Mk 6:3 = Jn 6:42; Mk 6:6 = Jn 4:48. Why would the disciple-editor have put the logion here? He obviously considers the enthusiasm of v. 45 as an inadequate display of faith based

[48] P. 124.

[49] Bultmann, 150[4], treats it as parenthetical, and translates the introductory verb in the pluperfect: "had testified." Lee, *art. cit.* (n. 24 above), 57, thinks that the sentence indicates that the author is referring to a phrase that he presumed the readers already know; the introductory *gar* is equivalent to "For you know. . . ."

[50] Also, in the best MSS of 4:44 there is no article before "Jesus," a usage strange for Jn.

[51] Lagrange, 124, mentions the possibility of a "tacit reference to the Synoptics." Wilkenhauser, 115, says that perhaps the verse is an addition of the editor. Of course, once again we may be dealing with a morsel of independent Johannine tradition that has certain parallels with the Synoptic tradition.

on signs (see v. 48: "Unless you see signs and wonders, you do not believe"). He shows his estimate of this faith by inserting v. 44[52] which becomes a general characterization of the Galilean lack of faith. If our suggestion is true, v. 44 has no chronological implications: the scene at the end of chap. 4 in Jn is not the equivalent of the final rejection of Jesus by the Galileans of Nazareth in the Synoptics; nor does v. 44 necessarily indicate that Jn's scene is chronologically posterior to the Synoptic scene.

Hence, even in such promising hints as Jn 2:12 and 4:44, we are deprived of any real means of synchronizing the two traditions. We may have to be content with the Synoptic and Johannine traditions as being solidly historical, but as not supplying us the means to write a scientific history.

THE DATE OF THE LAST SUPPER

The question of the date of the Last Supper has perennially vexed scholars. A dominating factor in its discussion is the Passover meal legislation of the Old Testament: the paschal lamb was to be slain on the afternoon of 14th Nisan, and to be eaten after sunset, which means the beginning of the 15th Nisan. (In all the following discussion it is essential to remember that, just as sunrise begins a new day in our solar calendar, so the moon governs the day in the Jewish lunar calendar.) For St. John (18:28), the evening of the Last Supper and the following day of the crucifixion were 14th Nisan, the day before the Passover meal of the Jews. The Synoptics (Mk 14:12), however, tell us that the Last Supper was the Passover meal; and thus the evening on which it was eaten and the following day of the crucifixion were 15th Nisan, Passover itself. The following seems to be the Gospel picture:

[52] Verses 43 and 45 connect very nicely without v. 44, and the *oun* of v. 45 makes much better sense.

	(Tues. night) Wednesday	(Wed. night) Thursday	Thurs. night Friday	Fri. night Saturday
	Betrayal (Mk 14:1) anointing (Mk; Jn has it on preceding Sat., 12:1)	Preparations for Passover Meal (Mk 14:12; Lk 22:7)	Last supper Arrest Trials Passion-death Burial	In the tomb
Synoptics			Passover	
John			Preparation Day	Passover

SOLUTIONS

While several solutions have been suggested, a favorite hypothesis has been to posit two different calendars: (*a*) the official Jerusalem calendar followed in Jn (for the priests are involved in Jn 18:28), whereby Jesus ate and died on 14th Nisan; (*b*) another calendar, followed privately by Jesus, whereby Passover fell one day earlier and thus His Last Supper was a real Passover meal, eaten according to this calendar on the evening beginning 15th Nisan. The real difficulty in this explanation is that the supposed calendar which Jesus followed exists only as a scholars' hypothesis. For some (Lagrange, Ricciotti) it was a calendar of the Pharisees as opposed to that of the Sadducees; for some it was a Galilean calendar. True, evidence exists for a series of different calendars in the past history of Israel, but were different calendars actually in use among the Palestinian Jews of our Lord's time?

Now, at last, we have clear proof of the existence and use of a different calendar among the Qumran Essenes in the first century A.D. The new calendar was partly known to us before the Qumran discoveries of 1947, for there were traces of a different calendar in Jewish apocryphal writings of the second and first centuries B.C., e.g., in the books of *Enoch* and *Jubilees*. The *Jubilees* calendar is a solar calendar (not basically a lunar calendar like the official Jewish calendar) based on a rough solar year of 364 days. This calendar has the unique advantage of being a perpetual calendar: *a certain date falls on the same weekday every year, e.g., 14th Nisan is always a Tuesday.*

Yet this strange calendar of *Jubilees* remained very much a literary calendar whose actual use could be doubted until the discovery of the Essene documents at Qumran. Among the material of cave IV, assigned for publication to Father Milik, are fragments of calendar documents (lists of feasts, lists of priestly courses). These unpublished fragments were among those assigned to the present writer to study for a concordance in Jerusalem in 1958. These confirm without a doubt that the solar calendar known from *Jubilees* was used by the Qumran Essenes. For instance, in the Qumran commentary on Habakkuk we hear of an attack by a Jerusalem priest on the community on the Day of Atonement (10th Tishri). Such an occurrence would have been improbable if the Qumran sect were following the official calendar of Jerusalem; no priest would be likely to violate this sacred day by leading a raid. But with their different calendar this was 10th Tishri only for Qumran, and an ordinary day as far as the wicked priest was concerned.

JAUBERT'S THEORY

Miss Annie Jaubert, a Catholic scholar at the Sorbonne who has done the most work on the *Jubilees* calendar, suggests that the origins of this calendar date back at least to the time of the Babylonian exile. She finds that it is presupposed in the detailed dates given in Chronicles, Ezra, Nehemiah, and in the priestly tradition of the Pentateuch (e.g., Lv 23:16 seems to indicate that the Jewish feast of Pentecost always falls on a Sunday, which is possible only in the solar perpetual calendar). The editing of these works is generally dated to the postexilic period (*ca.* fifth century B.C.). In fact, this solar calendar could not have been replaced in the Temple by the official lunar calendar of our Lord's time until the second century B.C. Father Milik suggests that the introduction of the lunar calendar into the Jerusalem Temple sparked the withdrawal of the Essenes into the Qumran desert.

Be that as it may, our main interest here is Jaubert's suggestion that Jesus followed this solar calendar in celebrating the Last Supper. If we presume the day began with sunset in the *Jubilees* calendar, Passover, or 15th Nisan, always fell on Tuesday evening–Wednesday. Therefore Jaubert suggests this chronology for Holy Week:

Tues.	Preparation for Passover (Mk 14:12–16)	Solar 14th Nisan
Tues. evening and night	Last Supper Passover meal (Mk 14:17) Arrest of Jesus (Mk 14:43) Inquiry before Annas (Mk 14:53a; Jn 18:13) Peter's denial (Mk 14:66) Jesus taken to Caiaphas (Jn 18:24)	Solar 15th Nisan (official 12th)
Wed.	First Sanhedrin trial (Mk 14:53b, 55)	
Thurs.	Second Sanhedrin trial (Mk 15:1a) Jesus before Pilate (Mk 15:1b) Jesus before Herod (Lk 23:6–12) Priests arouse people (Mk 15:11)	(official 13th)
Thurs. night	Pilate's wife's dream (Mt 27:19)	
Fri.	Before Pilate again (Mk 15:8; Lk 23:13) Barabbas incident (Mk 15:9) Condemnation, crucifixion, death (Mk 15:15 ff)	(official 14th)
Fri. evening	The official Passover meal; Jesus in the tomb	(official 15th)

Obviously this new chronology cannot be perfectly harmonized with either the Synoptics or John, all of whom *prima facie* have these events crowded into the twenty-four hours of one evening, night and day. For Jaubert, their accounts must represent a simplification and periscoping of events which historically were spread over three days. As she tells us, the primitive catechesis was much more interested in the substance of the events and their doctrinal import than in their exact chronology. Her theory, however, does satisfy the Synoptic evidence that Jesus ate a real Passover meal and John's evidence that He died the day before the official Passover.

ARGUMENTS IN FAVOR OF THEORY

Naturally Miss Jaubert does not propose this theory without evidence. Among her principal arguments are these:

1. The events narrated in the Gospels are very crowded if we try to include them within twenty-four hours; and this is especially true of the morning events. The Sanhedrin met at dawn (Mk 15:1). After this, the accusation before Pilate, the trip to Herod, the return to Pilate, the gathering of the crowds, the Barabbas incident, the scourging and the way of the Cross—all had to occur before noon when Jesus was crucified (Mk 15:33).

2. We have evidence in rabbinic law that to pass a death sentence, two sessions of the Sanhedrin were required on two separate days, neither of which should be the vigil of a feast. Since the night session (with Annas?) could not have been legal, the ordinary Gospel chronology allows only one official meeting and that on the vigil of the Passover (Jn) or, *mirabili dictu,* on Passover itself (Synoptics). Jaubert's chronology fulfills the rabbinic requirements.

3. On Friday morning Pilate's wife sent to him saying that she had dreamed of Jesus (Mt 27:19). This is difficult if Friday morning was the first time Pilate had dealt with Jesus (unless she was a very late sleeper!).

4. According to Jn 12:1, the anointing at Bethany was

six days before Passover. If, for John, Friday evening–Saturday was Passover, the anointing would have occurred the previous Saturday evening–Sunday (evidently Saturday, since Palm Sunday follows it in chap. 12). But for the Synoptics (Mk 14:1), the Bethany anointing was two days before the Passover. Only in Jaubert's chronology can this be harmonized, since in the solar calendar Passover was Tuesday evening–Wednesday, and two days before could be Saturday evening–Sunday.

5. Jaubert's chronology may have an echo in other New Testament evidence. Paul (1 Cor 11:23) refers to the Last Supper thus: "The Lord Jesus on the night he was betrayed [*tradebatur*] took bread"—Paul does not refer to the night before He died. Again, the Mass says, "pridie quam *pateretur*," not "before He died." Jn 13:1 refers to the Last Supper not as on the vigil of Passover, but simply as before Passover.

6. The most impressive argument of all is that there is a Christian tradition for the Last Supper on Tuesday. The *Didascalia Apostolorum,* a late second-century or early third-century document preserved in Syriac (and Ethiopic), speaks of Christ having eaten the Passover on Tuesday evening and of His arrest in the garden on Wednesday morning. The readers are told to fast on Wednesday and Friday for the Jews, because on Wednesday they arrested Christ and on Friday they crucified Him. St. Epiphanius (+ 403), who knew the *Didascalia,* supports the Tuesday Last Supper tradition. Victorinus Petaviensis (+ 304), who shows no knowledge of the *Didascalia,* also explains the Wednesday fast on the grounds of our Lord's arrest on that day.

This brief summary does not really do justice to the detail of Miss Jaubert's theory, whose work has been augmented by that of E. Vogt, S.J., former rector of the Pontifical Biblical Institute in Rome. The theory is so attractive that it has won at least sympathetic consideration among many writers, including Delorme, Cortes Quirant, Skehan, Walther, and Schwank. Certainly this much need be said: the theory can be reconciled with the New Testament evidence once we realize that the Gospels do not pretend to give a twentieth-century historical approach to the life of Christ. The quality of the Catholic scholars who favor Jaubert's thesis witnesses to the truth of her principle that the primary intent of the Gospels was not an exact chronology.

OBJECTIONS

However, other scholars have not been able to accept the Jaubert chronology, not on any grounds of Gospel inerrancy (which is not involved), but simply because of a different evaluation of the evidence. The present writer, while recognizing that the question is far from settled, finds himself in this camp, along with Benoit, Gaechter, Leal, Jeremias, and Blinzler. Briefly the objections are these:

First, in reference to the Christian tradition, we do not have the original Greek of the *Didascalia,* and while the Syriac translation has the tradition of a Tuesday Passover, the Ethiopic does not. Also, the *Didascalia* itself does not resort to calendar difference to explain the Tuesday Passover; it says that the legal Passover was to be Friday, but in their anxiety to put Jesus to death before His fellow Galileans could come up to the feast, the Sanhedrin moved up the Passover to Tuesday. The Wednesday fast is the real concern of the *Didascalia;* and one may well suspect that the idea of a Wednesday arrest arose as an *ad hoc* explanation of the fast, and that the Tuesday Passover was simply a corollary of this. In other explanations of liturgical usage, the *Didascalia* plays loose with history: to account for Christ's three days and three nights in the tomb, it reckons the noon hours on the cross on Friday as one day, and the darkness that came over the earth as one night, and then the return of light on Friday afternoon as another day—in the space of six hours it has accounted for two days and one night. We may suspect that its explanation of the Wednesday fast was just as fanciful. Judas betrayed

Christ on a Wednesday (Mk 14:10–11); could this have been confused with Judas' leading the priests to the garden of Gethsemane to arrest Jesus, and consequently that event placed on Wednesday? We should remember that we have earlier evidence of a Wednesday fast without such a fanciful explanation, and we have a number of first- and second-century writers who are quite content with the one-day chronology.

As regards the crowding of events (#1 above), admittedly the events are hurried in a one-day chronology, but not impossibly so. And was not haste of the essence? Jaubert's leisurely three days violate all the counsels of the priests to be careful in taking Jesus lest there be an uprising among the crowd. In the hurry of one morning Jesus was tried and crucified before His supporters in the crowd could cause trouble, but in three days all Jerusalem would have known.

We are not certain that the rabbinic law of two trial sessions (#2) was in effect as early as Christ's time. But, in any case, there are indications that the Sanhedrin did *not* wish to try Jesus formally and sentence Him. This is shown by the highly irregular witnesses (Mk 14:55–58), the abuse of the defendant (Jn 18:22), the fact that there was no strict blasphemy (Jesus did not use the divine name "Yahweh"), and the seeming failure to hand down a real sentence (only "he deserves death"—Mt 26:66). It was the intention of the Sanhedrin to put the onus of condemning Jesus on the Romans in case any trouble should arise later, and so they did not need to observe the rules of a formal trial.[53]

As to the dream of Pilate's wife (#3), John gives evidence that Pilate could have known of Jesus before Friday

[53] The recognition that the authorities of the Sanhedrin were active in the death of Jesus in no way contradicts the thesis that these authorities were *not* guilty of deicide (because they did not know Jesus was divine), or that the vast majority of Jews had no part in the crucifixion.

morning since he mentions a Roman cohort and tribune among those sent to arrest Jesus in Gethsemane on Thursday night (Jn 18:12). One can scarcely imagine such Roman action without Pilate's previous knowledge.

Miss Jaubert's evidence for the dating of the anointing at Bethany is truly striking (#4). Yet the fact remains that the Synoptics clearly place the anointing after Palm Sunday and not before it as does Jn. Her interpretation of Mk 14:1 as Saturday does not answer this objection. One may well wonder if it is not impossible to harmonize perfectly John and the Synoptics on this event without resorting to some theological motivation in situating the event.

The use of *pridie quam pateretur* in the Mass (#5) is very inconclusive: *pateretur* in the Mass means the whole process of the death of Christ, as the Creed witnesses: "*Sub Pontio Pilato passus et sepultus est.*" And so the citation does nothing to aid Jaubert's thesis.

Finally, there is a very strong objection to the theory that our Lord followed the solar calendar in eating the Passover meal three days before the official Passover. Adherence to a calendar was a test of religious orthodoxy, as the violence of the Essene adherence to their calendar shows. Calendars were not to be adopted or substituted at will. In all of the Gospels there is never a hint that Christ was guilty of heterodoxy in His observance of feasts. Rather, He appeared in Jerusalem at the time of the *official observance* of Passover (Jn 2:13), Tabernacles (Jn 7:2), and Dedication (Jn 10:22). It is unlikely that these feasts occurred at the same time in both the solar and lunar calendars, so our Lord must have been following a lunar calendar. In fact, the feast of Dedication never appears in the Essene solar calendar, for this was a Maccabean feast and Qumran disliked the Maccabees. Therefore, how can we say that Christ, after following the official calendar during His whole public life, suddenly adopted the Essene calendar before He died?

CONCLUSION

When all is said and done, we consider the Jaubert chronology as too radical a rearrangement for the evidence adduced. The simplest solution is to follow Jn's chronology, and admit that the Last Supper on Thursday evening was not a legal Passover meal since Passover did not begin until Friday evening. At the Last Supper, however, Christ deliberately imitated many of the details of a Passover meal (except the lamb) to show the connection of the Eucharistic sacrifice to the historic deliverance of the Jews from Egypt on the first Passover. In the Synoptic preaching tradition, by a simplification (remembering Jaubert's dictum that the Gospels were more interested in theology than in chronology) this meal with Passover features became a Passover meal; and from there it was just a step to the idea that the evening when the meal was eaten was the Passover.

BIBLIOGRAPHY

A. Jaubert, *The Date of the Last Supper* (French, 1957; English, Staten Island: Alba, 1965)

—— "Jésus et le calendrier de Qumrân," *New Testament Studies* 7 (1960–61), 1–30.

—— "Les séances du sanhédrin et les récits de la passion," *Revue de l'histoire des religions* 166 (1964), 143–169; 167 (1965), 1–33.

E. Ruckstuhl, *Chronology of the Last Days of Jesus* (German, 1963; English, New York: Desclée, 1965).

X

The Gospel Miracles

This article is an attempt to probe the preliterary relationships between the Synoptic tradition and the Johannine tradition. On first look the two traditions are startlingly different on the whole question of miracle. In the Synoptic tradition miracles are narrated one after the other in almost embarrassing profusion. Some 200 of the 425 verses of Mk 1–10 deal directly or indirectly with miracle, a statistic which means that almost one half of the Marcan narrative of the public ministry concerns the miraculous.[1] In Jn, on the other hand, we have seven miracles narrated during the public ministry.[2] The pressing of the crowds with their sick, the constant pleading for help, the wonder-struck awe, the excited reports of what has been done, in short the whole color of the Synoptic miracle narrative has faded in

[1] The figures are given by Alan Richardson, *The Miracle Stories of the Gospels* (London: SCM paperback ed., 1959), 36.

[2] Changing of water to wine at Cana (2:1–11); healing of the official's son (4:46–54); healing at Bethesda (5:1–15); multiplication of the loaves (6:1–13); walking on the water (6:16–21); healing the blind man (9) raising Lazarus (11).

Jn.[3] Rather, the miracles of Jn seem to serve primarily as a basis for long interpretative discourses. But not only the number and the circumstances of miracles differ in the two traditions. For Jn the might and wonder of the miracle seem to have been submerged in the concept of miracle as sign, a change which touches on the very nature and function of the miracle. Nevertheless, despite these obvious differences, we hope to show that, once we have made allowance for the peculiar genius of each tradition, their concept of miracle is not as diverse as might first seem.

From the time that Quadratus made apologetic use of the Gospel miracles in his *Apology to Hadrian* (c. A.D. 125) the interpretation of miracle seems to have been inextricably bound up with the defense of the Christian faith. While the apologetic usefulness of the miracle has had the advantage of leading the best theological minds in the Church to study and comment on it, nevertheless, this constant apologetic coloring of the exegesis of the Gospel miracles has been a mixed blessing. The history of the apologetic of miracles is too well known to present.[4] As exegetes we need but express our gratitude that the overemphasis on the transcendent value of the miracle (as an exception to "the laws of nature") has now given place among Catholic scholars to an emphasis on the religious context of the miracle and on its role as a sign.

With particular reference to the purpose and interest of our article, we might note that while the miracle is useful to apologetics as a guarantee of the credibility of revela-

---

[3] In Jn 7 and 8 we do get a picture of the excitement of the crowds, but this is not immediately connected to a miracle.

[4] For an excellent summary see John A. Hardon, S.J., "The Concept of Miracle from St. Augustine to Modern Apologetics," *Theological Studies*, 15 (1954), 229–257. Also Louis Monden, S.J., *Le miracle, signe de salut* (Desclée de Brouwer, 1960), 45–55 (he has an excellent bibliography on "miracle"). Modern opinions are clearly summarized in Robert Gleason, S.J., "Miracles and Contemporary Theology," *Thought*, 37 (1962), 12–34.

tion, this perfectly valid use of the Gospel miracles[5] must not lead us to the assumption that such an apologetic purpose dominated Jesus' own use of miracles. The question that concerns us in a purely scriptural study of the miracle is not how we can use the Gospel miracles in defending the faith but what role miracles played in the Gospel tradition. Once and for all, miracles are important external signs of revelation. But, beyond this, Jesus' miracles had a more primary, internal role *in His ministry* as acts through which He gave revelation; side by side, the word and the miraculous deed gave expression to God's entrance into time.[6] This is not novel once we realize that in the Old Testament Yahweh is pictured not only as a God who speaks (e.g., through the prophets) but also, nay chiefly, as a God who acts. His actions[7] in salvation history were

[5] The Vatican Council (*DB* 1813) has defined that miracles can be known with certainty and that they can be used to establish the divine origins of the Christian religion.

[6] The Hebrew term used for what we could call a miracle is *môpheth,* translated in the LXX by *teras.* (The Deuteronomist often adds a synonym to *môpheth,* namely *'ôth*—LXX, *sēmeion.*) As a translation, *teras* actually overplays the prodigy element in *môpheth,* for the Hebrew term refers to any symbolic act, e.g., of a prophet, and need not refer to anything extraordinary. When something extraordinary is described, *niphla'* can be added. It is interesting that the New Testament never uses *teras* alone to refer to the miraculous acts of Jesus and the Apostles, but always combines it with *sēmeion;* perhaps this is an attempt to avoid overemphasizing the prodigy element. *Teras* is used in secular literature, however, for the miracle worked by the Hellenistic wonder-worker (more frequently than *dynamis* or *sēmeion*). The word "miracle," from the Latin *miraculum* (never used in the New Testament), has not preserved the New Testament nuance of avoiding the prodigious element. See A. Lefèvre, "Miracle," in Vigoroux, *Dictionnaire de la Bible,* Supplément, 5, col. 1300.

[7] It is interesting that there are very few miracles worked by and for individuals in the Old Testament; rather God's miracles are centered on the whole people. Really, the only important

effective signs of His protection of His people; they accomplished what they signified. It is not surprising, then, that when God's Son came to establish God's dominion over men, He was also a God who acts as well as a God who speaks.[8]

I. THE SYNOPTIC DYNAMEIS

The ordinary term in the Synoptic Gospels for miracle is *dynamis,* an act of power. With Jesus, God's power erupts among men (Acts 10:38), and the entrance of God is centralized in one individual. The powerful divine deeds which were worked on a national scale in the Old Testament are now channeled through Jesus.

The Synoptic Gospels describe Jesus' ministry as one of announcing the coming of God's kingdom. The material which the Synoptists give us pertaining to the public ministry can be divided between preaching (mostly in parables[9]) and working miracles. This is in harmony with Peter's kerygmatic summary of the ministry in Acts 10:36–38 which mentions precisely preaching and healing (Acts 2:22 is more general: "mighty works and wonders and signs"). Therefore, it is clear that in the Synoptic Gospels Jesus' miracles are to be connected to the coming of the kingdom.[10]

There is no question that Jesus' miracles caused people

---

instances of private miracles are those of Elijah and Elisha in 1 Kgs 17–2 Kgs 13; these men heal, multiply food, and bring the dead back to life. This is why Jesus seemed like a second Elijah; see above, chap. VIII, n. 18.

[8] As Augustine puts it, *"Gesta Verbi sunt verba."*

[9] Mt, more than Mk or Lk, correctly characterizes many parables as parables *of the kingdom.*

[10] A. George, "Les miracles de Jésus dans les évangiles synoptiques," *Lumière et Vie,* 33 (1957), 7–24. Edwyn Hoskyns and Noel Davey, *The Riddle of the New Testament* (London: Faber paperback ed., 1958), 117–126.

to wonder and admire, and led many to faith. Nevertheless, it is evident that, at least in Jesus' mind, the element of proof or credential was not primary in the miracle, for He consistently refused to work a miracle simply as a proof.[11] Whether the request came from the devil, Herod, the Pharisees, or the people, Jesus would not perform miracles just to show that He was sent by God.[12] Since His miracles inevitably attracted attention, He sought to avoid this by performing His miracles privately, away from the crowd.[13] He minimized the purely prodigious element of the miracle which could not lead to understanding or faith. As He said, "If someone should rise from the dead, they will not be convinced" (Lk 16:31). He admitted that false prophets could work prodigies that would come close to deceiving even holy men (Mk 13:22–23).

The connection of the miracle with the coming of the kingdom lies in another direction. The miracle was not primarily an external guarantee of the coming of the kingdom; it was one of the means by which the kingdom came. In particular, Jesus' miracles were the weapons He used to

[11] The overemphasis on the apologetic aspect of the Gospel miracles has actually played into the hands of those who oppose the credibility of miracles. Bultmann's view is that the miracle stories have been added to the Gospels to gain understanding for Jesus as a wonder-worker: Jesus needed the same credentials as Apollonius of Tyana and the rabbinical wonder-workers. For a detailed critique of Bultmann's assumptions about the lack of historicity in the Gospel accounts of the miracles, see V. Taylor, *The Formation of the Gospel Tradition* (London: Macmillan, 1953), 119–136. (See n. 23 below.)

[12] Mt 4:5; Lk 23:6–12; Mk 8:11–13; Mt 12:38–42; Mk 15:31–32; Mk 6:1–6.

[13] Mk 7:33; 8:23; 9:25. As Ian Hislop, O.P., "Miracles and the Gospels," *Blackfriars*, 39 (1958), 57–60, points out, enthusiastic reaction to Jesus as a wonder-worker is on the same surface plane as reaction to Him as one possessed or mad. Both reactions are superficial; the astonishment has simply taken different directions.

overcome Satan.[14] The temptation story was set at the beginning of the public ministry in Mt and Lk to tell us that the coming of the kingdom involved a tremendous struggle with Satan. From the time of man's sin until the coming of Jesus, Satan had a certain dominion over nature and over man. He would not yield this dominion to God without a fight, a fight that culminated in Gethsemane and Calvary, the hour of the power of darkness (Lk 22:53).[15] So much of Jesus' energy and time was taken up in this struggle that He could virtually identify His ministry with the casting out of demons. As His ministry drew to a close, He said, "Behold *I cast out demons* and perform cures today and tomorrow, and the third day I finish my course" (Lk 13:32). The expelling of demons was the infallible sign of the coming of the kingdom: "If it is by God's spirit that I expel demons, then it follows that the dominion of God has at last overtaken you" (Mt 12:28). The reason for this is that in the New Testament demoniacal possession is not so much the result of a league with Satan as an expression of bondage under Satan's dominion.

In a wider field of application beyond that of demoniacal

[14] Although Satan entered Old Testament theology as a relatively latecomer, he assumed great importance in the last pre-Christian centuries. The New Testament picture is best summed up in 1 Jn 5:19: "The whole world is in the power of the Evil One." For the development of the concept of Satan's dominion see James Kallas, *The Significance of the Synoptic Miracles* (London: SPCK, 1961), 38–76. This can be supplemented from the Dead Sea Scrolls with their dualistic picture of a world divided into the dominions of light and darkness; see above chap. VII.

[15] In Jesus' ministry the two kingdoms are pitted against one another. This is the logic of Mk 3:22–27: Jesus' expulsion of demons is not a case of Satan's kingdom divided against itself, but of God's kingdom vs. Satan's. The stronger one (see Mk 1:7) has come to bind the strong man and take over his dominion. Satan recognized this: Mk 1:24 tells us the demons cried out, "What have you to do with us, Jesus of Nazareth? Have you come to destroy us?"

possession, sickness itself is part of the realm of Satan. We all know that in the Old Testament sickness and suffering were explained as the result of sin, and that this explanation was inadequate. However, this inadequacy does not vitiate the concept. Jesus Himself refused to draw any one-to-one equivalence between sickness or misfortune and actual sin: the fact that a man was sick or suffering did not prove that he (or his parents) had committed an actual sin (Jn 9:3; Lk 13:1–5). Nevertheless, it is good theology that human suffering is one of the consequences of original sin, that some sufferings are the penalties of actual sin. And Jesus' whole attitude toward sickness implies that it belongs to the disorder characteristic of the realm of evil and is intimately connected with sin. This is the real logic (often overlooked) in healing the paralytic as a sign that his sins are forgiven (Mk 2:1–12): if Jesus had power over one, He had power over the other.[16] It is this connection between sickness and evil that explains the frequency of possession in the Gospel narrative. Diseases that might be analyzed medically as epilepsy (Mk 9:14–29), or as arthritis (Lk 13:10–17), are directly connected with Satan and his kingdom. Indeed, the very vocabulary used to describe illness and healing seems to reflect a concept of sickness as almost personalized evil. In Lk 4:39 we hear that Jesus "rebuked" a fever, much as He would rebuke a demon.[17] Also, sickness is referred to as *mastix* (a castigation or whipping; Mk 3:10; 5:10; 5:29, 34), almost as if it were directly inflicted by Satan.[18] We may see this, too, in the use of "save" in reference to healing, a concept which we have overspiritualized. The term "save" includes not only spiritual regeneration, but also, and primarily, deliverance from the evil grasp of sickness, from the dominion of Satan

16 The same connection lies behind Jas 5:15: the man's sickness is removed and his sins are forgiven.

17 *Epitimaō:* for rebuking demons in Mk 1:25; 3:12; 9:25. Notice Mk 8:33: he *rebuked* Peter saying, "Get behind me, Satan!"

18 Kallas, *Significance*, 79.

—there is no dichotomy of soul and body in Hebrew thought; the whole man is saved.[19]

This concept of the Gospel miracle as an invasion of the kingdom of Satan and a means of establishing God's dominion affects other aspects of the Synoptic miracle narratives. Kallas[20] makes the plausible suggestion that the frequency of miracles worked on the sabbath day is not just accidental. Jesus' purpose in choosing the sabbath for His miracles was not just to raise a test case for the Law; rather, it was primarily to emphasize His miraculous work as a renewed creativity. God had rested from the work of the first creation on the sabbath; now He had resumed His creative work as He established His dominion, saved man from Satan, and re-created him in His own image.[21]

The ultimate expression of the miracle as the triumph of God's kingdom over Satan is found in Jesus' restoration of life to the dead.[22] Death, as a by-product of man's sin (Gn 3:19; 1 Cor 15:56), was a particularly strong element in Satan's dominion (1 Jn 3:14). As Paul puts it, "The last enemy to be destroyed is death" (1 Cor 15:26). Thus, in raising from the dead (Mt 9:18; Lk 7:12), Jesus

[19] See the use of "save" in Mk 5:23; 5:34; 6:56; 10:52. We should note, however, that the term "save" seems to have been used for deliverance from sickness in secular literature as well. See Arndt and Gingrich, *Lexicon*, 496. For a treatment of the question, see Richardson, *Miracle Stories of the Gospels*, 62.

[20] *Significance of the Synoptic Miracles*, 64.

[21] Mk 3:4 and esp. Lk 13:16: "Ought not this woman, a daughter of Abraham whom Satan bound for eighteen years, be loosed from this bond on the sabbath day?" It is quite obvious that in resuming the creative work on the sabbath, Jesus is tacitly asserting divine prerogatives (Mt 12:5–8).

[22] Notice the climactic position of death in the order of miracles in Mt 11:2–4: miracles dealing with the blind, lame, lepers, deaf, and the *dead*. These are the signs that Jesus is the stronger one who is to come (Mt 11:3 and 3:11). Jn, in situating the Lazarus miracle as the final and climactic miracle of the Gospel narrative, is a faithful interpreter of the New Testament appreciation of the importance of the raising of the dead.

manifests an especially strong intervention of *dynamis* and reveals that "God has visited his people" (Lk 7:16). The revelation of God's kingdom is even more obvious in the central miracle of the Gospel, the Resurrection of Jesus from the dead. It was this miracle, understood as the glorification of Jesus, that revealed that He was the Lord, Messiah, Savior, and King (Acts 2:32–33, 36; 5:31).

The explanation of some of the nature miracles also consists in seeing them as a revelation of God's dominion which is replacing that of Satan.[23] It is a commonplace that the Hebrew did not properly evaluate secondary causality, and that disasters caused by natural forces were often attributed directly to God or, later, to Satan. However, beyond this undeniable fact there is the valid theological observation that the sin of man did introduce certain elements of disorder into nature. Satan had established a certain dominion over all that creation which had been subordinated to man. Thus, as Paul tells us, all creation has been groaning in travail until the time of deliverance (Rom 8:22; 2 Pt 3:12–13). The great struggle of the last times will shake not only men's souls but also the very heavenly bodies as Satan is forced to give up his dominion over them (Mk 13:25; also Eph 2:2 where Satan is called "the prince of the power of the air"). In Jesus' announcement of the coming of God's kingdom, then, we would expect some sign that the powers of nature were being made subject through Jesus. In the words of Ps 8:7, "You have

[23] The nature miracles offer commentators a great deal of difficulty. Taylor's treatment of the miracle stories (*supra*, n. 11) is marred by his failure (136–141) to see the place of the nature miracles in the ministry of Jesus. However, Ph.-H. Menoud, "La signification du miracle selon le Nouveau Testament," *Revue d'Histoire et de Philosophie Religieuses*, 28–29 (1948–1949), 179, is correct when he states that the modern distinction between nature miracles and miracles worked on men is too rigorous. There is no real distinction in the Gospel treatment of the two types of miracles. See Wm. Neil, "The Nature Miracles," *Expository Times*, 67 (1956), 369–732.

given him rule over the works of your hands, putting *all things* under his feet."

A good example of the nature miracle as a victory over Satan is found in the stilling of the storm (Mk 4:37–41). When the raging of nature threatens to destroy the group in the boat, Jesus stands and rebukes (*epitimaō*) the wind, just as He rebukes sickness and demons. To the sea He says, "Be silent" (*phimoō* literally "to muzzle"), the same type of personal command that He gives to the demon in Mk 1:25.[24] And after His command the sea is tranquilized, much as a demoniac after the expulsion of the demon: nature has been restored to order. Perhaps a similar explanation is applicable to the walking on the water (Mk 6:45–52); in the Matthean account, at least, the miracle causes the disciples to recognize Jesus as God's Son (Mt 14:33).

Thus, many of the Gospel miracles (healing the sick, raising the dead, some nature miracles) reveal the triumph of God's kingdom by destroying Satan's hold on men and nature.[25] One part of this revealing function of the miracles lies in the fact that they fulfill Old Testament prophecies. Throughout the prophets we hear of a period of supreme divine intervention into the life of God's people, a period of overflowing divine mercy for those who have remained faithful. This will be the day when the Lord will comfort Zion and make her deserts into gardens (Is 51:3); imprisonment and suffering will come to an end (Is

[24] Perhaps there is a hint of the ancient mythological concept of the sea as the spawning place and special preserve of the evil monster. Certainly the idea was still alive in New Testament times (Ap 13:1).

[25] This is the only real significance of miracles which Kallas, *Significance,* allows. Thus he would tell us (92) that the multiplication of the loaves is a conquest of the disorder of nature which leaves men hungry. Again the miraculous catch of fish in Lk is seen as a reparation of nature's evil unproductivity. There is not the slightest indication of this in the Gospel text. Kallas is carrying a good theory too far.

61:1–3). Jesus presented His miracles as a fulfillment of
the prophesied deliverance. When the disciples of the Baptist came to ask Jesus if He was the one to come, He answered them in terms of the Old Testament prophecies.
His healing of the blind, the lame, the lepers, and His
raising the dead, and His preaching to the poor fulfill
Is 61:1–3 (good news to the poor; sight to the blind;
consoling the afflicted), Is 35: 5–6 (the blind see; the deaf
hear; the lame jump about), Is 26:19 (the dead rise). Of
course, Isaiah probably meant these things as a figurative
description of the messianic blessings, but Jesus is fulfilling
them literally.

At times this fulfillment of Old Testament prophecy seems
to become the prime purpose of the miracle. For instance,
the multiplication of the loaves, sparked by Jesus' compassion for the crowds (Mk 6:34), seems designed to show
God's care for His people and the abundance of His blessings are foretold by the prophets. The people were like
sheep without a shepherd (Mk 6:34); and, as Ez 34:11
had foretold, God Himself was pasturing them. The multiplication of food echoed back to the divine miracles of the
exodus and foreshadowed the messianic banquet.[26]

Here we come to an important step in our consideration of the Synoptic miracle. Hitherto we have been insisting that the miracles themselves were part of the coming
of the kingdom, especially inasmuch as they were acts of
divine power, opposing that of Satan. They were part of
the picture of divine intervention foretold by the prophets.
Yet, once we admit that certain miracles may have been
worked primarily to fulfill this Old Testament prophetic
picture, we are approaching another concept of miracle
as symbolic action. And we must admit that sometimes
in the Synoptic Gospels the main purpose of a miracle does

[26] Neil, *Expository Times,* 67 (1956), 372. Also, Menoud,
art. cit., 181, sees a reference to the liberation from need as
described in Ap 7:16–17.

seem to be symbolic. In the miraculous draught of fishes (Lk 5:1–11) there may be an element of divine compassion[27] toward the poor fishermen; but, as Lk 5:10 points out, the chief purpose of the miracle is the symbolism of the great numbers of men to be caught by the disciples as fishers of men.[28] Thus the miracle is a symbolic action prophetic of the nature of the kingdom.[29] The miraculous withering of the fig tree (Mk 11:12–14, 20–25) also seems to be a symbolic action prophetic of the rejection of Judaism. If, as a prophet, Jesus performed the healings, multiplications, and raisings of an Elijah, He also performed the symbolic actions by which prophets like Isaiah, Jeremiah, and Ezekiel illustrated their ministry.[30]

[27] Richardson, *Miracle Stories of the Gospels*, 29–30, stresses that we should not put too much emphasis on compassion as a motive for the Gospel miracles. However, there is a place for messianic compassion (as distinguished from mere humanitarian compassion) in the miracles.

[28] One may ask if there is not an element of the prodigious here: a miracle to impress the disciples and cause them to follow Jesus. However in Mk-Mt, which do not narrate the miracle, the disciples follow Jesus without having seen any prodigy at all. Some scholars hold the theory that Lk's miracle is the same as the one described in Jn 21, and that the postresurrectional setting in Jn is the more original position of the narrative. If this is true, there would be no need of impressing the disciples with Jesus' power after the Resurrection.

[29] Richardson, *Miracle Stories of the Gospels*, brings out very well the symbolic aspect of the miracles. At times, however, he exaggerates, and he seems to divorce the symbolism from the reality of the miracles. It is in reaction to Richardson that Kallas goes to the other extreme (*supra*, n. 25) of denying symbolism and writing it off as a Church creation.

[30] Perhaps symbolic action is the explanation of that very difficult miracle of the coin in the fish's mouth (Mt 17:24–27). At first this miracle seems to resemble very closely the action of a Hellenistic wonder-worker; but, as one of the three Petrine sections of Mt, it is probably connected to the theme of Peter's primacy.

If there are a few miracles in the Synoptic tradition whose main purpose is symbolism, there are many more where symbolism plays a secondary role.[31] For example, in the opening of the eyes of the blind, besides the above-mentioned deliverance from sickness and evil, we may see a symbolism of the spiritual opening of the eyes through faith in Jesus. At times this secondary symbolism is quite pronounced. Between two sections which describe how the disciples are slowly growing in faith (Mk 8:11–21 and 27–30), we find the narrative of the blind man who was healed by stages and only with difficulty (8:22–26). As Richardson[32] suggests, the miracle seems to symbolize the slowness of opening the ears to the meaning of the Gospel message. Certainly Jesus often hurled the challenge to hear, as if He were speaking to the spiritually deaf.

Was this secondary symbolism intended by Jesus, or was it a later insight of the Evangelists? We have no doubt that by a grouping such as that mentioned in Mk 8, the Evangelist has heightened the symbolism of the healing of the blind. Yet it would be hypercriticism to deny Jesus a symbolic use of His miracles. For instance, in the healing of the centurion's servant (Mt 8:5–13) and of the daughter of the Syrophoenician woman (Mt 15:21–28), the intention to make the miracle an occasion for teaching on the conversion of the Gentiles may well come from Jesus Himself. And, as we have pointed out, there are some miracles whose primary purpose seems to be symbolic,[33] and whose

[31] Of course, the distinction between primary and secondary purposes in a Gospel miracle is from our viewpoint. It is doubtful that either the Evangelist or Jesus Himself would have so distinguished; for them the symbolism would have been an essential part of the miracle.

[32] *Miracle Stories of the Gospels*, 84–85. We should note that this miracle is of indisputable antiquity. The use of spittle and the seeming difficulty encountered by Jesus seem to have embarrassed the authors of Mt and Lk who omit the miracle.

[33] It might be asked if the primary purpose of the Transfiguration were not pedagogic. Certainly it was an eruption of the

symbolism would therefore stem from Jesus Himself. Undoubtedly, in the kerygmatic use of Jesus' miracles in the early Church, there was a deepening and an extension of symbolism, but the road had been opened by the Master.

In summation, then, the Synoptic Gospels present the miracle as an instrument in the revelation of God's kingdom. Most of the miracles were actions[34] whereby the dominion of God was actually established over man and nature.[35] A few of the miracles were more symbolic in purpose, teaching men about the kingdom rather than directly bringing this kingdom about.[36] This symbolic aspect may be found on a secondary level in many other miracles which, besides establishing God's kingdom, helped to teach men about the demands and constitution of that kingdom (e.g., its relation to the Old Testament; its difficult demand for faith and cooperation; its demonstration of God's merciful love; its future extent and success). Thus the miracle stories were part of the *kerygma* and *didache* of the Synoptic tradition.

The acceptance of either or both of these aspects of the Synoptic miracle involved faith on the part of those who were the subjects or the witnesses of the miracle. For in-

---

divine *doxa* into the public ministry. Yet the heavy Sinai symbolism seems to be an attempt to draw the attention of the disciples to the appearance of God to Moses. The relation to Gethsemane, drawn out by Lk (9:32, 34b; 22:45), may stem from the Evangelist himself.

[34] Perhaps we may take a term from modern apologetics and call them sign-acts. Although the Synoptists do not call the miracles signs, the *dynameis,* in order to be effective, had to lead people to see the power behind the actions; they had to be signs.

[35] Since the miracle had such a vital role in the establishment and proclamation of the kingdom, small wonder that in sending out the Twelve (Lk 9:1) and the seventy (-two; Lk 10:17) Jesus specified the power to heal and exorcise as the essential part of their commission to preach the kingdom.

[36] These miracles might be called sign-symbols.

stance, the salvation from the power of Satan involved in
the healings is the result *both* of Jesus' action and of the
corresponding faith that it arouses. In fact, several times
Jesus attributes the salvation directly to the faith of the
person healed: "Your faith has saved you" (Lk 8:48;
17:19; 18:42). Faith calls forth the *dynamis* of Jesus (Mk
9:24; Mt 15:28; Lk 5:20; 7:9) because it represents a
readiness to accept God's dominion.[37] Indeed, faith can
put God's *dynamis* at the service of men so that they in
turn can work miracles: "All things are possible to him
who believes" (Mk 9:23; 11:22–23). As Fitzer[38] puts it,
faith is a sphere in which God's power comes to fruition,
and this power is seriously hindered by unbelief (Mk
6:5–6; Mt 17:19–20). In its variety this faith may vary
from initial trust in Jesus' power to a complete belief in
what He is.[39] Faith thrives and deepens and increases in
the presence of that exercise of divine power which is the
miracle.

II. THE JOHANNINE ERGA AND SĒMEIA

In our study of Jn we may proceed by first discounting
those differences from the Synoptic tradition which are
really only surface differences. The reduction of the number of miracles in Jn is guided in part by the stated purpose
of the Fourth Gospel. Jn 20:30–31 tells us that the signs
narrated were chosen from among many because they were
especially suited to encourage the faith of the reader.

[37] Here again the biblical approach to the miracle differs
from the apologetic: most often a Gospel miracle does not so
much lead to faith as presuppose it (at least initial faith). See
H. Holstein, S.J., "Le miracle, signe de présence," *Bible et Vie
Chrétienne,* 38 (1961), 49–58.

[38] G. Fitzer, "Sakrament und Wunder im Neuen Testament,"
In Memoriam Ernst Lohmeyer (Stuttgart, 1951), 180.

[39] The suggestion that the only type of faith involved in accepting miracles is that of trust in a wonder-worker is an oversimplification—Taylor, *Formation of the Gospel Tradition,* 132.

Nevertheless, in reducing the number of miracles (a tendency contrary to that of Mt and Lk which increase the number of miracles found in Mk), Jn further weakens any temptation to regard Jesus as a type of Hellenistic wonder-worker. The same effect is accomplished by the omission of most of the expressions of wonder and awe that usually accompany miracles in the Synoptic tradition.

In comparing Jn and the Synoptic Gospels on the type of miracle narrated, we do not find much difference.[40] The multiplication of the loaves, followed by the walking on the water, is found in both traditions; and the Cana miracle which is peculiar to Jn is a nature miracle of the same type as the multiplication.[41] The healing of the royal official's son (Jn 4:46–54) is probably the same miracle narrated in the Synoptics as the healing of the centurion's boy (Mt 8:5–13; Lk 7:1–10). The healing of the cripple at Bethesda (Jn 5:1–15), and of the blind man (9), and the raising of Lazarus (11) are individual examples of types known from the Synoptics.

It is on the meaning of the Johannine miracle that we must center our attention, and perhaps we may find a key to this in Jn's vocabulary. Although others (including the editor of the Gospel) refer to Jesus' miracles as "signs," Jesus Himself consistently refers to them as "works."[42] What is the origin of the Johannine term "works"? The

---

[40] L. Cerfaux, "Les miracles, signes messianiques de Jésus et oeuvres de Dieu, selon l'Évangile de saint Jean," *Recueil Lucien Cerfaux,* 2 (Louvain, 1954), 41–42.

[41] Besides the theme of messianic abundance, the theme of replacement of Jewish institutions also appears. Menoud, *art. cit.,* 182, points out that while, at first glance, the Cana miracle resembles that of pagan metamorphosis, it really fits into the theme of Jesus' ministry as a new creation. It is an act of revelation, not simply a prodigy.

[42] *Ergon* or *erga* is used of Jesus' doing His Father's work or the work He was sent to do some eighteen times. Only once do others speak of His "works" (7:3); the other seventeen times Jesus is using the term Himself.

term occurs only twice in the Synoptics for Jesus' miracles
(Mt 11:2; Lk 24:19); so, if the term is an authentic one
on the lips of Jesus, it is a case of Jn's preserving vocabulary
lost in the Synoptic tradition. An Old Testament background for the term may be found in the work or works of
God accomplished on behalf of His people, beginning with
creation and continuing with salvation history.[43] The use
of *ergon* for creation is quite prominent in LXX beginning with Gn 2:2. In salvation history a prominent example
of the *works* of God may be found in the exodus (Ex 34:10;
Ps 66:5; Ps 77:12; Dt 3:24 and 11:3—in the latter two
passages a variant reading with *terata*). It is interesting, in
this connection, that in Acts 7:22 Stephen calls Moses "a
man mighty in words and *works*." By the use of the term
"works" for His miracles Jesus was associating His ministry with creation and the salvific works of His Father in
the past: "My Father works up to now, and so do I work
as well" (5:17).[44] So close is the union of Jesus and the
Father in the works of the ministry that the Father Himself may be said to perform Jesus' works (14:10).

The concept of "work" in Jn is wider than that of miracles; in 17:4 Jesus can sum up His whole ministry as a
"work": "I glorified you on this earth by completing the
work you have given me to do." Not only are Jesus' miracles works; His words are works too: "The *words* that
I say to you people are not spoken on my own; it is the
Father, abiding in me, who performs the *works*."[45] Never-

---

[43] Cerfaux, *Recueil*, 2, 47.

[44] It is to be noted that the last passage is in the context of a
sabbath miracle. Thus Jn is in perfect harmony with the idea we
suggested above (n. 21) for the Synoptic Gospels, viz., working
miracles on the sabbath is a creative action.

[45] Jn 14:10. "Words" and "works" are companions in Jn;
this can be seen in Jn's custom of having a work followed by
an interpretive speech. We might note, with Gleason, *art. cit.*,
14, that the great works of God in the Old Testament are often
followed by an interpretation, e.g., the song of Ex 15 after the
crossing of the sea. Menoud, *art. cit.*, 185, points out the cor-

theless, miracles are prominent among the works given
Jesus by the Father to complete (5:36): "These very
works that I perform give testimony for me that the Father
has sent me."

Thus, while Jn does not present the ministry of Jesus
precisely in the Synoptic terms of announcing the coming
of God's kingdom, Jn does agree with the Synoptics in pre-
senting the miracles of Jesus as an integral part of the
ministry (or "work") and as a manifestation of God's
power.[46] The Synoptic emphasis is on God's power over-
coming that of Satan. Jn is quite aware of the opposition
of Satan (14:30; 16:33) and is even more dualistic than
the Synoptics. Yet the connection between the miracles and
the destruction of Satan's power is not emphasized in Jn.
The complete absence of exorcisms represents a remarkable difference from the Synoptic picture. In one place, however, Jn does seem to highlight death as almost a personal
force to be overcome. In the Lazarus story, in the presence
of death Jesus trembles angrily because of the emotions
that flare up within Him (11:33, 38: *embrimaomai*,
tarassō). It is interesting that we encounter similar expressions when Jesus is troubled (*tarassō*) at the presence of
Satan in Judas (13:21), and at the cleansing of a leper
(*embrimaomai*) in Mk 1:43.[47] If this vocabulary evidence

---

relativity of "word" and "work." Word reminds us that the
value of the miracle is not in its form but in its content; the
miraculous work reminds us that the word is not empty, but an
active, energetic word designed to change the world.

[46] Although Jn does not use the Synoptic term *dynamis* to
describe Jesus' works, Jn 5:19 comes close to the idea: "The
Son has no power (*dynatai*) to do anything on his own—only
what he sees the Father doing." Throughout Jn it is quite clear
that the Son acts with the same power as the Father.

[47] The sternness of Jesus with the leper can scarcely be explained except in terms of leprosy considered as the work of
Satan. Kallas, *Significance of the Synoptic Miracles*, 31, points
out that leprosy was a religious contamination, and a healed
leper was obliged to offer sacrifice signifying God's reacceptance

has any force, we might have one example of a miracle in Jn that is a direct attack on Satan.

The term in Jn used by others and by the editor himself to refer to Jesus' miraculous deeds is "sign." Once again we have a term not used by the Synoptics in the same way as in Jn. In the Synoptics we might distinguish two usages of "sign": (*a*) in an eschatological sense: the signs of the last times and of the parousia;[48] (*b*) of miracles demanded of Jesus as an apologetic proof by nonbelievers.[49] The latter use of signs has a pejorative connotation, for Jesus refuses to give such signs since they are requested by an evil and faithless generation. In Acts we encounter a third use of "sign": (*c*) "signs and wonders" have become a simple description of miracles.[50] In Acts 2:22 (under the influence of the Joel citation) Jesus is called a man attested by "mighty works and wonders and

of him into the community. Thus in healing leprosy Jesus was removing a curse which separated man from God's service.

[48] Mt 24:3, 24, 30. In 24:24 the familiar combination "signs and wonders" refers to the prodigies of the false prophets (see also 2 Thes 2:9; Ap 19:20). The eschatological use of "signs" stems from the prophetic books and the apocalyptic seers of the Old Testament (see Dn 3:99; 6:28), and is frequent in Ap. It is interesting that in Acts 2:19 Peter adds "signs" to the citation of the eschatological passage from Joel. Josephus, *Bell.*, 6:288–309, refers to the miraculous events connected with the fall of Jerusalem as "signs and wonders."

[49] Mt 12:38–39; 16:1–4; Lk 23:8 (see 1 Cor 1:22). This usage probably stems from the occasional Old Testament use of "sign" as a divine mark of credence, e.g., Tob 5:2 (Sin.): "What sign can I give him [that he may believe that you sent me as your representative]?" In a similar way the Pharisees are demanding Jesus' credentials. See D. Mollat, "Le semeion johannique," *Sacra Pagina* 2 (Paris: 1959), 213–215.

[50] For a history of this combined term see S. V. McCasland, "Signs and Wonders," *Journal of Biblical Literature*, 76 (1957), 149–152. This use in Acts may be the influence of septuagintal language on Luke; however, the use is Pauline too (Rom 15: 19; 2 Cor 12:12).

signs" (note that the standard Synoptic term for miracle, *dynamis,* is equated with *teras* and *sēmeion*).[51] "Signs and wonders" are also used to refer to the miracles of the Apostles,[52] as is "signs" alone.[53]

The comparison of these different New Testament usages of "sign" with that of Jn offers difficulties. While Jesus does not speak of His own works as signs, the use of that term by others is scarcely the same as its use by nonbelievers in the Synoptics (*b,* above). Only in Jn 2:18 and 6:30 where disbelievers demand a sign are we close to the Synoptic usage. More typically Johannine and less Synoptic is the case where people come to believe in Jesus because of the signs.[54] Nevertheless we should note that this is not a satisfactory form of belief, for Jesus speaks harshly of it (2:23–25; 4:48; 6:26). Evidently Jesus is not satisfied with having His miracles looked on as mere credential cards; He wants an understanding of what they reveal.[55] The most characteristic Johannine use of a "sign" is as a favorable designation of miracle, and this is very different from the Synoptic use. The Evangelist refers to Cana as the first of Jesus' signs (2:11), and to the healing of the official's sons as the second of the signs (4:54). He says that the Baptist worked no sign (10:41) while Jesus performed many (20:30). In 12:37 the Evangelist complains that the Jews had not believed even though Jesus had performed so many signs. Clearly, then, in many passages of Jn "sign" is the equivalent of miracle (with a certain deemphasis

[51] Also in 2 Cor 12:12; 2 Thes 2:9.

[52] Acts 2:43; 4:30; 5:12; 6:8; etc. (Rom 15:19; Heb 2:4).

[53] Acts 4:16, 22; 8:6 (8:13 with *dynamis*); Marcan appendix, 16:17, 20.

[54] Jn 2:23; 3:2; 6:2, 14; 7:31; 9:16; 12:18.

[55] Nevertheless, those who believe because they have seen signs have taken one step on the road to salvation; they are quite different from those who refuse to see, the willfully blind (3:19–21; 12:37–41). Those who demand signs in the Synoptic tradition (Mt 16:1–4) are close to being willfully blind in the Johannine sense.

on the prodigious aspect).[56] This usage is in part the same as that of Acts (*c*, above), although the Johannine tradition, with its distrust of the marvelous, disapproves of the combination "signs and wonders": "Unless you people can see signs and wonders, you will not believe" (Jn 4:48—only use).

The relation of the Johannine signs to the eschatological signs spoken of in the Synoptics (*a*, above) is interesting. Dodd's theory of realized eschatology in Jn is well known.[57] In Johannine thought the signs that are to mark the end of time are perhaps already found in Jesus' miraculous

---

[56] *Sēmeion* is a somewhat narrower term than *ergon;* it is not used of the whole ministry of Jesus. However, even words may be signs; e.g., in 12:33 (18:32) and 21:19 there is a statement which serves as a sign (*sēmainō*) of how Jesus or Peter is to die. This symbolic use is, C. H. Dodd claims, close to that of Philo who uses *sēmainō* of the symbolic significance of Old Testament passages (*The Interpretation of the Fourth Gospel* [Cambridge, 1954], 141–142). Yet, as he recognizes, the real parallelism is to prophecy.

Are there nonmiraculous signs in Jn? When the term *sēmeion* appears, *de facto* it refers to miraculous deeds. But Dodd suggests that the Evangelist considered actions such as the cleansing of the Temple as signs. Probably he did; the Jews did not, however (2:18). The fact that the cleansing of the Temple is followed by 2:23 which mentions that Jesus did many *signs* in Jerusalem is not probative, for 2:23–25 is simply an editorial transition to chap. 3; and 4:54 points to no sign between the two Cana miracles. Another candidate for a nonmiraculous sign might be 3:14–15 where the raising up of the Son of Man is compared to the serpent of the exodus narrative; the comparison is drawn from Nm 21:9, where (LXX) it is said that Moses set the serpent on a *sēmeion*.

[57] One cannot subscribe to the view that there is no final eschatology in Jn or that the passages referring to final eschatology (5:26–30) are intrusive interpolations made by an ecclesiastical redactor. Nevertheless, it is true that the burden of Jn's eschatology is realized. For examples see our pamphlet commentary, *New Testament Reading Guide*, #13 (Collegeville, 1960), 13.

signs.[58] This is not too far from Jesus' statement in Mt (12:39, 41) that no sign will be given except the sign of His own preaching, and that the signs of the times are already present to be interpreted by the Pharisees (Mt 16:3).

Thus there are some distant parallels in the New Testament for the Johannine use of "sign"; the main background for this use, however, seems to be in the Old Testament. In particular we should recall the signs wrought by God in the exodus story.[59] Exodus motifs are frequent in Jn;[60] and if the Evangelist saw that Jesus had replaced so many of the institutions of the exodus, it was no great step to see His miracles as signs corresponding to the signs by which God delivered Israel. We are told that God multiplied signs through Moses (Ex 10:1; Nm 14:22; Dt 7:19); yet the people refused to believe. In Nm 14:11 God asks, "How long will they not believe in me despite all the signs which I have performed among them?" This is very much like Jn 12:37, "Even though he had performed so many of his signs right in front of them, they refused to believe." Jn answers the problem with a reference to the arm of the Lord (Is 53:1) which had been at work in these signs. Dt 7:19 speaks of "signs, wonders, the mighty hand, the outstretched arm." Jn 20:30 ends the Gospel on the note of the signs Jesus had performed before His disciples, just as Dt 34:11 ends on the note of the signs and wonders which Moses performed before Israel. Nm 14:22 connects God's glory to His signs, two terms very characteristic of Jn. Just as God's signs showed His glory, so Jesus' signs showed His glory (2:11; 12:37, 41).

[58] Mollat, *Sacra Pagina,* 2, 216–217. In a similar vein 1 Jn 2: 18 seems to have fitted the notion of antichrist into realized eschatology: the antichrists are lapsed Christians.

[59] Mollat, *Sacra Pagina,* 2, 213–215; Cerfaux, *Recueil,* 2, 43.

[60] Theme of the new tabernacle (1:14); the paschal lamb (1:29; 19:14, 29, 36); bronze serpent (3:14); comparison of Christ with Moses (1:17; 5:45–47); the manna (6); the water from the rock (7:38–39); the feast of Tabernacles (7–8).

Both the Johannine terms for miracles, "works" and "signs," share as a background the Old Testament description of God who acts on behalf of man.[61] "Work" emphasizes more the divine perspective of what is accomplished, and is thus a fitting description for Jesus Himself to apply to His miracles. "Sign" expresses the human psychological viewpoint, and is a fitting description for others to apply to Jesus' miracles.

In this concave-convex description of miracle as "work" and "sign," we find that, as the background in the exodus story might lead us to expect, the Johannine tradition presents the miracle as a work of revelation which is intimately connected with salvation. Yet, while in the Old Testament the physical deliverance accomplished by God's work on behalf of His people is in primary focus (a deliverance with deep spiritual overtones, of course), in Jn the reference to spiritual deliverance is primary and the symbolic element is stronger. Here, again, Jn differs from the Synoptic tradition. As we have seen, most of the mighty deeds in the Synoptic Gospels are a direct part of the deliverance of the world from Satan; there is a symbolic element, but most of the time this is secondary.[62] In Jn, however, the

[61] Both the terms *ergon* and *sēmeion* occur in the accounts of the exodus; the Synoptic term *dynamis* is rare. [*Dynamis* is frequently used for "army, host"; but it occurs for God's powerful deeds only in Ex 9:16 (v.1.) and Dt 3:24 (LXX).]

[62] We made the allowance that some miracles in the Synoptic tradition have primarily a symbolic significance, e.g., loaves were multiplied to remind people symbolically of messianic abundance. In the case of such a miracle it seems that in Jn this primary symbolism becomes stronger, e.g., the people connect the multiplication with the expected messianic miracle of the manna (6:30–31) and see in Jesus the Mosaic prophet-to-come (6:14). Also the secondary symbolism is stronger. There is a hint in the Synoptics that the food was to be understood on a spiritual level (Mk 8:11–21) and even a hint of eucharistic symbolism (comparing Mk 6:41 with Mk 14:22). Both of these themes are developed at length in Jn 6. To take another case, if we compare Jn's account of the walking on

symbolic element has become primary. We do not mean that the material action, like healing, can be dispensed with, but that there is little emphasis on the material results and great emphasis on the spiritual symbolism. If Jesus heals the royal official's son and grants him life (*zaō* in 4:50, 51, 53), the commentary that follows this miracle and that of Bethesda[63] makes it clear that the life that Jesus communicates is spiritual life (5:21, 24). If Jesus restores the blind man's sight, the interchange that follows (9:35–41) shows that Jesus has given him spiritual sight and reduced the Pharisees to spiritual blindness. If Jesus gives life to Lazarus, the remarks of Jesus (11:24–26) show that the restoration of physical life is important only as a sign of the gift of eternal life. This Johannine attitude wherein the spiritual import of the miracle clearly dominates over the material effect is a natural consequence of Jn's incarnational theology. The Word has become flesh, and now flesh of itself avails nothing. The world of spirit has been brought into the world of time, and this penetration results in a transformation.

Perhaps the best Old Testament parallel for this dominant symbolism in the Johannine sign is the prophetic symbolic action.[64] The sign performed by the prophet (e.g., Is 20:3) was important only in what it graphically portrayed, e.g., God's coming judgment, or God's intervention. In Jn, with its partially realized eschatology, Jesus'

---

water with that of the Synoptics, we find that all the elements of amazement are lost in Jn, and that the divine title of Jesus (6:20) is highlighted.

[63] A. Feuillet, S.S., "The Theological Significance of the Second Cana Miracle," *Johannine Studies* (New York: Alba House, 1965), 39–51.

[64] While we say that the account of the exodus is the ultimate source for the Johannine concept of sign, we must also recognize the strong influence of the prophetic symbolic action. Mollat, *Sacra Pagina*, 2, 213; C. H. Dodd, "Le Kerygma apostolique dans le quatrième évangile," *Revue d'Histoire et de Philosophie Religieuses*, 31 (1951), 272.

symbolic actions not only prophesy God's intervention, but contain it. The physical health, sight, and life are accompanied by the gift of spiritual life and faith. Thus Dodd[65] is correct in referring to the Johannine miracles as *signa efficacia* (whereas we may classify the prophets' symbolic actions as *signa prophetica*). But to modify this terminology, we may call Jesus' miracles also *signa prophetica*. The prophetic aspect consists in this: the spiritual life and sight which have been attached to physical miracles during the ministry of Jesus will be poured forth without such intervention once Jesus is glorified and the Spirit is given. Thus the miracle is a sign, not only qualitatively (material standing for spiritual), but also temporally (what happens before *the hour* prophesying what will happen after the hour has come). That is why the signs of Jesus are concentrated in the first half of Jn; for once the hour has come (13:1), there is no more mention of Jesus' performing signs. It is in the period of the hour that His "work" is accomplished (17:4; 19:30); the hour is the watershed between the miraculous prophetic sign and the reality prophesied.[66]

By way of parenthetical remark, we might add that the prophetic element in the miraculous sign is what allows the Johannine narrative of the miracle to bear so often a secondary sacramental significance.[67] The sacraments are the great means of pouring out spiritual life once Jesus has been raised up. From His side come blood and water, the Eucharist and baptism (19:34); from the very heart of Jesus flows the water of the Spirit (7:38–39). The sacraments are the efficacious signs of the postascensional period, as the miracles are the efficacious and prophetic signs of the period before the hour has come.[68]

[65] *Ibid.*

[66] The hour refers to the passion-death-resurrection- (theological)-ascension of Jesus. It is the hour of His return to the Father, begun on Holy Thursday and completed on Easter Sunday.

[67] See above, chap. IV.

[68] P. H. Menoud, "Miracle et sacrement dans le Nouveau Testament," *Verbum Caro*, 6 (#24, 1952), 139–154, insists that

Returning to the primary symbolism of the Johannine signs, we can now understand the type of belief that is demanded in Jn of those who observe the signs. As we have mentioned,[69] there are two preliminary unsatisfactory stages in reaction to the signs:

a) That of those who refuse to see the signs with any faith, e.g., Caiaphas (11:47). Such people refuse to come to the light (3:19–20); it would have been better for them if their eyes were physically incapable of sight (9:41; 15:22). Their willful blindness can only be explained as a fulfillment of the lack of faith predicted in the Old Testament (12:37–41).

b) That of those who see the signs as wonders and believe in Jesus as a wonder-worker sent by God. Jesus regularly refuses to trust Himself to this type of faith (2:23–25; 3:2–3; 7:3–7) which is not real belief in what Jesus truly is.

But there is also a satisfactory reaction to signs:

c) That of those who see what is signified by the signs, and learn who Jesus is and what He has come to do, and so believe in Him (4:53; 6:69; 9:38; 11:40).[70] It is this comprehension of the sign that leads one to see the true

sacraments did not take the place of miracles because miracles are reported side by side with sacraments in the Acts. For Menoud sacraments refer back to the historical act of salvation and re-present it, while miracles (in the Church) announce eschatological fulfillment. All of this is true but does not concern the Johannine picture. As Menoud admits, "Thus the Johannine notion of sign establishes a relation between miracles and sacrament" (146). See Fitzer, *Lohmeyer Memorial*, 171–172: "The miracle is to be understood as the sign of the presence of God in Christ. The sacrament is to be understood as the sign of the presence of Christ in the Church."

[69] *Supra*, n. 55. O. Cullmann, "Eiden kai episteusen," *Aux sources de la tradition chrétienne* (Mélanges Goguel; Paris, 1950), 52–61.

[70] There are stages in this belief: the disciples who believed at Cana are still growing in faith in 6:60–71. Full faith comes only after the Resurrection (20:28).

glory of Jesus (2:11). And it is thus that the works that
Jesus performs give testimony for Him (5:36), and Jesus
can challenge men to put faith in His works (10:38).[71]
At the Lazarus miracle Jesus thanks the Father (11:41–42)
for the sign that will lead people to believe in Him as the
resurrection and the life.

Of course, there is a still higher type of faith which can
arrive at the identity of Jesus without the use of signs, that
of those who have believed without seeing (20:29). They
believe on the word of the Apostles (17:20), and Jesus
blesses them and prays that they may see His glory (17:24).

In this emphasis on faith as a necessary accompaniment
of the miracle Jn is in perfect harmony with the Synoptics.
We saw that in the Synoptic tradition faith is an active
partner with the miracle (i.e., the faith of the healed person is said to save); so in Jn faith is part of the *ergon*
(6:29): "This is God's work: to have faith in him whom
He sent."[72] In exalting a faith that has no dependence on
miraculous signs, Jn has moved out of the sphere of the
ministry of Jesus into that of the Church, and into the ultimate development of the sign, the sacrament.

Perhaps we might conclude our article by drawing together the conclusions of our comparisons:

1. The circumstances of the miracle are somewhat different in the two traditions. Jn gives very little emphasis to

[71] "Even though you will put no faith in me personally, put
your faith in these works so that you may come to know and
understand that the Father is in me and I am in the Father."
The most complete meaning of this is in sense (c), that the
Gospel miracles can lead men to believe, not only that Jesus
was sent by God, but just who He is. He is asking for belief in
His works, not solely as the credentials of a wonder-worker,
but as the revealing acts of one who is teaching. This is clear
if the whole verse is quoted and the proper emphasis is given
to the purpose clause which concludes the verse.

[72] See G. Bertram, *"Ergon," Theological Dictionary of the
New Testament* (Grand Rapids: Eerdmans, 1965), 2, 643.

circumstances that would highlight the miracle as a prodigy; and in so doing, Jn brings us more easily to the theological purpose of the miracles in Jesus' ministry.

2. The vocabulary for the miracle is different. Jn's *ergon* and *sēmeion* have Old Testament roots, and help to show the continuity between the Father's actions and those of Jesus. Once again the Johannine vocabulary avoids any stress on the prodigious.

3. In neither tradition are the miracles merely appendages to the ministry of Jesus, convenient credentials; rather they are an essential part of the proclaiming and introducing the kingdom of God (Synoptics) and of the work of Jesus given Him by the Father (Jn).

4. The predominant element in most of the Synoptic miracles is that of an action of divine power delivering man from Satan's evil grasp. The miracles are God's intervention on behalf of His people as foretold in the OT. The didactic or symbolic element in the miracle (what it tells about the kingdom) is secondary in most miracles. In Jn the symbolic element (what the miracle teaches about Jesus[73]) is predominant. The Johannine miracle is conceptually close to the prophetic symbolic action.

5. Faith is emphasized in both traditions, but in Jn this faith is more clearly distinguished from trust in the wonder-worker.

When we look over these comparisons, we realize that there are differences between the two traditions. The differences, however, are really differences of emphasis. The developments in the Johannine picture of the miracle are perfectly consonant with the stated purpose of the Gospel, i.e., to use the event of Jesus' life to give meaning to the faith of the later Christians.

[73] In Jn Jesus is the personification of God's kingdom. What the Synoptics say about the kingdom, Jn often applies to Jesus, e.g., the Johannine "I am" similes take the place of the Synoptic parables of the kingdom.

XI

John and the Synoptic Gospels: A Comparison

The relations between Jn and the Synoptic Gospels cannot be determined solely by studying whether or not the final author of Jn was familiar with Mk, Mt, Lk. There is also the problem of the interrelation of the two traditions, the Johannine and the Synoptic, in the formative period of the Gospel narratives. Our purpose here is to see if the two traditions have narrated the same basic historic incidents in very dissimilar ways. For our purpose we shall take four scenes presented as units in the Synoptics but whose members are seemingly scattered in Jn. We do not pretend that the same solution is possible or necessary in all four instances, but their collective impression is interesting.

I. THE AGONY IN THE GARDEN (MT 26:36–46; MK 14:32–42; LK 22:40–46)

The scene is found in all three Synoptics but not in Jn. If we inquire as to the historicity of Jesus' having suffered in Gethsemane, we may be relatively certain on purely scientific grounds that this is scarcely an invention of the Christian community after the Resurrection.[1] The Church has had a great deal of difficulty with the thought that Jesus was troubled in face of death.[2] One ancient explanation is that it was not a real agony that Jesus endured, but a show of weakness as bait for Satan—a trap to entice Satan into the final struggle. Modern orators do not do much better in explaining that the real source of Jesus' agony was the thought of the amount of sin in the world, or the thought of the souls to be lost.

Theological embarrassment is not the only argument militating against the invention of the scene. It also seemingly runs against the favorite early Christian theme of the Suffering Servant freely and willingly taking on Himself suffering for the sake of others. Neither is it likely that the unflattering portrait of the disciples who slept while their master suffered in agony was a free invention of the early Church. Finally, Jesus' anguish in face of death is further attested by Heb 5:7.

Granting then the basic historicity of the agony scene, we are concerned here with its content. There are two major problems: (*A*) there is a certain disagreement among the Synoptics as to what happened; (*B*) the only possible eyewitnesses were asleep at a distance.

Problem A. Lk gives us a one act drama in which Jesus goes off to pray by Himself and returns only once to find the disciples sleeping. Mk and Mt have three such acts.

It would be tempting simply to regard Lk's account as the more original. Yet, while reserving ultimate judgment on the one or the three, we should notice that in some

---

[1] R. Bultmann, *History of the Synoptic Tradition* (New York: Harper and Row, 1963), 267, describes it as "originally an individual story of a thoroughgoing legendary character." However, V. Taylor, *The Gospel According to St. Mark* (London: Macmillan, 1953), 551, defends the basic historicity.

[2] Cf. J. Schmid, *Das Evangelium nach Markus*, 4 ed. (Regensburger Neues Testament, 1958), 277. Early adversaries like Celsus and Julian the Apostate used it against Christianity.

ways Lk definitely modifies a more original account.[3] On
the other hand, in one additional detail, that of the angel
and the bloody sweat, Lk may be preserving an original
element.[4] When we turn to the three acts in Mk-Mt, we
do not find complete unanimity. In Mk 14:39 we are told
that when Jesus went off by Himself the second time, He
prayed saying the same words. But Mt 26:42 fills in the
prayer, and it is not the same as the first prayer (26:39).
Rather the second prayer of Mt is a definite development
toward resignation.[5] Again in the third act of the agony,
Mt seems to fill out Mk's account. Mk 14:41 mentions no
going away to pray a third time, but only a coming back
a third time to the disciples. Mt 26:44 mentions both the
third going away and returning, and even tells us again

---

[3] For instance, he does not mention: (*a*) Jesus' being dis-
tressed and troubled, as in Mk 14:33; Mt 26:27; (*b*) the appeal
to the disciples for consolation, as in Mt 26:40 (Mk 14:37):
"Could you not watch with me one hour?"; (*c*) the criticism of
the disciples that their flesh was weak (Mk 14:38; Mt 26:41);
in fact Lk 22:45 spares the disciples: "He found them sleeping
for sorrow."

[4] It is well known that many manuscripts omit Lk 22:43–44.
However, there seems to be a growing tendency to accept their
authenticity, e.g., *RSV, SBJ.* For a defense of authenticity, see
J. Schmid, *Das Evangelium nach Lukas,* 3 ed. (Regensburger
NT, 1955), 336. In relation to "the bloody sweat" we should
note that Lk does not say that Jesus sweat blood but that "his
sweat became like great drops of blood falling to the ground."
The implication *may* be that He sweat as profusely as if He
were bleeding.

[5] The final clause of Mt's second prayer, "Your will be done,"
is the same as a petition in the Matthean form of the Lord's
Prayer (Mt 6:10). It has often been suggested that the petition
of the Lord's Prayer was borrowed from the Gethsemane account. H. Schürmann, *Praying With Christ* (New York: Herder,
1964), 123, n. 192, makes the more likely suggestion that this
elaboration in Mt's Gethsemane account comes from the community formula of the Lord's Prayer (which is what Mt gives
us in chap. 6), and what we have is a once independent saying
used in two different settings.

that Jesus prayed ("saying the same words"—the phrase from Mk's second act).

Since we must admit some elaboration in the three-act presentation, Schmid[6] may be right when he suggests that the one act presentation is the more original (as in Lk, but without the Lucan modifications). Perhaps a standardization based on a parallel to the three denials by Peter has caused the Mk-Mt three-act formulation. Be this as it may, we wish simply to point out that the Synoptic presentation of what happened during the agony is not uniform, and in itself witnesses a certain freedom of treatment.

Problem B. Lk 22:41 has Jesus withdraw a stone's throw from (presumably all) the disciples. Mk 14:32 and Mt 26:36 have a preliminary withdrawal from the larger group of the disciples: "Sit here while I go over there and pray." And then, having taken three disciples with Him, Jesus further separates Himself from the three (Mk 14:35; Mt 26:39). Thus in Mk-Mt we have a more thorough separation than that of Lk's report.

All three Synoptics agree that the disciples, even the closest ones, fell asleep; and all the Synoptics place the scene at night. How then did they know what Jesus said and did? Of course there is no impossibility involved: Jesus could have told the disciples what He said and did after the Resurrection (the disciples had no time alone with Him from the agony scene until His death). Yet we must admit that this puts demands on the imagination, and that there is a difficulty in the Synoptic account. The Gospel, after all, is supposed to depend on eyewitness testimony (Acts 10:39); and where we have a scene not backed up by eyewitness account, we have a right to ask how this scene was composed.

While the garden scene in Jn 18:1–12 has no account of an agony, we find scattered in Jn fragments that closely resemble elements of the Synoptic scene.

a) The agony is the chief place in the Synoptic Gospels

6 *Markus*, 278.

that we hear Jesus use the term "hour" for the passion. In Mk 14:35 (only) Jesus prays that the *hour* might pass from Him. In Mk 14:41 and Mt 26:45 at the end of the agony scene the disciples are told that the *hour* has come. This use of hour is found over ten times in Jn to describe the whole complexus of the passion and elevation of Jesus, and its spiritual effects.[7]

b) In the Synoptic agony scene, Jesus says, "My soul is sorrowful unto death." In Jn 12 we have a dramatic scene introduced by the coming of the Greeks on Palm Sunday to see Jesus.[8] Jesus reacts to this news in 12:23 with the exclamation: "The hour has come"—the same expression we heard in the agony scene, as mentioned above.[9] Then, in this setting of the coming of the hour, Jesus expresses sorrow of soul: "Now is my soul disturbed."[10]

He continues with the prayer: "Father save me from this hour" (12:27). Mk 14:35 has Jesus praying that the hour may pass from Him; and Mk 14:36 (Mt 26:39; Lk 22:42) has: "Father . . . remove this cup from me." Returning to Jn 12:27 we find that Jesus refuses this prayer:

---

[7] See Jn 4:21; 4:23; 5:25; 5:28; 7:30; 8:20; 12:23; 12:27; 13:1; 16:25; 16:32; 17:1. In our opinion, this holds true for the Cana scene (Jn 2:4) as well. See W. Thüsing, *Die Erhöhung und Verherrlichung Jesu im Johannesevangelium* (Münster: Aschendorf, 1960), 92–96.

[8] The similarities between Jn 12:23, 27–30 and the Synoptic agony scene have been pointed out by J. H. Bernard, *The Gospel according to St. John* (*ICC,* 1928), II, 435–436. Also R. Bultmann, *Das Evangelium des Johannes,* 16 ed. (Göttingen: Vandenhoeck, 1959), 327, n. 7.

[9] Jn uses *elēlythen;* Mk 14:41 uses *ēlthen;* Mt 26:45 *ēggiken.* Jn 12:23 continues: "The hour has come for *the Son of Man* to be glorified." The Synoptics continue: "The hour has come; *the Son of Man* is betrayed into the hand of sinners."

[10] Jn 12:27 uses the verbal form *tetaraktai;* Mk 14:34 and Mt 26:38, seemingly citing Ps 42:6, use *perilypos.* Is it sheer coincidence that in this very verse of the psalm Jn's *tarassō* is in parallelism to *perilypos?* "Why are you sorrowful [*perilypos*], my soul, and why do you disturb me [*syntarassō*]?"

"Rather [*alla*] for this purpose have I come to this hour. Father, glorify your name." Mk 14:36 has: "Rather [*alla*] not what I wish but what you wish."[11]

In Jn 12:28–30 this submissive prayer is answered by a voice from heaven, speaking of the glorification of the divine name. Some among the crowd say that an angel has spoken to Him. In Lk's agony scene (22:43), an angel is sent from heaven to strengthen Jesus.[12]

Thus there are many parallels between Jn 12 (vv. 23, 27–30) and the Synoptic agony scene.

c) The agony scene in Mk-Mt ends with the words: "Rise, let us be going [*egeiresthe agōmen*]. Behold my betrayer [*paradidous*] is at hand" (Mk 14:42; Mt 26:46). This expression occurs in the Johannine account of the Last Supper (Jn 14:30–31): "The prince of this world is coming. . . . Arise, let us be going from here [*egeiresthe agōmen*]." It is interesting that Mk and Mt speak of the *paradidous* (Judas for them). In Jn, Satan is the real *paradidous,* for it is Satan who puts it into the heart of Judas to betray (*paradoi*) Jesus (Jn 13:2). Thus when Jn connects the "Rise, let us be going" to the coming of the prince of this world, we are not far from the Synoptic

---

[11] As mentioned in n. 5 above, in the second act of Mt's agony scene (26:42), we hear Jesus say, "Your will be done." In the Lord's Prayer, this parallels "Your name be sanctified" (Mt 6:9), which is virtually identical with Jn's "Glorify your name."

[12] Mt too has angels where later on in the arrest scene Jesus asserts His power to call on twelve legions of angels (26:53)— are these the servants of Jn 18:36: "If my kingship were of this world, my servants would fight"? Such a scholar as C. K. Barrett, *The Gospel according to St. John* (London: SPCK, 1956), 355, suggests that the angel of Jn 12:29 may be a recollection of Lk's angel in the agony. However, E. Osty has pointed out that the relations between Jn and Lk are very complex, and often not resolved on the basis of simple literary dependence. See "Les points de contact entre le récit de la Passion dans Saint Luc et Saint Jean," *Recherches de Science Religieuse* 39 (1951), 146–154.

statement in the agony scene that the *paradidous* is at hand.[13]

d) Still another parallel to an element of the Synoptic agony scene can be found in Jn 18:11. In Jn's description of the arrest in the garden, we are told that, after Peter struck off the servant's ear, Jesus told him to put his sword away (Jn 18:11; also Mt 26:52): "Shall I not *drink* the *cup* which the *Father* has given me?" All three Synoptic Gospels report Jesus' prayer in the first act of the agony in terms of the *Father's* removing the *cup* from Him. In the second act of the agony, the prayer reported only in Mt 26:42 contains these words: "If this cannot pass unless I *drink* it, your will be done."

So much for the parallels; how do we evaluate them? The first and easiest solution is that both traditions, the Synoptic and the Johannine, are faithfully recording just what happened, and the similarities are just the coincidental repetitions of ideas that occur in everyone's life. Another solution would be that the Synoptic account of the agony is historical, and that the Johannine tradition has dismembered it, scattering fragments through the Gospel. Those who believe that Jn is composed from sources would say that bits of Synoptic material have been ingested into the various Johannine scenes mentioned above.[14] Why

---

[13] Lk 22:53 makes explicit the presence of Satan behind Judas in Gethsemane: "This is your hour and the power of darkness." We might mention too that the section Jn 12:27–30 (treated under *b* above) continues right into the theme of the judgment of Satan in 12:31.

[14] So Bultmann, *Johannes,* 327, n. 7, and 489. Personally we believe that the final editor of Jn was familiar with Synoptic tradition as it appears in Mk (or perhaps the formative stages of Mk; yet the real parallels are to the Greek of Mk). But we do not believe that whole scenes of Jn were made up out of phrases borrowed from the Synoptic tradition. The parallels we have seen above and will see in the rest of the article are too subtle to be accounted for by such last-minute borrowings. Besides, here we are dealing with parallels to Mt as well, and

would Jn omit the scene? We might think perhaps to avoid any hint of weakness in a portrait of Jesus, and yet Jn 12:27 does not hesitate to report a troubling of soul. Also this solution favoring the Synoptic historicity has to face the two problems (*A* and *B*) which we encountered in the Synoptic tradition.

A third solution would be to give the priority to the Johannine tradition, and to hold that the scattering of these elements in Jn represents a more original picture. The Synoptic tradition of the agony would then represent a gathering of prayers uttered at various times in the public life of Jesus—a life which, after all, consisted in constant struggle with Satan and whose prayers would not be at all unfitting in the agony scene of preparation for the great struggle with Satan. Within the Synoptic tradition there would probably have been some real reminiscences of what Jesus actually prayed about in Gethsemane, but this skeletal framework would have been filled out from the broader material of the public life. This solution has the advantage of solving our Problems *A* and *B*. Of course, it would be acceptable only to those who look on the Johannine tradition as basically and ultimately stemming from an eyewitness.

II. THE CAIAPHAS TRIAL (MT 26:59–68; MK 14:55–65; LK 22:66–70)

The problem of the Jewish trials of Jesus is well known. Mk-Mt tell of a night trial before Caiaphas, and merely mention a morning session. Lk has no night trial and puts the Caiaphas trial in the morning. Jn has a night interrogation before Annas and merely mentions a morning presentation before Caiaphas (18:24, 28).

The various theories offered to harmonize these accounts lie beyond our scope. Personally we prefer the theory ad-

---

the evidence that the final editor of Jn knew Mt is very tenuous. See above, chap. IX, pp. 149–150.

vanced by Benoit[15] that there was an unofficial night interrogation (as in Jn) in which Christ was mocked; and then
in the morning (as in Lk) the official trial before Caiaphas
recorded in the Synoptic tradition. Our primary interest,
however, is in the absence of the Caiaphas trial in Jn.

Here again we face a twofold problem in the Synoptic
tradition of the trial: (*a*) lack of uniformity between Mk-
Mt and Lk; (*b*) the fact that the disciples were not eyewitnesses of the trial.

Problem A. Besides the discrepancy on the time of the
trial, there are certain differences between Mk-Mt and Lk
concerning the contents of the trial. Mk-Mt begin the trial
with a search for witnesses against Jesus and the interrogation of these witnesses. This leads to the saying about the
destruction of the Temple, and the high priest's demand
for an answer by Jesus to the testimony. All of this (Mk
14:55–60; Mt 26:59–62) is omitted by Lk.

Then Mk-Mt have one solemn question placed by the
high priest to Jesus concerning His being the Messiah, the
Son of the Blessed, followed by Jesus' answer. Lk 22:66–
70 has two questions and two answers. The rending of the
garments and the charge of blasphemy (Mk 14:63–64; Mt
26:65–66) are omitted by Lk. And the mockery scene
which immediately follows in Mk-Mt is placed by Lk elsewhere (Lk 26:63–65). Thus, in their report of the same
trial, the Synoptics are far from complete agreement on its
contents.

Problem B. The trial was held before the Sanhedrin;
the disciples were not present. Here, however, there is less
problem than in the agony scene. Jn 12:42 tells us that
many of the authorities believed in Jesus; and we know
specifically of Nicodemus, a Pharisee member of the
Sanhedrin (Jn 3:1) and of Joseph of Arimathea, another
Sanhedrin member (Mk 15:43). Any of these could have

15 "Jésus devant le Sanhédrin," *Angelicum*, 20 (1943), 143–
165. It was the vague memory of the unofficial night interrogation and the mockery that accompanied it that drew the official
trial before Caiaphas back into the night (as in Mk-Mt).

found out what happened and reported it to the disciples.[16] A curiosity among the disciples as to what happened at the trial is not at all unlikely.

Once again, although Jn omits the trial, we find elements parallel to the details of the Synoptic trial scattered through Jn.

a) The accusation made by the false witnesses in Mk-Mt centers around Jesus' claim of ability to rebuild the Temple: "I am able to destroy this Temple of God and to build it in three days."[17] We find the statement on the Temple in Jn 2:19: "Destroy this Temple, and in three days I shall raise it up." No matter whether we accept the Johannine or the Synoptic date for the cleansing of the Temple, it is perfectly logical that the statement on the Temple's reconstruction could have been made on this occasion as reported in Jn (such a claim is not likely to have been frequently repeated by Jesus). The form of the statement given in the Synoptic tradition by *false* witnesses may be a distortion of the more original Johannine form.[18]

It is interesting that Lk omits this part of the trial scene, even though the Lucan tradition knew of this Temple saying (Acts 6:14). Was it omitted as meaningless to Lk's Gentile audience, or for some reason did Luke think it did not belong in the trial?[19]

[16] Taylor, *op. cit.*, 563: ". . . knowledge of what happened, even if we allow for the absence of a biographical interest, must have been available."

[17] Mt 26:61. In Mk 14:58 we have the distinguishing adjectives "made with hands" and "not made with hands." Schmid, *Markus*, 282, treats these adjectives as added theological clarifications.

[18] The *"you* destroy" of Jn seems more original than the *"I* am able to destroy" of Mt. However, the Synoptic "build" is probably more original than Jn's "raise it up," a clause which leads into the theological explanation of the temple as Christ's body.

[19] It would be foolish to deny that the statement played some part in the Passion for it was turned against Jesus on the cross

b) As mentioned, Lk reports two questions placed by the high priest in the trial. The first is in Lk 22:67: "If you are the Messiah, tell us." In reply, Jesus says, "If I tell you, you will not believe. And if I pose a question you will not answer." We hear virtually the same dialogue in the Johannine description of a scene in the Temple at the feast of Dedication. In Jn 10:24 the Jews (i.e., the Jewish authorities—compare Mk 15:3 to Jn 18:31) press Jesus: "If you are the Messiah, tell us plainly." Jesus answers, "I told you and you do not believe."

The second question (Lk 22:70) is: "Are you the Son of God then?" Jesus answers, "You say that I am." This is the end of the questioning in the trial; there is no further need of witnesses. In Mk 14:64 and Mt 26:65 Jesus is accused of blasphemy. When we turn to Jn and read on in the Dedication scene, we find that the reaction of the Jews to Jesus' answer to their question on being the Messiah is to take up stones against Jesus for blasphemy (Jn 10:33—the only time *blasphemia* occurs in Jn). Jesus answers them (10:36): "Do you say . . . 'You are blaspheming,' because I said, 'I am *God's Son*'?" He then calls on His works for a witness to Himself.

Thus in close sequence in Jn we find roughly the same questions, answers, and reactions as in the Synoptic trial, with particular similarity to Lk's version.[20]

(Mk 15:29; Mt 27:40) where Lk omits it again. J. Blinzler *The Trial of Jesus* (Westminster: Newman, 1959), 101, n. 27, say that Lk omitted the statement in the trial because it had no decisive influence on the outcome. This explanation seems desperate.

[20] Osty, *art. cit.*, brings out the closeness of Lk and Jn in the Passion narrative; he finds forty individual points of contact although he misses the ones we have just given. Barrett, *op. cit.* 316: "John may be dependent upon Luke, but the whole of the present section recalls the Marcan trial before the high priest with its question, charge of blasphemy, and murderous attack." Also C. H. Dodd, *The Interpretation of the Fourth Gospel* (Cambridge University, 1954), 361–362.

c) In Jn 11:47–53 we find something resembling a trial before Caiaphas, even though Jesus is not actually present.[21] Some of the Jews report the Lazarus miracle to the Pharisees. This results in a Sanhedrin session (v. 47) where the high priest Caiaphas decides the course of action (v. 49); the decision is to put Jesus to death (v. 53). If we were to combine this material with that of Jn 10 above, we would have a scene virtually identical with the Synoptic trial. And we would even have a reference to the destruction of the Temple (11:48): "If we let him go on this way . . . the Romans will come and destroy our holy place (*topon*)."

d) There is one element in the Synoptic tradition of the trial that we have not yet discussed. In all three Synoptic Gospels Jesus cites Ps 110:1 (combined in Mk-Mt with Dn 7:13) in answer to His judges: "But I tell you, from now on you will see the Son of Man seated at the right hand of the Power, and coming on the clouds of heaven" (Mt 26:64; also Mk 14:62; the form in Lk 22:69 omits the last clause). In its context, it seems to be a reference to the parousia.

We have no exact parallel to this statement in Jn, but we might call attention to 1:51: "And he said to him [Nathanael], 'Amen, amen, I say to you [pl.!], you will see heaven opened, and the angels of God ascending and descending upon the Son of Man." Since Jesus had just spoken to Nathanael as "you [sg.]" in v. 50, we must admit that v. 51 poorly fits the sequence. Actually 1:50 could be joined to chap. 2 in Jn and fit perfectly; for 1:50 promises Nathanael that he will see greater things, and in the Cana miracle of chap. 2 the disciples do see the glory of Jesus (2:11). V. 51 serves only to interrupt this chain of thought.

Modern writers have suggested a connection between Jn

---

[21] Barrett, *ibid.*, 337, says the scene is of dubious historical value.

1:51 and Mt 26:64;[22] but in this they were anticipated by the ancient scribes. In some manuscripts[23] and also in the Peshitta Jn 1:51 reads: "Amen, amen, I say to you, *from now on* you will see . . ."; the *ap' arti* is borrowed from Mt 26:64.

Windisch,[24] in his study of Jn 1:51, mentions that this is really the only "Son of Man" saying in Jn that is not worked into a discourse. And too it is the only mention of an angelophany in the Fourth Gospel. Windisch suggests that this saying originally dealt with the parousia, and that it has been attracted to its present context by a certain surface similarity of 1:50, since both verses deal with a promise of seeing.[25] Of course, in the new context it is not theologically out of place since its eschatology now becomes realized. The words and works of Jesus in the following chapters serve as a manifestation of the Son of Man, and of His constant contact with heaven. These suggestions are worth considering for they would establish a contact of thought between this statement and the parousia promise of Mt 26:64 and parallels.

In conclusion, when we turn to evaluating the similarities between the Synoptic trial scene and the various passages in Jn, we are faced with the same possible solutions as in the agony scene. Here, however, we believe the *a priori*

[22] *Ibid.*, 155.

[23] Koridethi, Lake group, the Palatinus of the Old Latin, and von Soden's Koine group.

[24] "Angelophanien um den Menschensohn auf Erden," *Zeitschrift für die neutestamentliche Wissenschaft,* 30 (1931), 215–233.

[25] Of course, we must also remember that v. 51 may have been added here because it fits in well with the theme of Nathanael being "worthy of the name of Israel" (i.e., Jacob) mentioned in 1:47 ff. The Jacob's ladder background supplied by Gn 28:12 is obvious in 1:51.

We might mention that the theme of the angels in this verse fits in very well with Windisch's suggestion that the original theme was the parousia; the Son of Man is frequently pictured as returning accompanied by His angels (Mk 8:38; Mt 16:27).

likelihood of the disciples' knowledge of some details of the trial must be weighed. Whether or not inquiries by the disciples would have gained an exact knowledge of the fairly detailed and dramatic dialogue that we now have in the Synoptic tradition is another question. Perhaps a general knowledge of the basic charges made at the trial, e.g., the Temple statement, or the title "Son of God," has been combined with dialogue which actually occurred during the ministry and of which the disciples themselves were witnesses. Certainly the trial was not the first time such charges were made against Jesus. Thus Jn's presentation of the various elements which we have seen may be the historical background of the trial scene.

III. THE TEMPTATIONS OF JESUS (MT 4:1–11; MK 1:12–13; LK 4:1–13)

Jn's sequence of the events following Jesus' baptism does not parallel that of the Synoptic Gospels. In Jn Jesus returns to Galilee a few days after the baptism.[26] In the Synoptic tradition He is driven into the desert to be tempted by Satan for forty days, and only when this is over does He return to Galilee.[27]

Once again, in dealing with the historicity of the Synoptic tradition of the temptation scene, we are faced with two problems:

Problem A. The accounts of Mk and Mt-Lk are not in total harmony. Mk simply reports the fact of the temptation;[28] Mt-Lk, presumably drawing on the common non-

---

[26] Jn 1:43. The row of days in Jn 1, however, may well betray a theological interest rather than a historical one.

[27] This is after the Baptist's arrest (Mk 1:14; Mt 4:12). Jn does not report the Baptist's arrest until later (3:24).

[28] Mk 1:13 adds that he was with wild beasts. Some have seen here a (rather far-fetched) reference to Ps 91:13 which mentions the lion and the adder. The preceding verse of the psalm concerns the "angels having charge of you," etc.—the citation made by Satan in Mt 4:6; Lk 4:10–11.

Marcan source, describe the temptations. In this dramatic description, except for a shift of order in the three temptations, Mt and Lk agree closely. It is generally thought that by placing the temptation at Jerusalem last (Mt has it in second place), Lk is favoring the theological motif of gradual progress toward Jerusalem which dominates the order of the Third Gospel.

This is interesting for its shows a certain freedom in handling the details of the temptations to promote theological purpose. And indeed the primary purpose of the scene is certainly theological: placed before the ministry of Jesus, it shows that the whole ministry of Jesus will be a struggle with Satan, culminating in the final struggle of the Passion. Lk 4:13 brings this out nicely by reporting that Satan left Him "until an opportune time." It has also been pointed out that all three answers given Satan by Jesus are from Deuteronomy, and fit in well with the theological theme of matching Christ's forty days in the desert with Israel's forty years in the desert.[29]

Also we must admit a certain figurative element in the Synoptic description of the temptations. There is no mountain from which one can see the whole world (Mt 4:8); and we can scarcely believe that Jesus was physically placed on the pinnacle of the Temple (Mt 4:5) for all to see.[30] This does not, however, disprove the psychic reality of the temptations.

Problem B. The disciples were not eyewitnesses to the

---

[29] Jn may have a similar theme: the baptism of Jesus in the Jordan may represent a new crossing of the Jordan. See M. Boismard, O.P., *Du Baptême à Cana* (Paris: Cerf. 1956), 38 ff.

[30] Cf. J. Schmid, *Das Evangelium nach Matthäus*, 4 ed. (Regensburger NT, 1959), 67. Unfortunately, the study of the historicity of the temptation scene has been complicated in the past by attempts to prove from it false concepts of Jesus' lack of messianic consciousness. There is nothing in this scene to suggest that it gave birth to the messianic consciousness of Jesus; His answers portray Him as already quite aware of His special role.

temptation scene. This presents a grave difficulty in establishing the historicity of the scene. To overcome it, we would have to suppose that Jesus Himself narrated His temptations to the disciples in order to instruct them about their struggle with Satan. We can think of no other example in the Gospel of Jesus' personally baring His soul at such length to the disciples. And, of course, there is always the basic principle that the Gospel should represent the Apostles' preaching of that which they witnessed.

When we turn to Jn, we find no such direct dramatic encounter between Satan and Jesus; but we do find an interesting series of temptations faced by Jesus in cc. 6–7.

a) Jn 6:15. Jesus had just multiplied the loaves. In the Synoptic multiplication account, we are told that Jesus then made (*ēnagkasen*) His disciples get into the boat and leave (Mk 6:45; Mt 14:22), and that He then dismissed the crowd. No reason for the hasty and forced departure is given.

Jn alone explains what happened. Impressed by His physical miracle, the crowd was about to make Jesus king by force. Jesus withdrew from this attempt almost certainly because He would have nothing to do with a kingdom of this world (Jn 18:36). Basically the same situation arises again in the Johannine account of the Palm Sunday events. When the crowd goes out with palm branches to hail the King of Israel,[31] Jesus finds a young ass to ride upon. His action is designed to remind the people of Zechariah's promise (9:9) that the king was to be primarily one of peace and salvation, rather than one of political power.

---

[31] Jn 12:12–16. The description of the crowd reminds us of the political celebrations of the Maccabees (1 Mc 13:50–52; 2 Mc 10:7) and has definite political overtones. Cf. W. R. Farmer, *Journal of Theological Studies*, 3 (1952), 62–66. Also R. H. Lightfoot, *St. John's Gospel* (Oxford: Clarendon, 1956), 237–239.

While Satan is not specifically mentioned in these passages as the instigator of this attempt to make Jesus into a worldly king, we may well suspect that in Jn's thought such enticement lay in the sphere of the *prince of this world* (12:31; 14:30; 16:11) for to him belongs worldly sovereignty (1 Jn 5:19).

Turning to the Synoptic temptation scene, we find a similar attempt to make Jesus a political king as Mt's third temptation and Lk's second.

b) Jn 6:26–34. The crowd who witnessed the multiplication of the loaves the day before finds Jesus at Capernaum. They want more of this bread so that they will not have to work. Their ancestors had manna daily in the desert; if Jesus is a second Moses, can He not do as well or better?

In studying Jesus' reply, we should recall Dt 8:3: "He therefore let you be afflicted with hunger, and then fed you with manna, a food unknown to you and to your fathers, in order to show you that not by bread alone does man live, but by every word that comes forth from the mouth of the Lord." Although this text is not cited explicitly in Jn, Jesus is virtually commenting on it when He says that their fathers did not profit from the manna (6:49–50) and that they should turn from the physical bread which perishes (6:27) and does not produce life to the bread of life in which they must believe (6:35). Verse 45 seems to make it quite clear that this bread of life is God's teaching. Jesus is the incarnate *Word* of God, and as such is the true bread of life given from heaven by the Father (6:32–33).

We have a similar enticement to multiply bread in the first temptation by Satan in Mt-Lk. The answer given by Jesus in Mt 4:4 is a citation of Dt 8:3, opposing the word of God to natural bread. Again, of course, Satan does not directly enter in Jn's scene. Yet the opposition between the bread of life and that which leads to death (6:49–50) is in Johannine dualism part of the contrast between the realm of God the Giver of life (1:4) and that of Satan the murderer (8:44; 1 Jn 3:12).

c) Jn 7:1–4. Before the feast of Tabernacles, the brethren of Jesus, who still do not believe in Him, taunt Him. They ask Him what good are miracles done in the country district of Galilee. If Jesus wants a following, He should go up to Jerusalem and show Himself to the world. This challenge has basically the same theme as Mt's second and Lk's third temptation where Jesus is taken up to *Jerusalem* and invited to make a spectacle of Himself by jumping off the pinnacle of the Temple. In Jn 7:7 Jesus rightly connects this taunt with the evil world which in Johannine thought is Satan's domain.

The parallels between the scene of three temptations in Mt-Lk and the individual passages of Jn 6–7 are interesting.[32] They raise the question of whether or not the Matthean-Lucan common source has not filled in Mk's vague "he was tempted by Satan" with a dramatic synopsis of the type of temptations Jesus actually faced during His life. Certainly we are making no claim that Jn's scenes are the direct prototypes of the Synoptic temptations. But they do give examples of how the struggle between Satan and Jesus was fought out. Mt and Lk (or their common source) would be doing no injustice to historic fact if they dramatized such temptations within one scene, and unmasked the real tempter by placing these enticements directly in his mouth. They would be simply being guided by theological motive and a sense for figurative impact. Need we recall that elements of both the theological and the figurative must be admitted in the temptation scene of Mt-Lk, no

[32] P.-H. Menoud, *L'évangile de Jean* (Paris: Delachaux, 1947), 29, says that these parallels have been defended by H. Preisker, "Zum Charakter des Johannes-evangeliums," in *Luther, Kant, Schleiermacher in ihrer Bedeutung für den Protestantismus* (1939), 379–384. Preisker's article has not been available to this writer.

matter what we may judge of its exact historicity. We make
no claim for our suggestions other than that they might
help to solve the problems raised by the Synoptic account.

IV. THE CONFESSION OF PETER (MT 16:13–20;
MK 8:27–30; LK 9:18–21)

This scene occurs in both the Synoptic and the Johannine
traditions. It is important first to consider the general setting of the scene. Mk-Mt have two multiplications of loaves
and fishes, and the confession by Peter follows the second.
Lk has only one multiplication, and the confession by Peter
follows that. Thus:

Multiplication for 5000:
    Mk 6:31–44   Mt 14:13–21   Lk 9:10–17
Multiplication for 4000:
    Mk 8:1–10   Mt 15:32–39
Confession of Peter:
    Mk 8:27–30   Mt 16:13–20   Lk 9:18–21

It has been often suggested that the whole sequence of the
second multiplication in Mk-Mt is a doublet.[33]

When we turn to the setting of the Petrine confession in
Jn, at first sight the setting strikes us as different. The multiplication of the loaves in Jn 6 is the occasion of a long
discourse on the bread of life of which the Synoptic Gospels know nothing. Yet if we make allowance for the fact
that Jn, like Lk, has only one multiplication, we find an
interesting sequence which is not unlike Mk's.[34] We shall

[33] For a discussion, see Taylor, *Mark,* 628–632. Also see
above, chap. IX, p. 202.

[34] This was pointed out in part by Bertil Gärtner, *John 6 and
the Jewish Passover* (Lund: Gleerup, 1959), 12. If this sequence is true, it vitiates Bultmann's rather arbitrary dismem-
berment of the chapter.

use the Greek enumeration of verses for the end of Jn 6
(Greek 6:52–71 = Vulgate 6:51–70).

Multiplication for 5000:	Jn 6:1–15	Mk 6:31–44
Walking on the sea:	16–24	45–54

(then skipping to after Mk's second multiplication in
8:1–10)

Request for a sign:	25–34	8:11–13
Discourse on bread:	35–59	14–21
Confession of Peter:	60–69	27–30
Passion theme; denial:	70–71	31–33

This sequence has not been given sufficient attention in de-
termining the relation of the Johannine and the Synoptic
traditions, nor in the question of evaluating the second multiplication in Mk-Mt.[35]

In considering the confession of Peter in itself, we notice
that within the Synoptic tradition Mk and Lk agree closely,
while Mt alone has the "Petrine Primacy" section (16:17–
19). Since Cullmann's[36] treatment of this section, there is
a wider acceptance of its authenticity among non-Catholics.
On the other hand, some Catholic scholars (along with
Cullmann)[37] question whether the promise of building the
Church on Peter was made on this occasion.

[35] The fact that Jn 6:7 and Mk 6:37 (alone of the Synoptic
Gospels) both mention 200 denarii as the price of bread for the
crowd is often used as an example of the familiarity of the author of Jn with the Marcan tradition. This would make the
omission of the second multiplication in Jn even more significant.

[36] *Peter,* 2 ed. (Philadelphia: Westminster, 1962), 164–217.

[37] *Ibid.,* 184. D. M. Stanley, S.J. *The Gospel of St. Matthew*
(Collegeville: Liturgical Press, 1960), 58. P. Benoît, *Exégèse
et Théologie* (Paris: Cerf, 1961), II, 295. J. Schmid, *Das
Evangelium nach Matthaus* (Regensburg: Pustet, 1959), 247.
An especially interesting defense of this view is found in E.
Sutcliffe, "St. Peter's Double Confession in Mt 16:16–19,"
Heythrop Journal 3 (1962), 31–41. Any doubts about the
orthodoxy of the suggestion that possibly the promise to Peter

Now let us turn to an examination of the confession of
Peter as it appears in the Synoptic and the Johannine
tradition:

a) In all the Synoptic Gospels the section begins with
Jesus' question: "Who do men say that I am? [Mt: that
the *Son of Man* is?]" The answer shows that men have not
as yet understood who Jesus is, nor His true mission.

The scene in Jn 6:60–69 might at first glance seem very
different. The disciples (here a larger group than the
Twelve) have not understood the discourse on the bread
of life. Jesus speaks to them of the *Son of Man* ascending
to where He was before, but they still do not believe. The
Evangelist (v. 64) tells us that Jesus knew from the first
who those were that did not believe. Thus, although the
material is different, the opening theme is the same as that
of the Synoptics: the general disbelief of men and the
failure to understand Jesus.

In the Synoptic Gospels, after this general failure to com-
prehend, Jesus turns to His disciples: "But who do *you* say
that I am?" In Jn 6:67 Jesus says to the Twelve, "Do *you*
also wish to leave?" In both traditions it is Peter who takes
it on himself to answer for the others. In Mk 8:29 he
says, "You are the Messiah [or anointed one; Lk 9:20:
the Messiah of God]." In Jn 6:69 he says, "You are the
holy one of God."[38]

Thus the similarities between the Johannine scene and
that part of the account shared by all the Synoptic Gospels
are quite close.

---

was uttered on another occasion than that of Caesarea Philippi
now seem to have been resolved, for in reference to Mt 16:13–
20 Bernard Cardinal Alfrink states in *Biblica* 43 (1962), 259:
"I do not believe either that the faith is any more endangered
if one maintains that one or other verse of this passage (for
example, the beatitude of v. 17, *'Beatus es Simon Bar Jona'*)
was in fact spoken by Our Lord on another occasion and not
at that precise moment."

[38] This is the correct reading. The Vulgate reading, "You are
the Messiah, the Son of God," has been influenced by Mt 16:16.

b) We come now to the special "Petrine Primacy" section of Mt. For Mt 16:16 Peter's confession includes not only the messiahship of Jesus ("anointed one") but also that He is the "Son of the living God."[39] Let us note two points in the Matthean section that follows:

First, flesh and blood have not revealed this to Peter but direct intervention of the Father (16:17). Is it just coincidental that in Jn's scene in 6:60–69 we hear of the inability of flesh to produce faith? In response to the general disbelief, Jesus warns the disciples (6:63): "It is the Spirit that gives life; the *flesh* is of no use." And 6:65 stresses that no one can believe in Jesus unless he is enabled to do so by *the Father*.

Second, in Mt 16:18 Simon Bar-Jona's name is changed to Peter with a play that he is the rock (*kepha*) on which the Church will be built. Jn is the only other Gospel to give us a scene in which Simon's name is changed to Peter.[40] It is back in the first week of the public ministry (1:41–42). Andrew comes and tells Simon, "We have found the Messiah (which means 'anointed one')." And Jesus, seeing Simon, says, "So you are Simon Bar-John. You shall be called Cephas (which means Peter)." Notice these details: the changing of the name follows the recognition of the "anointed one"; the Bar-Jona/Bar-John similarity; the reference to the Aramaic word for Peter. They point up the closeness of the Matthean and Johannine scenes.[41] Of

[39] Normally we would consider this as simply another messianic title, not necessarily implying divinity. But the enthusiasm of Jesus' reaction to this confession seems to imply more.

[40] We doubt that Mk 3:16 should be cited on a par with Mt and Jn in this connection. Mk's "Simon, whom he surnamed Peter," occurs in a list of names, and seems to record simply that Simon had a second name, as do the lists in Lk 6:14 and Mt 10:2.

[41] Perhaps we should add a note on Jn 1:51 which we have already discussed. This mention of the angels ascending and descending on the Son of Man follows shortly after the Petrine scene of Jn 1:41–42. In Mt 16:27, shortly after the Petrine

course, the changing of name in Jn is intended to be
prophetic of Peter's future role, and presumably that role
will have something to do with "rock," but that is not
made explicit as in Mt.

Hence, while Jn 6 has similarities to the general Synoptic
material on the confession of Peter, the parallel to Mt's
additional material is in both Jn 6 and Jn 1. We have mentioned that some hold that the present location of the
Petrine name-changing in Mt is not original, but we would
be hasty to jump to the conclusion that Jn's position is
more original. In Jn 1 we have a whole list of titles which
show the gradually deepening insights of the disciples into
Jesus' mission: Teacher in 1:38; Messiah in 1:41; Prophet
like Moses in 1:45; Son of God and King of Israel in 1:49.
This arrangement looks artificial, and runs against the
Synoptic theme of belated messianic recognition. Therefore, at least the setting of the changing of Simon's name
in Jn 1 does not appear to be original.

c) To throw a little more light on this question we shall
have to go farther afield. We hope the reader will allow us
this luxury. The "Petrine Primacy" passage of Mt 16 is
one of three Petrine sections preserved only by Mt. The
other two are 17:24–27 (the finding of the coin in the
fish's mouth), and 14:28–33 (Peter's walking on the sea).
We are interested in the latter. Of the three Gospels that
narrate how Jesus came to the disciples walking on the
sea (Mk, Mt, Jn), only Mt tells how Peter vaguely recognized Jesus standing at a distance on the water. He said
(Mt 14:28): "Lord, if it is you, command me to come to
you on the water." At Jesus' command, he got out of the
boat to go to Jesus; but, when his faith failed, he cried out,
"Lord, save me." Jesus did so, although He rebuked Peter
as a man of little faith.

It is curious that Mk and Jn, who know of the storm

---

scene of Mt 16:16–19, we hear of the Son of Man coming
with His angels in the glory of His Father. Jn 1:51 is almost a
blending of Mt 16:27 and 26:64. See Bernard, *John,* I, 68–69.

at sea, omit this episode. Perhaps, as with the "Petrine Primacy" section, Mt may be including an incident here which occurred at another time. Jn 21:7 ff. has a scene which somewhat resembles the Matthean scene. The disciples are in a boat; Jesus is at a distance standing on the shore. When the disciple whom Jesus loved recognizes Jesus ("It is *the Lord.*"—notice that "Lord" occurs in Mt 14:28), Peter jumps out of the boat and goes to Him. No miraculous walking on water, however, is mentioned. The ensuing conversation on feeding the lambs of Christ is regarded as the reconciliation of Peter after his threefold denial.

Could Jn and Mt be giving us parts of the same scene? Certainly some of the dialogue of Mt's scene is better understood after the Resurrection. The cry "Lord, save me" (Mt 14:30) would be doubly significant, as would also the Lord's rebuke (14:31): "O man of little faith, why did you doubt?" This would also explain the reaction of the other disciples in the boat (14:33): "Truly you are the Son of God."

The scene in Jn 21 contains a miraculous draught of fishes. This does not appear in Mt, but it does appear in Lk. Mk 1:16–20 and Mt 4:18–22 describe the call of the first disciples at the Sea of Galilee. Lk 5:1–11 describes the same scene but with the added detail of a miraculous draught of fishes. In its present context in Lk, the scene creates problems. For Mk-Mt the scene at the lake is the very first time Jesus has encountered Peter; it is followed by the healing of Peter's mother-in-law. Lk is not happy with this arrangement and places the healing of Peter's mother-in-law first. But even the shift in sequence does not account for Peter's reaction to the draught of fishes. He falls down at Jesus' feet (Lk 5:7—presumably in the boat!) saying, "Depart from me for I am a sinful man, O Lord." If Lk's scene is really the same one as Jn describes,[42] these words would again have more meaning after Peter's denial and after the Resurrection.

[42] Cf. Barrett, *John*, 481.

May we then be dealing with a large Petrine scene of which parts are found in Jn 21,[43] Mt 14:28–33, and Lk 5: 1–11? And should we perhaps include Mt 16:16–18? As we have mentioned in n. 37, many Catholic scholars regard this "Petrine Primacy" passage out of place at Caesarea Philippi, and one of the suggestions made is that it is post-resurrectional. Time does not permit us to treat of the subject here, and so we refrain from expressing any opinion of our own on the subject. But, if the postresurrectional suggestion of these scholars should prove correct, the promise of making Peter the foundation of the Church and of giving him the keys would be paralleled by the grant of shepherdship in Jn 21:15–17. This might also be the historic occasion of the changing of Peter's name at his confession of Christ as "the Son of the living God" (Mt 16:16).

Obviously these are but speculations that cannot be proved. Yet, if there is any truth in them, it is Jn who once again has supplied the basic historic framework. Along with Mk and Lk, Jn would be correct in confining the confession of Peter after the multiplication of the loaves to a recognition of the fact that Jesus was sent as God's anointed or holy one. The confession of divinity by Peter (Mt—if we take "Son of God" in its fullest sense) and his consequent reward of preeminence (Mt and Jn) would all come after the Resurrection.

CONCLUSION

When we come to sum up, to a certain extent we must let the individual sections speak for themselves. They are only unproved suggestions, and they do not all lead us to the same conclusion. Probably the relations between the

[43] We should note that Jn 21 is a peculiar segment of Johannine tradition, seemingly added after the main Gospel outline was completed. Its origins are not clear. Cf. M. E. Boismard, O.P., "Le chapitre XXI de Saint Jean," *Revue Biblique*, 54 (1947), 472–501. Also see above, p. 120, n. 26.

Synoptic and Johannine traditions are too complicated to be unraveled satisfactorily after nearly two thousand years. But if there is any one common denominator, if there is a collective impression, as we promised, it is that when the two traditions differ, we are not always to assume facilely that the Synoptic Gospels are recording the historic fact and that Jn has theologically reorganized the data. In the cases we have studied, an interesting case can be made out for the basic historicity of the Johannine picture and for theological reorganization on the part of the Synoptic Gospels. We are coming to realize more and more that the critics have played us false in their minimal estimate of the historicity of the Fourth Gospel.[44]

[44] For an interesting picture of the greater respect for the historicity of Jn in modern literature, see A. M. Hunter, "Recent Trends in Johannine Studies," *Expository Times,* 71 (1960), 164–167 and 219–222. Also see above, chap. IX.

Part Two

Section 3

Important Passages in the Synoptic Gospels

XII

The Pater Noster as an Eschatological Prayer

In recent years there has been a great deal written on the Pater Noster (henceforth PN).[1] Much of this literature has stressed the eschatological interpretation of the prayer as its more original meaning in the early Church. We wish to present here the case that can be made for such an interpretation.

At the outset we should make clear that by "eschatologi-

---

[1] The most valuable work is that of Ernst Lohmeyer, *Das Vater-unser*, 2 ed. (Göttingen, 1947); also available in English, *Our Father* (New York: Harper, 1966). All references in this text are to the German edition. For a Catholic treatment, Josef Hensler, *Das Vater-unser* (*NT Abhandlungen* 4/5; 1914), is still the most complete, especially in textual problems, but it is dated in its interpretations. More recent works include: J. Alonso Díaz, "El problema literario del Padre Nuestro," *Estudios biblicos*, 18 (1959), 63–75; Heinrich Schürmann, *Praying With Christ* (New York: Herder & Herder, 1964). H. Van den Bussche, *Le Notre Père* (Brussels, 1960); A. Hamman, *La prière I: Le Nouveau Testament* (Tournai, 1959), Part 3 of chap. 1; J. Jeremias, "The Lord's Prayer in Modern Research," *Expository Times*, 71 (1960), 141–146.

cal" we refer to the period of the last days, involving the
return of Christ, the destruction of the forces of evil, and
the definite establishment of God's rule. We are defining
the limits of our use of the word because in a broader sense
the whole Christian period can be called eschatological,
since God's kingdom has already been partially established
in this world through Jesus, who by His death and Resurrection has won a victory over Satan. In this broader sense,
the PN could be interpreted of the everyday aspirations
and needs of the Christian and still be called eschatological.[2] What we hope to show, however, is that the petitions
of the PN do not refer to daily circumstances but to the
final times.

Also, our interest is confined to the meaning that the PN
had for the early Church (as witnessed, in particular, in
Mt) after the Resurrection of Jesus. What shades of meaning the prayer had when Jesus first spoke it before His
death,[3] or what the disciples understood at that time, lie
beyond the scope of our investigation.

[2] Thus there is no distortion, but merely a broadening of
scope, if, in the Christian use of the PN, the petitions which
originally referred to the coming of the last days were soon
adapted to daily life.

[3] Van den Bussche, *op. cit.,* has done some investigation along
this line. For instance, the petition "May your name be sanctified," uttered during the lifetime of Jesus, may have referred to
the glorification to be achieved in His death and Resurrection
(see Jn 12:28). The viewpoint would naturally be changed
after these events.—This confining of our interest to the early
Church's understanding of the PN applies also, of course, to the
question of eschatology. We shall cite texts that the early Church
applied to the final coming of Christ, without *necessarily* implying that Jesus Himself was referring to His final coming
when He uttered those statements. John A. T. Robinson, A.
Feuillet, and others maintain that many of Jesus' statements
about His return referred originally to the destruction of Jerusalem, but in the early Church they came to be applied to the
final Parousia.

There are certain introductory problems to be treated briefly before we can discuss the petitions themselves. We may begin with the question of the different forms of the PN. Of the two forms of the prayer found in the Gospels, Lk's is considerably shorter than Mt's. The form found in the *Didache*[4] is longer than Mt's by a doxology at the end. Recent scholars have come surprisingly close to agreement on the origin of the different forms. It is generally held that the short Lucan form most closely represents in the number of its petitions the form of the prayer as historically spoken by Jesus.[5] The principle behind this solution is that it would be very difficult to conceive that the Lucan tradition would have dared to excise petitions from a longer form, for the prayer, being Jesus' own, took on a sacred character which would have discouraged such omissions. It is much more likely that the Matthean tradition represents a prayer to whose original petitions have been joined other sayings of Jesus.[6] This is a well-attested phenomenon in Mt, for Mt's eight beatitudes (as compared to Lk's four) and Mt's long Sermon on the Mount (as compared to Lk's shorter Sermon on the Plain) represent conflations of material.

---

[4] Because of its antiquity, the *Didache* must be considered an important witness to first-century Christian usage. J. P. Audet has given us the most recent and comprehensive work on the *Didache* (*La Didachè: Instructions des apôtres;* Paris, 1958), and he would date it (199) somewhere between A.D. 50–70, as a contemporary of the earlier Gospels. This may be too early, but a date much later than the beginning of the second century seems unlikely.

[5] Any theory that the PN was spoken by Jesus twice, once as in Lk, and once as in Mt, is not worthy of serious consideration (even though it was held by Origen). Besides exemplifying an impossible solution to the relation between the Synoptic Gospels, it would imply that the disciples forgot what Jesus told them and had to learn the prayer over again.

[6] Actually, as we shall see, the Matthean petitions not found in Lk (3 and the second part of 6) have parallels elsewhere in the Gospels.

	MATTHEW 6:9–13	LUKE 11:2–4	DIDACHE 8:2
Title	πάτερ ἡμῶν ὁ ἐν τοῖς οὐρανοῖς	πατερ	πατερ ημων ο εν τω ουρανω
Petition 1	ἁγιασθήτω τὸ ὄνομά σου	αγιασθητω το ονομα σου	αγιασθητω το ονομα σου
Petition 2	ἐλθέτω ἡ βασιλεία σου	ελθατω η βασιλεια σου	ελθετω η βασιλεια σου
Petition 3	γενηθήτω τὸ θέλημά σου ὡς ἐν οὐρανῷ καὶ ἐπὶ γῆς		γενηθητω το θελημα σου ως εν ουρανω και επι γης
Petition 4	τὸν ἄρτον ἡμῶν τὸν ἐπιούσιον δὸς ἡμῖν σήμερον	τον αρτον ημων τον επιουσιον διδου ημιν το καθ᾽ ημεραν	τον αρτον ημων τον επιουσιον δος ημιν σημερον
Petition 5	καὶ ἄφες ἡμῖν τὰ ὀφειλήματα ἡμῶν ὡς καὶ ἡμεῖς ἀφήκαμεν τοῖς ὀφειλέταις ἡμῶν	και αφες ημιν τας αμαρτιας ημων και γαρ αυτοι αφιομεν παντι οφειλοντι ημιν	και αφες ημιν την οφειλην ημων ως και ημεις αφιεμεν τοις οφειλεταις ημων
Petition 6	καὶ μὴ εἰσενέγκῃς ἡμᾶς εἰς πειρασμὸν ἀλλὰ ῥῦσαι ἡμᾶς ἀπὸ τοῦ πονηροῦ	και μη εισενεγκης ημας εις πειρασμον	και μη εισενεγκης ημας εις πειρασμον αλλα ρυσαι ημας απο του πονηρου
Doxology			ὅτι σοῦ ἐστιν ἡ δύναμις καὶ ἡ δόξα εις τους αιωνας

NOTE: In the versions of Luke and the Didache, the accents are supplied only where the words differ from the version of Matthew, omitted where they agree with Matthew.

However, we now recognize that the case of the PN was probably not a simple question of literary editing. We are dealing with a prayer that was recited frequently by the early Christians[7] and thus became a part of the Christian liturgy. Therefore, what Mt may well be giving us in Greek is the form of the PN recited in the churches of Syria (it is with this area that the first Gospel is usually associated). Here the Aramaic tongue of Jesus was the spoken language, and it is of importance that Mt's PN can be rendered back into good Aramaic poetry.[8] Thus the addition of other petitions of Jesus to an originally shorter PN may have been the work of the liturgy.

On the other hand, while Lk's tradition preserves the shorter and more original outline,[9] the Gentile churches whose tradition Lk represents have also had their influence. The wording of the Lucan petitions has been adapted to their use, understanding, and outlook, and consequently is further away from the original Aramaic words of Jesus than is Mt's wording. Therefore, while modern scholarship favors the Lucan number of petitions as more original, it generally favors the Matthean wording of the petitions. The theory of liturgical influence would also explain the addition of the doxology in the *Didache*. No one doubts that this work contains liturgical instructions and descriptions; and if Audet is correct in locating its origins at Antioch,[10] it is another example of the Syrian liturgy,

---

[7] *Did*, 8, 3 instructs the Christians to say the PN three times a day.

[8] As given in Lohmeyer, *op. cit.*, 15, and Jeremias, *art. cit.*, 143. For Lohmeyer, there are a title and five two-line units in the Aramaic.

[9] Lk's form can also be rendered in Aramaic (if we make allowance for Lk's Grecisms), but with a different poetic pattern consisting of a title and seven one-line units; cf. Lohmeyer, *op. cit.*, 16.

[10] *Op. cit.*, 208–209. The introduction to the PN in *Did*, 8, 2 tells the Christians to pray as the Lord has asked "in His Gos-

whence its closeness to Mt. Jewish prayer formulae generally end in a doxology, and this Jewish usage would have had its influence on the large number of Jewish Christians in the Syrian churches. Consequently, the PN of the *Didache* may represent a liturgical adaptation to a familiar prayer pattern.

The liturgical use of the PN has, in fact, colored its whole history.[11] It is found in that part of the *Didache* directed to those who are already church members, coming after the baptismal ceremony of chap. 7 and before the Eucharistic ceremony of chap. 9. In Africa it was taught to baptismal candidates eight days after the Creed; and Tertullian, who gives us our earliest commentary on the PN,[12] may in part be giving us a baptismal explanation. Cyril of Jerusalem[13] approached the prayer as part of a commentary on the Eucharistic liturgy for those who had been baptized. This liturgical usage is important, not only in explaining the evolution of different ancient forms of the prayer, but also in understanding forms in use today. As we discuss the petitions, we shall see that the standard English form of the PN scarcely renders justice to the Greek of Mt. These observations may tend to produce in the reader the type of reaction so common in regard to the modern advances in Scripture studies: "Don't tell us they want to change the Our Father now!" But the

---

pel"; thus the *Didache* may represent the same general church as Mt's Gospel.

[11] We draw heavily here on T. W. Manson, "The Lord's Prayer," *Bulletin of the John Rylands Library,* 38 (1956), 99–113, 436–448, who gives a history of the liturgical usage of the PN. He suggests that the rarity of references to it in the early writers may be explained by the feeling that it was a Christian prayer not to be shared indiscriminately. In the Mass we still approach it warily: "Taught by our Saviour's command and formed by the word of God, we *dare* to say."

[12] *De oratione* (*PL* 1, 1149 ff.).

[13] *Catechesis* 23 (=*Mystagogica* 5), "De sacra liturgia et communione" (*PG* 23, 1117 ff.).

reader should remember that not one of the traditional versions of the PN in English,[14] French,[15] German,[16] or for that matter in Latin,[17] is a real translation from a critical Greek text. These versions are liturgically hallowed prayer forms, and the liturgies have exercised a certain freedom in relation to the Gospel text.[18] In suggesting a more accurate translation of the Greek text, then, we have no intention of suggesting a change in the prayer formula.

In regard to the freedom exercised in treating the PN, we might now turn to the context of the prayer in Lk and Mt, for this context bears on the question of prayer formula. Lk (11:2–4) situates the PN in the journey to Jerusalem,[19] shortly after the Mary-Martha story. Jesus told Martha, "One thing is needful." Perhaps in the Lucan schema the PN is to be the example of the "one thing," namely, prayer. The disciples ask Jesus: "Lord, teach us to pray, as John taught his disciples." Jesus says, "When you pray, say . . ." Is He giving them a fixed prayer formula such as the Jews had?[20] The very fact that there

[14] The standard English form employs the concluding doxology; cf. n. 135 below.

[15] Cf. n. 121 below.

[16] Cf. n. 56 below.

[17] Our Latin formula does not entirely agree with the Vulgate of Mt, for we use *quotidianum* instead of the Vulgate *supersubstantialem;* cf. the discussion of *epiousios* under Petition 4.

[18] For other examples see nn. 65 and 71 below.

[19] This Perean section of Lk is a collection of miscellaneous material; and Lk 11:1–13 gathers together several separate sayings pertaining to prayer and petition. There is a ninth-century tradition that identifies the site where the PN was said with the Garden of Olives. For the probable reason see Petition 3.

[20] In treating the PN we shall have occasion to refer to these Jewish prayers. Hamman, *op. cit.*, 98–99, has a convenient table of them, and our citations may be found there unless otherwise indicated. Two of these prayers deserve special mention: (1) The *Qaddish;* Jewish tradition connects this doxology with Johanan ben Zakkai and Aqiba; this would mean that its primitive form was in use in first-century Judaism. (2)

appear two variant forms of the PN in the Gospels sug
gests that He was not. All that Jesus may have intended
was that the PN, with its brevity and complete dependence
on God, serve as a model for the spirit of Christian
prayer. Of course, the Christian liturgies soon turned i
into a formula.

Mt (6:9–13) places the PN in that great collection o
material which constitutes the Sermon on the Mount. The
original outline of the section can be traced through the
sayings on alms, on prayer, and on fasting in 6:2, 5, 16
all three attacking hypocrisy. The saying on prayer (6:
5–6) served as a magnet to attract other sayings on prayer
including the criticism of Gentile prayer (6:7–8) and
the PN, thus giving us a small collection of Jesus' thoughts
on prayer. The immediate introduction to the PN is "Pray
then like this . . ." which again is not to be interpreted
as referring to a fixed formula.

What is interesting is the fact that the disciples felt the
need of asking Jesus how to pray, or that Jesus gave them
a model of prayer.[21] This indicates a realization that the
traditional Jewish prayer formulae were no longer ade
quate for the followers of Jesus. From the time of His
introduction by John the Baptist, Jesus had stood for a
certain newness in religion. When His observances were
compared to those of the Pharisees, He had said that one
should not put new wine into old wineskins (Mk 2:22)
In the very Sermon on the Mount which frames the PN
He had shown His freedom with regard to the Torah by
repeating over and over, "You have heard it said, bu
I say . . ." Now, if Jesus presented Himself as the repre

The *Shemoneh 'Esreh* or eighteen benedictions; this obtained
its final form after the destruction of the Temple in A.D. 70
but had its origins earlier.

[21] In both Mt and Lk the PN is directed, not to the crowd
but to the intimate followers of Christ, a group that the Mat
thean setting characterizes as the salt of the earth and the
light of the world (5:13–14), a group separated from the scribe
and Pharisees (5:20) and from the Gentiles (5:47).

sentative (and, indeed, the incarnation) of a new way of approaching God, it was only logical that He would have a new way to pray to God. Thus, while many of the phrases of the PN may be found in contemporary Jewish prayers,[22] there is a new spirit that invests the "Lord's Prayer." The Jewish prayer formulae, depending heavily on the Old Testament, were for the community of Israel, which regarded God's manifestation of Himself to their fathers as the definitive way of approaching God. The PN is a prayer for the Christian community,[23] for those who believe that Jesus is the way to God and that the new and final dispensation has come.

This concept of the PN as a prayer of the Christian community is essential to our interpretation. Even after Jesus left His followers and returned to His Father, His image remained, not only as a model, but as the object of all hope. He had spoken frequently of His return and of its suddenness, and that return occupied the imagination of the Christian communities, as 1 and 2 Th and 1 Pt attest. On their lips, we believe, the prayer given them by Jesus was an expression of their yearning for His return and for the ultimate fulfillment of the things He had promised.[24]

[22] In general, however, the petitions of the PN are shorter than those of the more wordy Jewish prayers, and its title is simpler ("Father").

[23] That it is a community prayer is obvious from the first person plural which appears throughout. When an individual prays it, he prays it in the name of the community. And it is a Christian prayer; for, despite the vague modern use of "the fatherhood of God," it is the New Testament outlook that only those have God as a Father who recognize Jesus as His Son. Therefore, the PN must be interpreted more through parallel ideas found in the Gospels than through the Old Testament or through Jewish writings. Tertullian is right when he calls it "a brief form of the whole gospel."

[24] As Lohmeyer (*op. cit.,* 11) phrases it, the PN serves as "the basic prayer for the eschatological community of disciples, not a prayer . . . for the necessities of everyday life, but for the needs of a disciple's life in the eschatological period." And,

Let us now turn to this prayer as it was repeated in the early Christian community whose traditions find their voice in Mt. For our study we shall divide the PN into a title and six petitions (two sets of three each).[25]

TITLE

Mt: *Our Father who are in heaven* (pl.)
Lk: *Father*
Did: *Our Father who are in heaven* (sing.)

Jesus' uses of *abba* (the Aramaic word for "father"[26]), without modifier, in addressing God is distinctive.[27] It was so distinctive that it was remembered in the early Church, so that Paul could write to the Galatians and to the Romans and cite the Aramaic term to these Greek speaking communities.[28] The use of "Father" for God was, of course, known both to pagan ("Father Zeus") and Jew. However, the contemporary Jewish prayers tended

---

as he adds, the present period when the community of disciples is hidden and inconspicuous will soon pass and the eschatological light of the last times will dawn. In Mt's setting of the PN we hear (6:6) that we should pray in secret, and then will come the Father's reward. The PN is the prayer for that reward.

[25] The traditional (e.g., Luther) division into seven petitions is not satisfactory, for the two parts of 6 belong together. For the reconstructed divisions of the original Aramaic, see nn. 8 and 9 above.

[26] Jeremias, *art. cit.*, 144, claims a diminutive and caritative force for *abba*, almost equivalent to "daddy." Nevertheless, *abba* is the normal word for "father," and the philological efforts to explain it as a diminutive are not convincing.

[27] E.g., Mk 14:36: "*Abba*, Father, all things are possible for you" (the parallel in Mt 26:39 reads "My Father"); Mt 11:25-26 (=Lk 10:21): "I thank you, Father, Lord of heaven and earth." Also, "Father" is found in Lk 23:34 and 46, and *passim* in Jn.

[28] Gal 4:6: "God has sent the Spirit of his Son into our hearts crying, '*Abba! Father!*'" Also, Rom 8:15.

to use the Hebrew term *ab* and to accompany it by a possessive such as "our"—thus, "Our Father," *abînû*.[29] They did not use the Aramaic *abba* without qualification.

From this we may suspect that in "Our Father"[30] Mt is giving us an adaptation of the more original Lucan "Father" to the standard Jewish prayer formula.[31] Besides the employment of the Aramaic term, there was something distinctive about the very connotation of Jesus' use of "Father." In the Old Testament, God was thought of as the Father of the people Israel, and Israel (as long as it remained faithful) as God's child.[32] In the New Testament,

[29] *Shemoneh 'Esreh* 6: "Forgive us, our Father, for we have sinned." *Seder Elij*, 7 (33): "Our Father, who is in heaven." When the Aramaic is used, it is also in the form "Our Father," *abûnan*.

[30] The term *"our* Father" is not too frequent in the rest of the New Testament, except for the opening addresses of the Pauline Epistles, e.g., 1 Cor 1:3.

[31] This is not certain, however, for there are several other factors to be considered: (1) While Mk does not record the PN, Mk 11:25 is reminiscent of it: "And whenever you stand praying, forgive . . . so that *your* Father *who is in heaven* may also forgive you your trespasses." This verse in Mk is closer to Mt's form of the PN than to Lk's. (2) The Lucan form of the title, besides having no "our," has no "who are in heaven." Yet a few verses later, Lk 11:13 seems to recall the latter phrase: ". . . how much more will the *heavenly* Father give the Holy Spirit to those who ask him." By a type of inclusion, this verse might be considered an indication that the word "heavenly" was originally in the title of the PN. (3) In Jewish Aramaic *abba* means both "father" and "my father." Lohmeyer, *op. cit.*, 20, cites a place where it seems to stand for "our father." Thus, a case might be made for the idea that Lk and Mt are giving us variant translations of the same Aramaic substratum; however, this is quite unlikely, and Lohmeyer himself rejects the suggestion.

[32] Nm 11:12; Dt 32:6; Is 63:16. At times this sonship is especially centered on the king, but as the representative of the people (Ps 2:7). Ps 89:26 promises an intensification of this Davidic sonship in the final days of Israel's history. In the last

God's Fatherhood is not put on the basis of a national covenant, but on the basis of union with Jesus, who is God's Son in a special way.[33] He alone can call God "my Father" in the proper sense; those who unite themselves to Him share His power to do so through God's gift.

This New Testament concept of God's Fatherhood and Christian sonship gives an eschatological tone to the title of the PN;[34] for if we examine the Synoptic Gospels carefully, we find that becoming sons of God is something that happens in the last days and in the heavenly kingdom.[35] Lk 20:36 says that there will be no marriage in

---

books of the Bible and in the intertestamental literature, the concept of divine sonship becomes more eschatological and is on the verge of breaking its national barriers: e.g., Wis 5:5; Ps Sol 17:30; Jub 1:23–25.

[33] This is implicit in the whole New Testament view of the redemption. Explicitly, we may quote 1 Jn 5:1: "Everyone who believes that Jesus is the Christ is a child of God"; and Gal 3:26: "For in Christ Jesus you are all sons of God through faith."

[34] It has been objected that the title "our Father" should not be considered reciprocal, and that, therefore, in studying it we should not consider texts dealing with divine sonship, but only those dealing with God's Fatherhood. Such a division, however, is foreign to New Testament mentality; e.g., Rom 8:14–15 clearly connects sonship and Fatherhood.

[35] Here there is a certain divergence in New Testament thought; for, on the other hand, Paul and John treat sonship as a gift already conferred (in Paul's thought, by adoption [Gal 4:5]; in John's thought, by divine begetting [Jn 1:12–13; 3:5; 1 Jn 3:9; also 1 Pt 1:23]). This is an aspect of "realized eschatology." We believe that both views of divine sonship stem from the mind of Christ. The Synoptic view (which dominates our interpretation of the PN, since that prayer is found in the Synoptic Gospels) would represent an emphasis more popular when the hope of the Second Coming was more vivid and imminent; the other view is more sophisticated and would be better appreciated when the concept of the Second Coming began to play a less dominating role. Both views are true: we are God's sons now through sanctifying grace; but this sonship

the next age because those who are worthy to attain that age "cannot die any more, since they are equal to angels and are *sons of God*." Again, Lk 6:35 promises a heavenly reward to those who love their enemies: "Your reward will be great, and you will be *sons of the Most High*." The beatitudes promise heavenly rewards[36] to various groups among the followers of Jesus; the peacemakers are blessed, "for they shall be called sons of God" (Mt 5:9). In the explanation of the parable of the weeds in the field (Mt 13:37–43), we find that at the close of the age, when the angels are sent forth, there is a separation between the sons who enter the kingdom of their Father (vv. 38, 43) and the sons of the Evil One.

Hence, if in the PN the Christians can address God as "Father," it is because they are anticipating their state of perfection, which will come at the close of this age. They are anticipating the coming of God's eschatological kingdom, which is already incipient in the preaching of Jesus.[37]

---

will be perfected in ultimate union with God. And both Paul and John recognized this: cf. Rom 8:23: "We ourselves who have the first fruits of the Spirit groan inwardly as we wait for adoption as sons, the redemption of our bodies"; 1 Jn 3:2: "We are God's children now; it does not yet appear what we shall be; but we know that when he appears, we shall be like him."

[36] It may be objected that these rewards belong to the after-life, but not to the end of the world. However, it should be remembered that in Jesus' preaching there is virtually no emphasis on the next life as distinct from the final coming of God's kingdom; He constantly pictures judgment, not in terms of a particular judgment, but in terms of a general judgment. That an equation between heavenly reward and the Second Coming persisted in the early Church is seen in 1 Thes 4:13, where the Thessalonians are troubled because Christians are dying and yet Christ has not come back—what happens to them? The notion of a particular judgment and heavenly reward immediately after death is a solution to this problem.

[37] Johannine realized eschatology carries the relation between Jesus' ministry and the coming of the kingdom almost to the

It is no accident that in the beatitudes mentioned above,
the parallel to the promise that the peacemakers shall be
called the sons of God is the promise that the poor in spirit
shall inherit the kingdom of God. And so, the community
that says the Our Father is not the Jewish nation but the
poor, the sick, and the needy who accept Jesus' preaching
of the kingdom, a kingdom prepared by the Father through
Jesus (Lk 22:29–30).

In Mt's title there is a second qualification of "Father,"
i.e., "who are in heaven."[38] Here again Mt is close to Jewish prayer formulae which use "heavenly"[39] as an honor-
ific qualitative to give God His proper place and to distinguish Him from "our father Abraham." Lohmeyer,[40]
however, suggests that in Mt this is no mere formalism, but
rather a sign of the eschatological times when God's
presence is no longer localized in a place like Sinai, Zion,
or Gerizim. As Jesus said to the Samaritan woman (Jn
4:21), "The hour is coming when you will worship the
Father neither on this mountain [Gerizim] nor in Jerusalem."

Having now seen that the title of the PN already places
us in the anticipation of the last days, let us turn to the
first group of three petitions.

---

point of identity. Jn has no parables of the kingdom, only
parables of Jesus (the living bread, the vine, the shepherd, the
seed in the ground). In a way, for Jn, Jesus represents the kingdom or dominion of God; and so reaction to Jesus constitutes
judgment (Jn 3:19–21; 5:24), just as, for the Synoptic Gospels,
judgment is connected with the ultimate coming of God's kingdom.

[38] Mt uses the plural *ouranois,* which is closer to Semitic
usage, for in Hebrew the word for "heaven" is plural. *Didache's
ouranō* is less original.

[39] This adjective and the phrase "in heaven" are simply
variant translations. Semitic is deficient in adjectives, and there
is no Aramaic adjective for "heavenly"; a phrase must be employed.

[40] Cf. *op. cit.,* 39–40. We are somewhat doubtful whether
this should be pressed.

FIRST PETITION

Mt, Lk, *Did: May your name be sanctified.*

As a preface, we should notice that grammar itself unites these three petitions. The verb that stands at the head of each is in the third person aorist imperative (passive in 1 and 3). The interpretation of this Greek form involves two important notes. First, the aorist in Greek is not normally used for a continuing process (e.g., a day-by-day sanctification). It has a once-and-for-all aspect, an *Einmaligkeit*, as the Germans call it. Second, this peculiar passive form in New Testament Greek does not necessarily convey a passive meaning, for it is frequently used as a surrogate for the divine name.[41] We remember that out of a sense of reverence the Jews avoided the divine name, so that in the New Testament, instead of "May God do something to somebody," we often find "May something be done to somebody." This seems to be especially common in sayings dealing with divine eschatological activity.[42]

Coming now to the first petition, we find that it is not a new concept; for the *Qaddish* resembles it very closely: "May His great name be magnified [and sanctified] in the world." But when we try to uncover the exact meaning of this petition of the PN, we are faced with a problem: Is

[41] A more frequent surrogate in Aramaic is to use the third person plural for the divine name, but there are few examples of this in the New Testament. Lk 6:38 has an example of both surrogates: "Give, and it will be given [*passive*] to you; they will put [*third pl.*] into your lap a good measure." Another example of the third plural may be Lk 16:9.

[42] Schürmann, *op. cit.*, 118, n. 92, points this out, but without examples. We find this usage in the parables in the general statements on divine rewards and punishments (at judgment), e.g., Mt 25:29 (=Lk 19:26): "To everyone who has, more will *be given* . . . from him who has not, even what he has will *be taken* away." (Also, Lk 10:20; 12:48b; 18:14b; Mt 22:14.)

the primary agent in the sanctification man or God? Many writers, including St. Augustine and Luther, have understood it as a prayer that men would come to bless God's name.[43] Yet the fact that this petition is a prayer addressed to God suggests that it concerns divine action, a request for God to make manifest the sanctity of His own name. A study of the Old Testament background and the New Testament parallels makes the latter interpretation, we believe, virtually certain.[44]

As is well known, the name in Hebrew thought is virtually equivalent to the thing itself. The divine name, then, reflects what God is (with the special aspect of intelligibility to man).[45] When we turn to sanctity, the other term in our petition, we find that only God is holy in Himself. For the Hebrew mind, all other things are holy only because they have been set aside for worshiping God (e.g., the cultic holiness of the Temple) or because they are connected to God's holiness in a special way. Thus Israel is holy because God has chosen Israel as His people; or, as Lv 11:45 puts it, "You are holy because I am holy." God has engaged His sanctity in the protection of Israel and is thus the Holy One of Israel (Ps 89:18 and Is *passim*). By manifesting His power through action in Israel's history,[46] God may be said to sanctify His name or vindicate His

---

[43] There is backing for this notion in the Bible, of course. The second commandment concerns keeping holy God's name. Also, Is 29:23; Mt 23:39.

[44] It is held by Lohmeyer, Van den Bussche, Schürmann, Hamman, Jeremias, etc.

[45] If we interpret the basic divine name "Yahweh" as "He who causes to be," this name is related to the creation of the universe and man.

[46] The initial sanctification of the divine name is in creation; providence, especially in sacred history, is its continuation; and the end of the world will be its culmination. All of these have as a counterpart that acknowledgment of sanctity which is God's glory. As Lohmeyer, *op. cit.,* 48, phrases it, God's glory is His revealed holiness; His holiness is His hidden glory.

holiness.[47] Now at times Israel proved itself unworthy and profaned God's name. In face of this, God promised through the prophets that He would renew Israel, giving it a new spirit, and would thus "vindicate the holiness of his great name" (Ez 36:22–27). Thus there is good background in the Old Testament for seeing the sanctifying of God's name as a divine action.

In the New Testament, God manifests His holiness and sanctifies His name in Jesus, who is the Holy One of God (Mk 1:24; Jn 6:69)[48] who comes in the name of the Lord (Mk 11:9). He was sanctified and sent into the world (Jn 10:36), and He makes God's name known (Jn 17:26).[49] The most revealing text in this regard is found at the end of Jesus' public ministry (Jn 12:28). Feeling that His hour is at hand—the culminating hour of return to the Father in passion, death, resurrection, and ascension —Jesus cries out, "Father, glorify your name." (This verse is the closest parallel in the Gospels to our petition,[50] and we see that it concerns God's glorifying His own name.) The answer comes back from the Father: "I have glorified it and will glorify it again." We should notice the past and future tenses. The past (aorist) tense seems to cover the glorification of the divine name through Jesus' earthly work; the future seems to cover the glorification that will be effected in Jesus' return to the Father and the sending

[47] Ex 33:19; Ez 20:41; 39:27.

[48] Also, Acts 3:14; Ap 3:7; and perhaps 1 Jn 2:20.

[49] *Did*, 10, 2: "We give you thanks, O holy Father, for your holy name which you have made dwell in our hearts, and for the knowledge . . . which you have revealed to us through Jesus."

[50] "Sanctify" (*hagiazein*) and "glorify" (*doxazein*) are synonyms. Cf. Lv 10:3: "I will show myself holy [*eqqādēsh-hagiasthēsomai*] among those near me; and before all people will I be glorified [*ekkābēd-doxasthēsomai*]." Also, Is 6:3: "Holy, holy, holy [*hagios*], Lord of Hosts; the earth is full of your glory [*doxa*]".

of the Spirit (see Jn 16:14).[51] Thus the ultimate sanctifi
cation of the divine name is still to come: the glorification
accomplished by the Spirit will include the guidance of th
Church toward the last times and the final struggle with
Satan (as the whole of 1 Jn makes clear, especially chap
5).

With this background we can now understand the peti
tion "May your name be sanctified." The passive is a sur
rogate for the divine name, and the *Einmaligkeit* of the
aorist is to be given its full force.[52] It is a prayer that
God accomplish the ultimate sanctification of His name
the complete manifestation of His holiness, the last of His
salvific acts. As we shall see in Petitions 2 and 3, this
sanctification consists in the final coming of God's king
dom and the perfection of the plan that God has willed
Only the last days will see that vindication of the holines
of God's name promised by Ezekiel to the new Israel.[53]

By way of addenda, we might mention that it has been
suggested that there is an immediate connection between
the title "Father" and this first petition, and that the par
ticular aspect of the divine name involved here is that of
Father.[54] In other words, the Christians are praying that

[51] See Wilhelm Thüsing, *Die Erhöhung und Verherrlichung
Jesu im Johannesevangelium* (Münster, 1960), 193–198.

[52] Cf. Hamman, *op. cit.*, 107: this is the one historic act that
affects all history.

[53] In holding that this petition refers primarily to God's work
not man's we do not wish to exclude human cooperation. God
manifestation of the sanctity of His name and man's recognition
of this sanctity are two sides of the coin. This Christian com
munity that prays for God to sanctify His name consists of
the elect who have been called through Jesus Christ "from
ignorance to the full knowledge of the glory of His [God's
name" (i *Clem. ad Cor.*, 59, 2). They are exhorted "to be
obedient to His most holy and glorious name" (*ibid.*, 58, 1
Yet it should not be forgotten that the *metanoia* which pro
duces such obedience is the work of God as well as of man.

[54] Cf. Lohmeyer, *op. cit.*, 55; Manson, *art. cit.*, 437–438. But
Schürmann, *op. cit.*, 23, denies it on the grounds that *abba*

God will manifest His holiness as Father and hasten the perfection of their sonship which is to come in His kingdom. This suggestion is very hard to prove, but it would have some interesting corollaries. First, it would explain why the petition concerning the divine name is the first petition, coming right after the title.[55] Normally, we would have expected the petition on the coming of the kingdom (Petition 2) to have had priority, for the notion of the kingdom is of far greater importance in the Synoptic tradition than is that of the divine name. Second, this suggestion would cement the first and second petitions even closer together. We have mentioned, in treating the term "Father," that the Fatherhood of God is closely connected to the coming of God's eschatological kingdom. If, then "Father" and all its implications constitute the divine name to be sanctified in the first petition, we have a very close parallel to the second petition, which concerns the coming of the kingdom. This parallelism is already foreshadowed in Zech 14:9:

And the Lord will become *King* over all the earth;
on that day, Yahweh will be one, and His *name* will be one.

SECOND PETITION

Mt, Lk, *Did: May your kingdom come*[56]

This petition, too, has its echo in the *Qaddish* (following the petition on the divine name cited above): "May He

---

not really a divine name. There is, however, a close association of *abba* and "name" in "Father, glorify your name" (Jn 12:28).

[55] Schürmann, *op. cit.*, 28, explains the sequence between Petitions 1 and 2 thus: the first is wider than the second and should logically come first.

[56] The only valid variant is that the *Didache* and some manuscripts read *elthetō* in place of *elthatō*, thus correcting the Koine form with its second aorist base and first aorist ending; there is

establish His kingdom in your days." There is little doubt
here that God is the primary agent in causing the kingdom
to come. The real problem is whether this petition of the
PN deals primarily with a question of everyday growth
of the kingdom[57] or with the definitive reign of God at the
end of the world.[58] On a purely grammatical basis, the
aorist is more favorable to the latter.[59]

The Old Testament does not precisely speak of the coming of God's kingdom, but it does promise a universal
kingship of God (Jer 10:7, 10; Mal 1:14). Is 24:23 connects the signs of the last times, like the darkening of the
sun and moon, with the reign of the Lord of Hosts on Mt
Zion and the manifesting of His glory. Dn 7:18 has the
saints of the Most High receiving the kingdom after all the
earthly kingdoms have passed away. Thus, already in the
Old Testament, divine kingship has eschatological overtones.

In the New Testament, the establishment of God's kingdom[60] is to a certain extent identical with Jesus' coming

---

no difference in meaning. Codex Bezae of Lk (followed by German church use) reads: "May your kingdom come *upon us.*"
This is probably dictated by a feeling that *elthatō* is too abrupt
without a complement. The same difficulty is witnessed in the
Latin, where some of the Old Latin manuscripts read *venia*
and the Vulgate reads *adveniat.*

[57] Either in terms of increased numbers through missionary
efforts or in terms of individual growth in grace.

[58] Tertullian chose this eschatological view, as did many
Latin Fathers under the influence of the translation *adveniat.*
Chrysostom and some later interpreters, like Luther and Calvin
applied the petition to a twofold coming, in time and in eternity. Lohmeyer, *op. cit.,* 69–70, gives a good refutation of this
view.

[59] The *Didache* (10, 5) gives the eschatological aspect when
it asks that the Church be gathered from the four corners into
the kingdom, "for yours is the power and the glory." The last
clause shows a connection of this verse with the PN.

[60] It is well known that the Gospel notion of "kingdom" has
different aspects. Frequently the word means "dominion, sov-

for His ministry opens with the announcement that the kingdom of God is at hand.[61] Yet, if Jesus through His word and work established God's dominion on this earth, the fullness of that kingdom cannot come until Jesus returns again to destroy the prince of this world.[62] As long as Satan has power in this world, God's dominion is not perfected (Lk 4:6; 1 Jn 5:19).

We believe that the petition "May your kingdom come" concerns this final coming of God's kingdom. Actually, the expression "kingdom come" does not occur frequently in the Gospels; but when it does, it refers primarily to the eschatological coming.[63] We have "coming" and "kingdom" joined in Mk 9:1: "There are some standing here who will not die before they see the kingdom of God come with power" (the parallel in Mt 16:28 interprets this eschatologically: ". . . before they see the Son of Man coming in His kingdom"). At the Last Supper (Lk 22:18) Jesus says: "I shall not drink of the fruit of the vine until the kingdom of God comes."[64] While not using *erchesthai*,

---

ereignty, rule," something more dynamic than static. Yet at other times it refers to a place or state which one can enter into (Mt 5:20), which can be shut (Mt 23:14), of which one can have the keys (Mt 16:19).

[61] Mk 1:15; Mt 4:17; 10:7; 12:28.

[62] There is a continuity between the two stages of the kingdom. As Hamman, *op. cit.*, 111, remarks, "Christian eschatology does not come after Christ's coming, but begins with it." Also, see Van den Bussche, *op. cit.*, 65–66.

[63] The same verb "to come," *erchesthai*, is part of such eschatological time indications as "The days are coming" (Amos 4:2; Lk 17:22; 21:6; 23:29) and "The hour is coming" (Jn 4:21, 23; 5:25; 16:25). Lohmeyer, *op. cit.*, 62–64, has an excellent treatment of the Hebrew concept of "coming." It is not simply a question of coming about, but implies the divine action of bringing about, of realizing something in the realm of time.

[64] Other examples of "kingdom" and "coming" are Mk 11:10 and Lk 17:20. The prayer of the bandit crucified with

Lk 21:31 is interesting; in speaking of the signs of the last days, it says: "When you see these things take place, you know that the kingdom of God is near."

When the Christian community utters the second petition of the PN, it is identifying itself with the divine plan. The Christians are not primarily asking that God's dominion come into their own hearts (as the variant in footnote 54 suggests), but that God's universal reign be established—that destiny toward which the whole of time is directed.

Again by way of addenda, we might mention a Lucan variant of this petition. In place of "May your kingdom come," some manuscripts[65] read "May your [Holy] Spirit come upon us and purify us." This equivalence between the Spirit and the kingdom is not un-Lucan. In Acts 1:6–8, when the disciples ask about the coming of the kingdom, Jesus answers them in terms of the coming of the Holy Spirit.[66] Yet this Eastern variant reading in the PN is almost certainly a development from the use of the PN at baptism, the sacrament of the giving of the Spirit and of purifying. It is a good example of the freedom felt in the liturgical employment of the prayer, and of the gradual loss of eschatological import.

Jesus (Lk 23:42) should probably be read: "Jesus, remember me when you come in your kingdom."

[65] 162, 700, Gregory of Nyssa, Maximus the Confessor, Marcion. In a famous controversy Harnack supported this reading, while von Soden rejected it. More recently, R. Leaney, "The Lucan Text of the Lord's Prayer," *Novum Testamentum* 1 (1956) 103–111, defended the reading again.

[66] Also, compare Mt 7:11, "How much more will your Father who is in heaven give good things to those who ask him," with Lk 11:13, "How much more will the heavenly Father give the *Holy Spirit* to those who ask him."

THIRD PETITION

Mt, *Did: May your will come about on earth as in heaven*

The verb is *genēthētō*, an aorist passive. The English translation "be done" is too restrictive, for again the passive can be a surrogate for the divine subject. The Latin *fiat* is much more satisfactory. And again the *Einmaligkeit* of the aorist favors one supreme moment rather than a gradual process.

The petition is not found in Lk; indeed, the vocabulary is distinctively Matthean.[67] The same petition appears again in Mt's version of the Agony in the Garden[68] and forms Christ's prayer when He withdraws from the sleepy disciples a second time (Mt 26:42). Since in the Marcan parallel to this verse (Mk 14:39) we have only the general statement, "He prayed saying the same words," we may suspect that Mt is using the petition to fill in the actual words of the prayer.[69] Thus the stray logion "May your will come about" is employed twice in Mt to fill out sequences.

The problem in interpreting this petition concerns its subject. Is this a request that men will come to obey, i.e.,

[67] The aorist passive of *ginesthai* is not found in Jn, and only once in Mk and Lk (and there it is a quotation from the LXX shared by Mt). Mt has seven other occurrences.

[68] The closest parallel to the Synoptic agony scene in Jn is 12:23, 27–30, and it is curious that it is there we have the Johannine parallel to the first petition of the PN ("Father, glorify your name"). Cf. above, chap. XI, division I.

[69] As Schürmann, *op. cit.*, 123, n. 192, points out, the theory that the author has borrowed the logion from the Gethsemane scene and introduced it into the PN is to be rejected; there is as much evidence for its being secondary in the one place as in the other.

to do, God's will?[70] Tertullian thought so, as did many of
the Latin Fathers. And it may be pointed out logically that,
if the second petition concerns the establishment of God's
kingdom, this petition concerns the preparation of man's
heart for that kingdom.[71] On the other hand, we may ask
if in this petition, as in the previous petitions, it is not
primarily a question of God's action, of God bringing about
His own will on earth and in heaven.

In deciding the question, we must recognize that God's
"will" has several meanings.[72] We usually think of it in
terms of commandments to be obeyed, but it also covers
God's plan for the universe.[73] New Testament writers use
the term God's "will" for God's design of salvation effected
through Jesus and extended to men through the Apostles.
Eph 1:5–12 lays this plan out before our eyes and speaks
of it as the choice (*eudokia*) of the divine will (v. 5),
the mystery of the divine will[74] (v. 9), the plan (*boulē*)
of the divine will (v. 11).

[70] As Lohmeyer, *op. cit.,* 79, points out, if we are going to
speak in biblical terms, we should speak of doing God's will
rather than of conforming our wills to God's. That men must do
God's will is found all throughout the Bible, e.g., 2 Mc 1:3;
Jn 9:31; Mt 7:21; Heb 13:21; and in the rabbinic writings,
e.g., R. Eliezer (*ca.* A.D. 90) prayed to God: "Do your will in
heaven on high, and give a patient disposition to those on earth
who fear you."

[71] Tertullian is even more logical in inverting the order of
the petitions to have the will done on earth before the kingdom
comes.

[72] The Greek *thelēma,* being a substantive in *–ma,* tends toward a passive meaning, i.e., "what is wished, the object of the
will." Aramaic *re'ûtâ* and Hebrew *rāsôn* are more active, including the notion of desire, good pleasure, that is found in
the Greek *eudokia.*

[73] This includes both creation (Ap 4:11) and providence
(Mt 10:29).

[74] This is an echo of Jesus' own words in Mt 11:25–26:
"You have hidden these things from the wise and the clever,
and revealed them to infants; yes, Father, for this was your
will (*eudokia*)."

In this plan Jesus is the primary instrument of God's will. "I have come down from heaven, not to do my own will, but the will of him who sent me" (Jn 6:38; also, Heb 10:7–10). The Agony in the Garden represents a great crisis in the implementation of the divine will. The words we hear there cannot be interpreted simply in terms of the obedience of the human will of Christ to the divine will. "Abba, Father, . . . not what I will, but what you will" (Mk 14:36) concerns the salvific plan of God. It was necessary that Jesus should suffer and enter into His glory (Lk 24:26–27).

God's will also concerned the selection of men to spread the effects of Jesus' salvific death and resurrection to all men. If Jn 6:38 says that Jesus has come to do God's will, the next verse explains this will: it is that Jesus should not lose those whom the Father has entrusted to Him.[75] Thus, later on, the choice of men like Paul is part of the divine will: "Paul, called by the will of God to be an apostle of Jesus Christ."[76] The Apostles know God's salvific will (Acts 22:14) and have the duty of putting it into effect.

The ultimate goal of this plan is the redemption of the universe, the subjecting of all things to the Father's will in the Person of Jesus Christ (Eph 1:20–22), for it is to Jesus that all power in heaven and on earth has been given (Mt 28:18). We may now see the full impact of the third petition of the PN: "May your will come about *on earth as in heaven*." If God created heaven and earth ac-

---

[75] Besides phrasing the mission of Jesus in terms of doing God's will, Jn also reports it in terms of manifesting God's name (17:6) and of establishing the kingdom (18:37)—thus the terms of the first three petitions of the PN. And just as the preservation of the disciples is connected to doing God's will in 6:38–39, so it is connected to manifesting His name in 17:6.

[76] 1 Cor 1:1 and the opening of many of the Epistles. From this we may suspect that many of Paul's statements about doing God's will do not refer simply to obedience but to furthering God's salvific plan, e.g., Acts 21:14, where he says "The will of the Lord be done" in reference to his trip to Jerusalem.

cording to His will (Gn 1:1; Ap 4:11), that will concerns the ultimate perfection of heaven and earth.[77] As Col 1:20 phrases it, it is God's pleasure to reconcile to Himself all things whether on earth or in heaven, through Jesus Christ. God's will shall have come about when there is a new heaven and a new earth, when the heavenly city comes down and weds itself to the people of God (Ap 21:1–3).[78]

And so, in uttering this petition of the PN, the Christian community is praying that God will bring about the eschatological completion of His salvific plan.[79] The coming about of God's will is basically the same as the establishment of His kingdom, and, indeed, as the sanctification of

[77] "Heaven and earth" is a Hebrew expression for "world" or "universe" (there was no single Hebrew noun for world until a relatively late period). The suggestion that this petition of the PN means that men are to obey God's will as the fixed planets of heaven is to be rejected. We might note that in Petition 3 "heaven" is the singular and not in the plural as in the title. The singular is a Septuagint usage, not a Hebrew one; but it may have been preferred here as a better combination with the singular "earth," to give the impression of parts of a whole.

[78] We have been avoiding a difficulty in the last clause of the petition. In place of "on earth *as* in heaven," some manuscripts omit the "as" and read "in heaven *and* on earth" (Bezae, Old Latin, and Old Syriac; Tert.). There is a difference of meaning. In the former, heaven seems to be held up as a model for earth, i.e., God's will is already done in heaven, and may it now come about on earth in similar manner; so Schürmann, *op. cit.*, 124, n. 194. (See Ap 12:7–12, where Satan has been thrown out of heaven, and now only his power on earth remains.) In the latter, and in some interpretations of the former, God's will is to come to completion both in heaven and on earth. The context is really insufficient for a decision, but the totality idea does seem to dominate the New Testament eschatological expectation.

[79] Again, while putting the primary emphasis in the petition on God's action, we do not mean to exclude man's cooperation with God's plan. The one implies the other to a certain extent.

His name.[80] The first three petitions are really expressing only different aspects of the same basic thought, namely, the eschatological glory of God. Petition 1 on the name emphasizes more the internal aspect of this glory; Petition 2 on the kingdom emphasizes more its external aspect; and Petition 3 on the coming about of God's will on earth as in heaven emphasizes the universality of the divine glory.[81]

FOURTH PETITION

Mt, *Did: Give us today our future* [?] *bread*
Lk: *Keep on giving us daily our future* [?] *bread*

With the fourth petition we begin the second half of the PN. The predominant verbal person in the last three petitions in Mt shifts to the second person of the aorist imperative active; and whereas "your" dominated the first three petitions, the last three are dominated by "our" and "us." The last three petitions are longer than the first three.

Up to this point there has been reasonable agreement among recent Catholic writers on the eschatological interpretation of the PN. Here, however, most[82] change over to interpreting the PN in terms of daily needs, pointing out that the end of the third petition has brought us down to

[80] A close study of Phil 2:9–10, Mk 3:35, Mt 21:31 and 18:14 will show how the ideas we encountered in the PN (Fatherhood, sonship, name, kingdom, will) are closely intertwined in New Testament thought.

[81] Schürmann, *op. cit.*, 124, n. 194, is probably correct in rejecting the suggestion that the phrase "on earth as in heaven" modifies all three petitions, in idea if not grammatically.

[82] Van den Bussche, Schürmann, Hamman, Schmid (*Das Evangelium nach Matthäus*, 4 ed. [Regensburg, 1959]). They point out, however, that the daily needs are eschatological in the broad sense we mentioned at the beginning of this paper. Lohmeyer really blends both interpretations. Jeremias is the closest to our view, but without our Eucharistic emphasis.

earth. This would have a logically compelling force if all of the last three petitions dealt with the daily situation rather than with the eschatological. However, as we shall see, the sixth and final petition is certainly eschatological (as most of these same writers admit), and the fifth is very likely eschatological. A noneschatological interpretation would leave the fourth isolated among all the other petitions.[83] But, in our opinion, a good case can be made for interpreting this petition eschatologically.

When we speak henceforth of the fourth petition, we are confining ourselves to the Matthean wording. Lk's present imperative is definitely continuative and noneschatological. Mt's aorist imperative receives its justification from its parallelism with the aorist imperatives of Petitions 5 and 6.[84] In like manner, Lk's "daily" (*to kath' hēmeran*) is distributive and noneschatological.[85] The best interpretation of the Lucan rendering is that, with the passing of the tension about the Second Coming (or in communities where such tension was not overly prominent), the eschatological interpretation of the PN yielded to the more pressing daily outlook. The Lucan emphasis on the poor of this world as the recipients of the Gospel message is well known (see chap. XIV, below); and among such, the eschatological aspect of the prayer for bread could soon lose its primacy.

The real key to the meaning of this petition lies in the

---

[83] The fact that the fifth and sixth petitions are connected to one another and to the fourth by "and" is a sign that they have common interests.

[84] The difference of meaning exists in the Greek; the presumed Aramaic original (*hab*) would have no such definite time implications.

[85] It is a Lucan expression, found in Lk 19:47 and Acts 17:11, but not in Mt, Mk, or Jn. A good example of Lk's preference for "daily" is found in the logion on taking up the cross (Mt 16:24; Mk 8:34; Lk 9:23); only Lk has the expression "to take up the cross daily (*kath' hēmeran*)."

adjective that modifies "bread,"[86] the word *epiousios*. In the third century the word puzzled Origen (*De oratione* 27, 7), who could find no example of it in other Greek writers. Seventeen centuries later we are not much better off.[87] Our only real help is etymology, and even here we are faced with two basic possibilities:

1. To derive the word from *epi* plus *einai* (the verb "to be").[88] (*a*) This could mean bread for the existing day, therefore "daily," as in the phrase *epi tēn ousan* (*hēmeran*). The *quotidianus* of the Old Latin (Itala) represents this.[89] (*b*) Or it could give the meaning of bread for being, for existence (*epi ousia*), i.e., the bread needed to live. The Peshitta translates it "for our need." And St. Jerome's *supersubstantialis* in Mt (he gave *quotidianus* in Lk) may have this derivation as a basis—*epi = super; ousia = substantia*.

2. To derive the word from *epi* plus *ienai* (the verb "to go, come"). This would mean the bread for the coming day, for the future. The phrase *hē epiousa* (*hēmera*) means "the morrow." St. Jerome (*In Matth*. 6, 11) says that in the Gospel of the Hebrews (an apocryphal Semitic gospel)

---

[86] The importance of "bread" in this petition is highlighted by the fact that it comes first in the sentence; in all the other petitions the verb comes first.

[87] The appearance of *epiousios* in the Lindos inscription (A.D. 22) from Rhodes has now been disproved; cf. B. Metzger, in *Expository Times*, 69 (1957), 52–54. The only other serious contender is the Hawara papyrus (fifth century A.D.), where in a list of distributions *epious . . .* appears. The broken word *might* be the equivalent of *diaria* in Latin lists, and refer to the day's provisions. However, the papyrus is very late; and the reading cannot be checked, for the papyrus is now missing. Its editor, Sayce, was not a particularly meticulous workman.

[88] As Hensler, *op. cit.*, 11, points out, however, this combination should not result in the hiatus we find in *epiousios*.

[89] Matthew Black, *An Aramaic Approach to the Gospel and Acts*, 2 ed. (Oxford, 1954), 153, maintains that the Aramaic original read "Give us our bread day by day."

he read *"Māḥār, quod dicitur crastinum, id est futurum."*[90]
The Bohairic and Sahidic and Marcion seem to agree with
this derivation.[91]

Now those who interpret the petition noneschatologically
follow the former derivation. They make this a prayer of
daily need on the part of the Christian community. Christ
had instructed His followers not to worry about the morrow (Mt 6:34) but to throw themselves on divine providence. His closest followers had been told to travel without provisions (Mk 6:8). He had thus created a community
of poor who depended on God for their needs. In this
petition they turn to their Father for their bread, the basic
necessities of life.[92] Schürmann[93] thinks of this petition
especially on the lips of those whose preaching of the
kingdom allowed them no time to earn even the basic necessities. One Old Testament passage always cited in favor
of the noneschatological interpretation is Prv 30:8, which

90 The value of the Gospel of the Hebrews in this connection
is disputed. In general, it was probably a retroversion of Greek
into Semitic, and therefore worth no more than the original
author's guess on the meaning of the Greek. But Jeremias, *art.
cit.,* 145, claims that in the case of a prayer like this the author
may not have translated, but simply have given the Aramaic
form used in the liturgy of his church. This would give *māḥār*
independent value.

91 The Curetonian Syriac may have worked from this derivation too, but in a different sense: it reads "continual," which
might stem from a derivation of "always coming." Lohmeyer,
op. cit., 99, suggests another derivation which would connect
it with "daily." D. Y. Hadidan, in *New Testament Studies,* 5
(1958), 75–81, shows that there is Armenian support for this
Old Syriac reading.

92 Hebrew *leḥem* can mean "bread" or can refer to food in
general. The Greek *artos* is not really so general. Where *leḥem*
means "food" rather than just "bread," the LXX frequently
translates it, not by *artos,* but by *trophē,* e.g., Ps 136:25. Therefore we should be cautious in generalizing the meaning of
"bread" in the PN.

93 *Op. cit.,* 59.

in Hebrew reads: "Feed me with the bread which is need-ful for me (*leḥem ḥuqqî*)." But it should be noted that in the LXX this verse offers no parallel to the PN at all: "Prescribe for me what is necessary and what is sufficient"; it does not even mention bread.

Those who favor the eschatological interpretation of this petition prefer the second derivation of *epiousios,* which makes the petition a request for the bread of tomorrow, the bread of the future. We may agree that the Christian community was marked with poverty; but we believe that in this need the Christians yearned, not for the bread of this world, but for God's final intervention and for that bread which would be given at the heavenly table. In the Gospels, God's supplying men with food is frequently in terms of an eschatological banquet:

Lk 14:15: "Blessed is he who shall eat bread in the kingdom of God."

Lk 6:21: "Blessed are you that hunger now, for you shall be satisfied"; as mentioned, the rewards of the beatitudes are heavenly ones.

Mt 8:11: "Many shall come from East and West and sit at table with Abraham, Isaac, and Jacob in the kingdom of heaven."

Lk 22:29–30: "As my Father appointed a kingdom for me, so I appoint for you to eat and drink at my table in the kingdom."

Ap 7:16: a picture of heaven in which the saints hunger no more.

We notice that the bread of the kingdom is promised to the Christians; therefore they could petition for it as *"our bread."* The request for it "today" expresses the urgency of the eschatological yearning of the persecuted and im-poverished Christians.[94] And their prayer is phrased in

[94] As Lohmeyer, *op. cit.,* 105, puts it, in the light of God's eternity "today" is the short period of time before man's es-chatological future.

terms of the *Einmaligkeit* of the aorist: Give us this once
and final time.

The Old Testament background for this interpretation
is interesting. The real parallel for "Give us today our
bread for tomorrow" is the description of the manna in
Ex 16:4: "I will rain *bread* from heaven for you . . . a
day's portion every day," and in Ps 78:24: "And he *gave*
them the *bread* of heaven." Remember that Moses told
the people that the manna would come on the *morrow:*
"At twilight you shall eat flesh, and in the morning you
shall be filled with bread; then you shall know that I am
the Lord your God." That the manna was heavenly bread,
the bread of angels, would make it a good figure of the
bread of the heavenly future for which the Christians
yearned.

And Jesus Himself made this connection. When the Jews
asked Him for a miraculous earthly bread for which they
would not have to work, Jesus answered them by citing
the manna text of Ps 78: "It was not Moses who gave
the bread from heaven; my *Father gives* you the *bread*
from heaven" (Jn 6:32). This is very close to the fourth
petition, which asks the Father to give us bread.[95] And
we see clearly that Jesus is speaking of no material bread,
for He Himself is the bread: "I am the bread of life; he
who comes to me shall not hunger" (Jn 6:35). As the
discourse that follows shows, He is the bread in a twofold
sense:[96] as the incarnate teaching (Word) of the Father[97]
and as the Eucharist. In the latter sense, as the Eucharistic
bread from heaven, He promises that whoever eats of
His flesh will be raised up on *the last day* (6:54; Vulgate,

[95] There is another echo of the PN in this section of Jn;
see the discussion of 6:38 in relation to Petition 3.

[96] See the discussion in our pamphlet commentary on Jn,
No. 13 in the *New Testament Reading Guide* (Collegeville,
Minn., 1960), 40–42. Also see chap. V, above.

[97] Notice that Is 55:10 already connects the descent of God's
word with the giving of bread.

55). Thus Jn joins with Paul (1 Cor 11:26) in seeing the Eucharistic bread as an eschatological pledge.

There is good reason, then, for connecting the Old Testament manna and the New Testament Eucharistic bread with the petition of the PN. Just as the Jews of the Old Testament received in the desert bread from heaven every day, so the Christians in the brief "today" which separates them from eternity are given by their Father a bread from heaven which is pledge of their future bread in the kingdom. To confirm this connection between our petition and the Eucharist, we might remember that the expression "to give bread (*arton didonai*)" is a rare one in the Gospels.[98] It occurs in the Bread of Life discourse in Jn, as just mentioned, and in two other important places: the multiplication of the loaves and the Last Supper. At the Last Supper, Mk 14:22 reports, "Taking *bread,* he blessed and broke and *gave* it to them." The multiplication scene in Mk 6:41 (8:6) has virtually the same words, probably by way of pointing out the multiplication as Eucharistic anticipation (Jn 6 makes this explicit).[99] Thus, in asking the Father "Give us our bread," the community was employing words directly connected with the Eucharist. And so our Roman Liturgy may not be too far from the original sense of the petition in having the PN introduce the Communion of the Mass.

In our interpretation of this fourth petition, therefore, it is just as eschatological as the first three. Only, where the first three petitions dealt with God's role in the last times, this petition deals with our role. This change of emphasis carries into the fifth petition; and while the fourth deals

[98] Lohmeyer, *op. cit.,* 93–94, gives a history of the phrase. In the early historical books of the Old Testament it is used secularly; but in the prophetic and wisdom books it takes on a religious sense: God giving bread to men (Ps 146:7) and men giving it to their fellowmen by divine command (Prv 22:9).

[99] The expression occurs again in the postresurrectional meal of Jn 21:13; in the Lucan postresurrectional meal (24:30) we have *epididonai* with *arton.*

with the positive aspect of our role (participation in the heavenly banquet), the fifth treats the negative aspect (pardon before God's judgment).

FIFTH PETITION

Mt: *And forgive us our debts as we have forgiven our debtors*
Did: *And forgive us our debt as we forgive our debtors*
Lk: *And forgive us our sins, for, indeed, we ourselves forgive our every debtor*

An introductory "and" assures the connection with the fourth petition. In all three forms the petition begins with the aorist, which again, if we wish to be consistent, bears the note of *Einmaligkeit*, "Forgive us this once." And Mt continues in the aorist, "as we have forgiven." We translate in the past, but it is not the tense that we mean to emphasize,[100] only the singleness of the action. It covers the summation of a lifetime, treated as one action before God's judgment seat. Both Lk and the *Didache* use a present tense.[101] This is probably the same tendency away from eschatology which we encountered in the Lucan version of the fourth petition. (Below we shall see a further reason for their present tense.)

The Matthean use of "debts"[102] has a Semitic flavor;

---

[100] Jeremias, *art. cit.*, 146, suggests a present tense which renders the aorist equally well: "as we herewith forgive our debtors."

[101] The *aphiomen* (a present form as if from an –ō verb) of Lk appears in certain manuscripts of Mt: Bezae, Wash., Korideth; the more classical present of the *Didache*, *aphiemen*, appears in the Koine manuscripts of Mt. The Sahidic, Bohairic, Vulgate (*dimittimus*), and Curetonian Syriac have a present tense for Mt. The reading in L is *aphiōmen*, which seems to be a futuristic use of the subjunctive (and seems to have support in the Syriac of Aphraates): "as we will forgive."

[102] Mt has the plural of *opheilēma*; the *Didache* uses the singular of *opheilē*. The words have the same meaning; both

for, while in secular Greek "debt" has no religious coloring, in Aramaic *ḥôbâ* is a financial and commercial term that has been caught up into the religious vocabulary. Perhaps it served to point up the personal nature of the offense involved in sin, as compared with the impersonal notion of trespass or transgression against divine law. Lk's "sins" might be an adaptation to a Gentile audience.[103] The idea of remitting (*aphienai*)[104] debts which appears in our petition is also more Semitic than Greek, for "remission" has a religious sense only in the Greek of the LXX, which is under Hebrew influence.

The prayer to God for forgiveness is in itself, of course, nothing new. The author of Ps 25:18 cries out: "Forgive all my sins." Sir 28:2 instructs: "Forgive your neighbor's injustice; then when you pray, your own sins will be forgiven." The sixth blessing of the *Shemoneh 'Esreh* reads: "Forgive us, our Father, for we have sinned."[105] However, as we shall see, this petition does take on a certain newness in the light of Christianity.

The urgency that we encountered in the fourth petition ("today") is transmitted to the aorists of the fifth petition, for the Christians lived in expectancy of imminent divine judgment. The return of Christ to make reckoning had been

---

are found in Koine Greek; the latter especially in the papyri and ostraca; the former also in Hellenistic literature (so Lohmeyer, *op. cit.*, 111). *Opheilē* appears in the parable of the king forgiving his servants. Mt 18:23–35.

103 Yet Lk uses the word "debtor" in the second clause of the petition (thus favoring the originality of "debts" in the first clause) and also in 7:41.

104 The whole religious background of the petition points to a real forgiveness, a real remission, of debts, and not a simple overlooking of them; for what the petitioner asks is a restitution of the original state of God's favor. The Latin *dimitte* is not too precise a translation.

105 Also, the rabbinic sources quote Gamaliel II (*ca.* A.D. 90) to the effect that God is merciful to men when men are merciful to others (Strack-Billerbeck 1, 425).

pictured to them as something sudden.[106] In this anticipation of judgment, they utter a petition for a complete forgiveness of sin. And it is interesting to see how often in the Gospels forgiveness of debts or sins is connected with the judgment. In the Sermon on the Mount, which is also Mt's setting for the PN, we hear (5:23–25) that the Christian should be reconciled to his brother who has something against him, ". . . lest your accuser hand you over to the judge, and the judge to the guard, and you be put in prison. Truly, I say to you, you will never get out till you have paid the last cent." Again, Lk 6:37 has a parallelism between judgment and forgiveness: "Judge not and you will not be judged . . . forgive, and you will be forgiven." The best illustration of our petition is the parable of the Unforgiving Servant (Mt 18:23–35). The king who wishes to settle debts with his servants is obviously God, and the atmosphere is that of judgment. The parable points out that God's forgiveness of the servant has a connection to that servant's forgiveness of his fellow servant. When this brotherly forgiveness fails, he is given to the torturers until he pays his debt.[107]

This leads us to the second clause of our petition: "as we have forgiven our debtors" (or "as we now forgive our debtors"—one action).[108] Once more, the Gospel background of fraternal obligations favors an eschatological interpretation, for the failure to deal properly with one's

[106] The master returns suddenly to his servants (Lk 12:37, 46); the Lord requires the rich barn builder to hand over his soul "this very night" (Lk 12:20).

[107] Perhaps we could cite here the parable of the Talents; for, while the servants are not judged on failure to pay debts, they are judged on obligations in the broad sense. Mt 25:30 points to an interpretation of the judgment as spiritual. We remind the reader of what was said in n. 36 about particular judgment.

[108] This is the only instance in the whole PN of action on the Christian's part; its anomalous nature must mean that it is really integral to the petition.

brother is frequently spoken of in terms of judgment. The description par excellence of the Last Judgment is Mt 25: 31–46, which describes the sentence being passed before the throne of the Son of Man. The criterion of judgment is precisely our dealings with one another. In the same mood, Mt 5:21–22 lists faults against one's brother which make one liable to judgment and hellfire. In the Lazarus story (Lk 16:19–31), the eternal judgment against the rich man is based on his enjoyment of wealth, instead of employing it in what Lucan theology emphasizes is the only proper way: giving it to the poor.

For a deeper appreciation of the eschatological nature of the fifth petition, however, we must investigate further the whole concept of forgiveness. The reason that the Christian can even pose this petition is his consciousness of the Fatherhood of God. Even in the Old Testament the picture of a forgiving and merciful God is that of a Father (Ps 103:13). But this is brought to the fore in the New Testament, as we see in the Lucan parable of the Prodigal Son (Lk 15:11–32). The son has sinned and is not worthy to be called a son; but the father forgives him and rejoices that his son, who was dead, is alive again. In the Matthean parable of the Unforgiving Servant, already cited, we should notice the moral at the end: "So also my heavenly *Father* will do to everyone of you, if you do not forgive your *brother* from your heart" (18:35). Here the Fatherhood of God is invoked against the lack of forgiveness.

It is, then, to the Father, addressed at the beginning of the PN, that the Christian directs his call for forgiveness. But, as we have pointed out, in the Synoptic view the fullness of God's Fatherhood and the status of sonship is not realized until the kingdom has come. And so it is by anticipation of his eschatological state that the Christian can confidently beseech God for the final pardon of debts.[109] Indeed, it is only at the judgment that all his debts will be

---

[109] The same Father who will give bread to His children in the heavenly banquet will forgive them.

apparent. He will sin many times a day until the moment of his death; and if we take "debt" in a wider sense than sin (as we probably should), his dependence on God for all that he is and has will continue to the last day. Then he will come before his Father like the servant of Mt 18:24–25, without the means to pay.[110]

And the clause on forgiving one's own debtors also gains meaning in the light of the Fatherhood of God. Any man can speak of "sins" or "offenses" against his fellowman but how can he call these "debts"? As Lohmeyer[111] has so ably pointed out, it is really only in a society of brothers, where there is a right to brotherly love, that offenses are properly debts. And this is especially true in the Christian society, where brotherly love is the charter commandment which distinguishes it from other groups, and marks its affiliation to its Founder (Jn 13:35). No wonder that Mt 18:15 discusses a Christian's sin in these terms: "If your *brother* sins against you . . ." In the second half of our petition, then, the forgiveness of our "debtors" refers to the forgiveness of those bound to us as brothers under the Fatherhood of God; and it too anticipates the eschatological state of divine sonship.

This understanding obviates a famous difficulty. The Matthean version, "Forgive us our debts as we have forgiven our debtors," sounds like a *do ut des* clause, a type of bargain with God (especially if we put too much emphasis on the time value of the second clause). The Lucan form of the petition may be an attempt both at better Greek and at avoiding this difficulty: "Forgive us our sins, for,

---

[110] Naturally, we do not exclude divine forgiveness in this life; but to communities expecting an imminent return of the Son of Man, forgiveness at that moment would be the vital issue. Even in our less eschatologically minded theology, we recognize that ultimate pardon is not given in this life, but when the soul comes before God's judgment seat. There are punishments due to sin that are left when the sin is forgiven here below.

[111] *Op. cit.,* 128 ff.

indeed, we ourselves forgive our every debtor."[112] Perhaps,
too, the variant forms mentioned in n. 101 above are
prompted by this difficulty. But when the petition is properly understood, there is no *quid pro quo*, nor is there a
question of the priority of human forgiveness.[113] The Matthean "as" simply means that the human forgiveness is the
counterpart of the divine.[114] In the last days the followers
of Christ will receive the fullness of divine sonship. Their
forgiveness of one another as brothers and their forgiveness by their Father are both parts of this great gift.[115] In
the fifth petition of the PN they stand by anticipation before
the throne of God;[116] and they request the supreme and
final act of fatherly forgiveness, even as they extend the
complete and final act of brotherly forgiveness. This forgiveness in both directions removes all obstacles to the perfect community of the heavenly banquet table for which
they have asked in Petition 4. The fifth petition is the acting
out of the Last Judgment as described in Mt 25:34: "Come,

---

112 Actually the *hōs* of Mt and the *kai gar* of Lk may be
variant translations of Aramaic *kedî*, which is vague. Lk's
"every" is an example of the Lucan tendency toward totality
found elsewhere; e.g., Mt 5:42 has: "Give to him who begs
from you," while Lk 6:30 has: "Give to *everyone* who begs
from you."

113 Mt 5:23 insists that we are to be reconciled with our
brother *before* making our offering to God. But in Mt 18:29
the test of forgiving a fellow servant is put on the servant who
has been *already* forgiven by his master.

114 1 Jn 4:20 catches this nuance: "He who does not love
his brother, whom he has seen, cannot love God, whom he has
not seen."

115 The correlativity of the two actions is nicely expressed
by Mt's aorist tense in both clauses. In part, the correlativity is
based on the fact that a sin against the brother is a sin against
the Father.

116 It must be remembered that in the first three petitions
the Christians have asked for the last days (which include the
divine judgment); they are now prayerfully dealing with the
consequences of their own request.

O blessed of my *Father,* and inherit the *kingdom* prepared
for you from the foundation of the world, for I was hungry
and you gave me food."[117]

SIXTH PETITION

> Mt, Lk, *Did: And do not lead us into trial*
> Mt, *Did:*   *but free us from the Evil One*

Thus far in the PN, the Christians have urgently peti-
tioned God's triumph and have dealt with their own role
in that triumph, both positive and negative. Now the only
remaining object of eschatological prayer is the terrible
obstacle that separates the Christian from that triumph,
namely, the titanic struggle between God and Satan which
must introduce the last days.

Once again, the aorist tenses[118] do not favor the interpretation of this petition in terms of daily deliverance from
temptation. And, indeed, such an interpretation has produced a theological difficulty, for the prayer would then
seem to imply that it is God who is responsible for temptation. It is true that the Old Testament speaks of God
tempting people, but normally in the sense of testing.[119] In
a late book like Sir (15:12) there is a reaction against
the inference that God is responsible for human failing. In
the New Testament, Jas 1:13 is lucid: "Let no one say

[117] Notice all the connections to the PN in this verse: the
title (Father); Petition 2 (the kingdom); Petition 3 (the divine
will: prepared from the foundation of the world); and the present petition (a favorable judgment based on dealings with our
brothers).

[118] The verb "lead" is aorist subjunctive; in Koine the pro-
hibitive subjunctive is frequently used for the negative imperative, and consequently this verb is the equivalent of the aorist
imperatives which surround it.

[119] Cf. Gn 22:1; Ex 15:25; 2 Chr 32:31. Hebrew *nissâ* has
a connotation of "test"; Greek *peirazein* can also have this
connotation.

when he is tempted, 'I am tempted by God.' . . . He himself tempts no one." Why, then, do we have the Christians asking their Father not to lead them into temptation? We see in the patristic phrasing of this petition attempts to avoid the difficulty. Tertullian says it means: Do not allow us to be led into temptation by him who tempts.[120] He thus makes Satan the tempter, not God. Other Fathers add an explanatory clause based on 1 Cor 10:13: Do not lead us into temptation which we cannot overcome.[121]

We can avoid these desperate explanations,[122] however, if we realize that we are not dealing with a question of daily temptation (which, after all, is the lot of the Christian and must be endured: Jas 1:2, 12) but with the final battle between God and Satan.[123] The word for "trial, temptation" here is *peirasmos*. While this word can refer to ordinary temptation,[124] it also has a specialized reference

[120] Codex Bobbiensis and the Itala show this influence: "ne passus fueris induci nos in temptationem." Also, Marcion and Dionysius of Alex. (cf. Lohmeyer, *op. cit.,* 135).

[121] Cf. Chromatius of Aquila (*PL* 20, 362); Jerome (*PL* 25, 485); Augustine (*PL* 34, 1284); and various Eastern liturgies. The French version of the PN shows these tendencies: "ne nous laissez pas succomber à la tentation."

[122] No real justification can be found for them. Some would justify the translation "allow us to be led" on the grounds that the original was an Aramaic aphel (= Hebrew hiphil) of *'ālâ,* and that the aphel, while normally causative ("cause to go"), can be permissive (very rarely). This is desperate; and, in any case, the Greek shows that the Evangelists did not understand the Aramaic in a permissive sense. See Lohmeyer, *op. cit.,* 137.

[123] So Lohmeyer, Van den Bussche, Schürmann, Hamman, Jeremias. Some stress the special peril of apostasy in this final trial.

[124] E.g., Lk 8:13 as a parallel to Mk 4:17; also, Gal 6:1. Of course, the everyday *peirasmos* is already a part of the struggle which will climax in the final *peirasmos,* just as Christ met the *peirasmos* by Satan after forty days in the desert as the first step in the struggle which was to lead to Gethsemane.

to the final onslaught of Satan.[125] Ap 3:10 contains a promise of Christ: "Because you have kept my command and stood fast, I will keep you from the hour of trial (*peirasmos*) which is coming on the whole world, to try those who dwell on earth." We see another instance of this in the Gethsemane scene (where we have already found parallels to the PN). Christ has accepted the chalice of suffering; the face-to-face battle between Him and Satan has begun. In the person of Judas,[126] Satan is entering the garden; and it is the hour of the power of darkness (Lk 22:53; Jn 14:30). At this moment Jesus tells His disciples: "Pray that you may not enter into trial [*peirasmos*]" (Mk 14:38; par.). He would spare them this great crisis in the struggle with Satan (Jn 18:8). It was only natural that the Christian community should take this instruction to pray and apply it to the final trial.

Are we, then, to think that the Christian community, which suffered so much for Christ, was not willing to face the final battle with Satan? Reflection shows us that there is no question of timidity here, but real insight into the nature of this terrible struggle to come. Paul warned the Ephesians (6:12–13) that they were not fighting against flesh and blood, but against a whole array of superhuman powers, and that it would take the whole armor of God to withstand them. True, Christ defeated Satan in principle on the cross; but before Satan would release his hold on this earth, there would come such tribulation as has not been seen since the world's creation. As Christ Himself admitted, if the Lord had not shortened the days of this tribulation, no human being would be saved.[127] But He

---

[125] Satan is the "tempter" in the New Testament: Mt 4:3; Lk 22:31; 1 Cor 7:5. The emergence of the devil in the later period of Old Testament theology solved the problem of who did the tempting.

[126] Lk 22:3; Jn 13:2, 27.

[127] Is this the fear of Lk 18:8: "When the Son of Man comes, will he find faith on earth?"

added by way of encouragement that the days have been shortened for the sake of the elect (Mk 13:19–20). And the text of Ap 3:10, cited above, shows Christ promising to keep His faithful Christians from the trial. Therefore, asking for preservation from the final diabolic onslaught is simply following Christ's directions.

The eschatological interpretation of our petition becomes all the more likely now that the Qumran literature has thrown some light on the theological views of the Jewish world in which Jesus lived.[128] We find the Essene community living in fearful anticipation of the attack of the forces of Satan. Sons of light themselves, and under the aegis of the spirit of truth, they have already drawn up their battle plans for meeting the sons of darkness under Belial, the spirit of perversion. This angel of darkness is already trying to lead them astray by persecution and affliction (1QS 3:22–25), but God is on their side. He has set a time limit to Satan's activities in the world (1QS 4:16–19). When it is up, the battle will be engaged, and Belial's authority will be destroyed (1QS 4:20). The Christian community had an eschatological outlook not too far from that of the Essenes.

The second part of the sixth petition (in Mt and the *Didache*) offers a perfect parallel to our interpretation of the first part. The reader is familiar with the translation "Deliver us from *evil*." The Greek *apo tou ponērou*, however, while it could mean "from evil," could also mean "from the Evil One." In general, the Western Fathers support the former translation,[129] and the Greek Fathers, along with Tertullian, support the latter.

In New Testament usage, when *ponēros* means "evil" in

[128] See Karl G. Kuhn, "New Light on Temptation, Sin and Flesh in the New Testament," in *The Scrolls and the New Testament*, ed. K. Stendahl (New York, 1957), 94–113.

[129] This is under the influence of the very ambiguous Latin translation "a malo," which suffers from Latin's lack of an article.

the abstract, the word "all" usually appears before it.[130] On the other hand, *ho poneros* is definitely a title for Satan.[131] In the parable of the Sower and the Seed, Mt 13:19 speaks of "the Evil One" who comes and snatches the seed from man's heart. And in Mt 13:38 the weeds of the Darnel parable are "the sons of the Evil One, and the enemy who sowed them is the devil." 1 Jn 5:18 assures us that the Evil One does not touch him who is born of God. In reference to the Parousia, 2 Thes 3:3 says: "The Lord is faithful: He will strengthen you and guard you from the Evil One." This is like Jesus' prayer to His Father in Jn 17:15: "I ask that you keep them from the Evil One."[132]

One of the main reasons for translating *poneros* as "evil" in the abstract has been its parallelism with *peirasmos*, thought to mean "temptation." Yet, once we realize that *peirasmos* means the final trial brought on by Satan's attack, a personal interpretation of *poneros* is most fitting. The introductory "but" suggests that this last clause is

---

[130] E.g., Mt 5:11: ". . . when men utter all kinds of evil [*pan poneron*] against you." Also 1 Thes 5:22; 2 Tm 4:18; *Did*, 10, 5. In other cases the context clearly implies the abstract, e.g., Acts 28:21 and Rom 12:9.

[131] This concept of Satan is the product of a dualistic tendency. The term is not used in the Old Testament, but we come close to it in the dualistic Qumran world, where Satan is the spirit of deceit and wickedness. The title "Evil One" for Satan is the counterpart of Mt 19:17, where we hear of God as the "one alone who is good."

[132] The Greek is *terein ek tou ponerou*. The expression *terein ek* is found in only one other place in the New Testament, namely, Ap 3:10, the very passage we have been quoting in relation to *peirasmos:* "I will keep you from the hour of trial." Thus we have two Johannine clauses which form a nearly perfect parallel to the two clauses of our petition. Other passages that might be quoted for *poneros* as "Evil One" are Mt 5:37, 39 (see Lohmeyer, *op. cit.*, 151); 1 Jn 2:13–14; 3:12; Eph 6:16. While one or the other of our examples might be challenged (since in some of them it is not impossible that *poneros* is abstract), their overall effect is conclusive.

climactic: if the Satanic trial is mentioned in the first clause, the prince of darkness makes his entrance in the second clause. Also, the verb *ruesthai* (once more in the aorist), in the sense of "tear free from," fits well with a personal interpretation.[133] The whole world is in the power of Satan (1 Jn 5:19); but the Christian has the promise that through God's begetting he will be protected from the Evil One (5:18), and this is what prompts him to utter the petition of the PN. Faced with the awesome power of the strong one, the Christian begs for the help of a stronger (Mt 12:28-29). He has asked for the coming of his Father's kingdom, but he knows that in that decisive moment the sons of the Evil One will be drawn up against the sons of the kingdom (Mt 13:38). And so he begs his Father, not only to spare him the trial of that terrible struggle, but also to wrench him free from the power of Satan.[134]

As we come to the end of our interpretation of the PN,[135] we can see how coherently the eschatological viewpoint binds together the petitions into one picture. The Christian community of the first century, anxiously expecting the Second Coming, prays that God will completely glorify His name by establishing His kingdom, which represents the fulfillment of the plan He has willed for both earth and heaven. For its portion in this consummation of time, the community asks a place at the heavenly banquet table to break bread with Christ, and a forgiveness of its

[133] It implies a certain motion of deliverance and is a good contrast for the "lead us into" of the first clause.

[134] Paul sees this already partially realized (Col 1:13): "He has delivered us from the dominion of darkness and transferred us to the kingdom of his beloved Son."

[135] We do not intend to treat the doxology found in the *Didache:*"For yours is the power and glory forever." With the addition of "kingdom," this doxology is found in certain manuscripts and versions of Mt (Wash., Korideth, Ferrar group, Koine, Curetonian Syriac, Peshitta, Sahidic—there are slight variations). This early liturgical addition, patterned on the Jewish doxologies, has 1 Chr 29:11, 30 as one of its sources.

sins. A titanic struggle with Satan stands between the community and the realization of its prayer, and from this it asks to be delivered.

Already in the Lucan form of the PN, as we have said, the intensity of eschatological aspiration has begun to yield to the hard facts of daily Christian living. It is a sign of the genius of this prayer, taught by the divine Master, that it could serve to express such different aspirations. Nevertheless, as we say the prayer nineteen centuries later, now completely enmeshed in the temporal aspect of the Christian life, it would, perhaps, profit us to revive in part some of its original eschatological yearning. Even if we choose to relegate the last things to a minor tract in theology, the return of Christ comes persistently closer each day. The PN, said as a fervent *maranatha*, would not be an inappropriate welcome.

XIII

Parable and Allegory Reconsidered

The study of the parables of Jesus has been one of the most active branches of Gospel exegesis in the twentieth century. A distinctive characteristic of this modern parable exegesis has been its rejection of the allegorical interpretation of the parables which dominated patristic and medieval commentaries. Bernhard Weiss and Adolf Jülicher[1] set the tone in their sharp and almost absolute distinction between parable and allegory. Jülicher, in particular, drawing on the canons of Greek oratory, regarded allegory as a sophisticated literary figure which the simple preacher of Galilee could not and did not use. As a result, any allegory found in the Gospels can almost automatically be considered as a Church creation, and not the authentic words of Jesus.

While there has been some uneasiness about Jülicher's Germanic precision, his rejection of allegory has had great influence in modern works of the parables.[2]

---

[1] B. Weiss, *Das Markusevangelium und seine synoptischen Parallelen* (Berlin, 1872). A. Jülicher, *Die Gleichnisreden Jesu* (Freiburg-i.-B., 1898–1899), 2 vols.

[2] With various modifications: A. T. Cadoux, *The Parables of Jesus* (London, n.d.), c. 3. C. H. Dodd, *The Parables of the*

First, we are told that the parables have one or, at most, two points to make. The details of the parable are only part of the dramatic machinery and have no meaning in themselves; nor are the characters of a parable to be identified allegorically. Let us give some examples. Jeremias[3] maintains that in the parable of the Prodigal Son the father does not stand for God. And in the original form of the parable of the Wicked Vinedressers the servants sent to the vineyard were not the prophets, nor was Jesus the son who was killed.[4] These would be allegorical identifications and have no place in a parable.

Second, this rejection of allegory has also had its influence on Johannine studies. The Jesus of Jn does not speak in parables, but in metaphors and allegories: "I am the vine, you are the branches" (Jn 15:5); "I am the sheepgate" (Jn 10:7); "I am the good shepherd" (Jn 10:11). Once again, if we follow the principle of rejecting allegory, these figures must be evaluated as the work of the Evangelist rather than of Jesus.

Third, it is also the prejudice against allegory which is chiefly responsible for the rejection of the explanations of the parables offered in the Gospels. Three parables are accompanied by specific explanations: the Sower and the Seed (Mk 4:13–20 and parallels); the Tares or Darnel (Mt 13:36–43); the Fish Net (Mt 13:49–50). These explanations are largely allegorical for they interpret the in-

---

Kingdom (London, 1935), 11–23. B. T. D. Smith, *The Parables of the Synoptic Gospels* (Cambridge, 1937), 21–25 (his view is quite modified in theory; more radical in practice). Charles W. F. Smith, *The Jesus of the Parables* (Philadelphia, 1948), 24–27. J. Jeremias, *The Parables of Jesus,* Eng. trans. of third German ed. (London, 1954), 16–18.

[3] *Op. cit.,* 103: "Thus the father is not God, but an earthly father; yet some of the expressions used are meant to reveal that in his love he is an image of God."

[4] *Ibid.,* 56–57.

dividual details and characters of the parable. Therefore they are rejected by many scholars as commentaries of the early Church (we shall discuss their corroborating arguments below).

We suggest that this point of view badly needs a reexamination. Jülicher, despite many exaggerations, rendered exegesis a service, and we do not wish to deny it. The patristic method of treating the parables allegorically had a purpose: as long as the Scripture was the basic catechism of the Church, all theology had to be found in Scripture. If Gregory the Great wished to preach a homily on the five external senses and the two faculties of the soul, what more natural than to turn to Mt's parable of the Talents, five, two, and one? However, while recognizing that such a method of exegesis (or eisegesis) had its role in teaching the faith to many, we need not seek its return.

Nevertheless, Jülicher's total rejection of allegory is an oversimplification. Fiebig and Hermaniuk[5] have shown in detail that there is no really sharp distinction between parable and allegory in the Semitic mind. In the Old Testament, the apocrypha, and the rabbinic writings, *mashal* covers parable and allegory and a host of other literary devices (riddle, fable, proverb, etc.). Therefore, there is no reason to believe that Jesus of Nazareth in His *meshalim* ever made a distinction between parable and allegory. He was a popular teacher and would naturally favor simple stories, so we need not look for the complicated allegories that the Fathers found. But simple allegory, and metaphors already familiar to His hearers from the Old Testament—these lay within his illustrative range. In fact, turning the tables on the Jülicher school, we may well ask: Would a popular teacher be able to disassociate himself completely from familiar metaphor and speak in pure

[5] P. Fiebig, *Altjüdische Gleichnisse und die Gleichnisse Jesu* (Tübingen, 1904), and *Rabbinische Gleichnisse* (Leipzig, 1929). M. Hermaniuk, *La Parabole Évangélique* (Louvain, 1947).

parables? As Michaelis[6] has pointed out, the theoretical schema of the "pure parable" breaks down in actual gospel investigation.

This is being increasingly recognized in modern writing.[7]

First, as to the point we mentioned above, the details of a parable do have meaning. In the reviews of Jeremias' book on the parables scholars like Benoit and C. F. D. Moule[8] insist that certain of the parables cry out for an allegorical interpretation of their details. In the example of the Prodigal Son the common Jewish reference to God as Father would make an allegorical identification of the father in the parable perfectly intelligible. We may grant that, for the sake of the story, God is portrayed as an earthly father; but, as Matthew Black has insisted,[9] this is so close to allegory as to make no difference. And in the parable of the Wicked Vinedressers, *doulos* is so frequent a Greek Old Testament term for the prophet that we feel Jeremias is missing the obvious when he refuses to see the servants of the parable as representing the prophets. We admit that Mt 21:35–36 may be carrying the allegory further in having two sendings of the servants and thus, perhaps, mak-

[6] W. Michaelis, *Die Gleichnisse Jesu*, 3 ed. (Hamburg, 1956), 15: "The pure parable is not so often encountered as one might think; and this fact should be noted in considering the parables of Jesus." J. J. Vincent, "The Parables of Jesus as Self-Revelation," *Studia Evangelica* (Berlin, 1959), 82: "Some kind of allegory is scarcely avoidable in any kind of comparison."

[7] An earlier rebel against the Jülicher tradition was A. H. McNeile, *The Gospel according to St. Matthew* (London, 1915), 186. V. Taylor, *The Gospel according to St. Mark* (London, 1953), 210: "The shade of Jülicher must not affright us from admitting allegory when we see it."

[8] P. Benoit in *Revue Biblique*, lv, 1948, 594–599; Moule in *Expository Times,* lxvi, 1954–1955, 46–48.

[9] M. Black, "The Parables as Allegory," *Bulletin of the John Rylands Library*, xlii, 1959–1960, 284. Also, see Vincent, *art. cit.*, 85–88.

ing reference to the former and latter prophets. But this is merely crossing the "t"s and dotting the "i"s of what Jesus meant.

Second, the whole question of the Johannine metaphor is being reconsidered. Msgr. Cerfaux[10] has shown that the Johannine "I am" statements (the vine, the sheepgate, the good shepherd) have a basic connection to the Synoptic parabolic theme of the kingdom, for in the Jesus of Jn the kingdom is present. The very same vineyard, gate, and shepherd comparisons occur in Synoptic parables. Thus neither in content nor in pedagogic method are the Johannine metaphors unworthy of Jesus the preacher. John A. T. Robinson[11] has studied the metaphors which open chap. 10 of Jn (the "Good Shepherd" chapter) and has suggested that at their root lie parables which have every chance of being authentic.

Third, and it is here that we wish to go into detail, even the three allegorical explanations of the parables are finding their way back to critical acceptability. While it is true that only these three parables get a detailed explanation, J. A. Baird[12] has used statistical evidence to show that Jesus did explain His parables (often by brief indications). In particular, Baird insists that He explained the parables concerning the kingdom to His disciples. *A priori,* then, there is nothing suspicious about the explanation of a parable. Parables were meant to make understandable and to illustrate; but there is a very consistent emphasis in the Gospels that not all the aspects of the kingdom could be easily grasped by everyone, and so explanations had their place.

[10] "La thème littéraire parabolique dans l'Évangile de saint Jean," *Recueil Lucien Cerfaux* (Louvain, 1954), II, 17–26.

[11] "The Parable of John 10, 1–5," *Zeitschrift für neutestamentliche Wissenschaft,* xlvi, 1955, 233–240.

[12] "A Pragmatic Approach to Parable Exegesis," *Journal of Biblical Literature,* lxxvi, 1957, 201–207.

The allegorical explanation of the parable of the Tares or Darnel has been carefully reexamined by De Goedt.[13] It is true that Jeremias[14] makes the claim that on the basis of vocabulary this explanation cannot have come from Jesus, but must have come from Matthew himself. But, according to De Goedt, the vocabulary studies of Jeremias are not as convincing as might first seem: many of the standards of comparison are inadequate. The explanation in its present form may well have been rewritten by Matthew as an adaptation to the situation of the early Church, but the essence of the allegorical explanation stems from Jesus Himself. Michaelis[15] is essentially of the same view.

We would like to take up the question of the allegorical explanation of the parable of the Sower and the Seed. In many ways this is the most important Gospel explanation of a parable; in fact C. W. F. Smith suggests that it supplied the Evangelists with the idea of explaining parables.[16] Even Matthew Black,[17] who recognizes that there are allegorical details in the parable of the Sower and the Seed, seems to write off the Gospel explanation as the work of the early Church. We would join ourselves to recent writers[18] who, while recognizing that the explanation of the

[13] "L'explication de la parabole de l'ivraie," *Revue Biblique,* lxvi, 1959, 32–54.

[14] *Op. cit.,* 64–67.

[15] *Op. cit.,* 49–52.

[16] *Op. cit.,* 89; and Jeremias, *op. cit.,* 67, n. 35.

[17] *Art. cit.,* 278. In this he is not far from the approach of J. Weiss, "Die Parabelrede bei Markus," *Studien und Kritiken,* lxiv, 1891, 289–321. His father, B. Weiss, had rejected all allegory in the parable; J. Weiss maintained that there was allegory in the original parable, but not that allegory given in the Gospel explanation.

[18] See L. Cerfaux, "Fructifier en supportant (l'épreuve), à propos de Luc, viii, 15," *Revue Biblique,* lxiv, 1957, 481–491. M. Didier, "Les paraboles du semeur et de la semence qui croit

parable has been adapted to the situation of the early Church, believe that there can be found underlying the Gospel explanation an allegorical explanation by Jesus Himself.[19] Indeed, the Gospel explanation does little more than expand Jesus' explanation to meet a new situation.

There are five principal reasons for questioning the authenticity of the Gospel explanation of the parable (references, unless otherwise indicated, are to verses in Mk 4):

a) The real purpose of the parable is to underline the abundance of the harvest. The explanation concentrates on unimportant details of the story and gives no major emphasis to the harvest.

b) A large number of details in the parable receive an allegorical explanation, e.g., the seed, the soils, the birds. This seems a bit too complicated for Jesus' simple preaching.

c) There is an unevenness of style in the explanation (Loisy has remarked that no other section of the Gospel is so awkward literarily and logically). For instance, in v. 15 the word is sown among the people along the path; but in vv. 16, 18, and 20 the various groups of people are themselves sown, not the word.

d) The vocabulary of the explanation betrays the usage of the Church as seen in the Epistles.

e) The whole explanation seems to imply a situation in which there is a Christian community—an anachronism when placed in Jesus' mouth.

Let us consider these points one by one:

a) It does seem clear that the principal point of the

---

d'elle-même," *Revue Diocésaine de Namur*, xiv, 1960, 185–196. A. George, "La parabole des semailles," *Sacra Pagina* (Paris, 1959), II, 163–169.

[19] Between the parable (Mk 4:1–9) and its explanation (4:13–20) are three verses on the reason for speaking in parables. We regard these verses as composed of several *logia* of Jesus, and probably an intrusion here—cf. E. Siegman, "Teaching in Parables," *Catholic Biblical Quarterly*, xxiii, 1961, 161–181. These verses have no real bearing on the authenticity of the explanation.

parable is the abundance of the harvest, which is a symbol of the miraculous fruitfulness of the kingdom. Yet that does not mean that the details of the parable cannot have meaning. The major part of the parable itself is concerned with the fate of the seed that did not produce. Proportionately, if we place the explanation side by side with the parable, the explanation gives no more attention to the fate of the lost seed than does the parable itself, and it gives the same amount of attention to the harvest as does the parable. The objection given above, then, is really no more than an expression of an *a priori* assumption that the details of a parable are just dramatic machinery and have no meaning in themselves.[20]

b) When we analyze what details are allegorically interpreted in the Gospel explanation, we note that only the seed itself and its four fates are allegorized. There is no identification of the sower. The three percentages of the harvest (thirty, sixty, one hundred) receive no interpretation as they did in the patristic period.[21] Thus there is no real comparison between the relatively simple Gospel explanation and the more complicated allegories given by the Fathers.

c) The very unevenness of style indicates that the Evangelist was not composing the explanation with absolute freedom. If the explanation were a complete literary fiction, we would expect smoothness and uniformity. The unevenness probably results from the adaptation of an earlier explanation, the order of which the Evangelist felt a certain responsibility to preserve.

d-e) These objections form the real argument against the authenticity of the Gospel explanation of the parable, and we shall have to treat them in detail. From the outset we wish to make it clear that we believe that the explanation

---

[20] Black, *art. cit.,* 278, stresses this point.

[21] For Jerome (Migne, *PL* 26, 89) the 100 percent = chaste women; the 60 percent = widows; the 30 percent = married. For Augustine (*PL* 35, 1326), the 100 percent = martyrs; the 60 percent = widows; the 30 percent = married.

as it now appears is addressed to an organized and existing Christian community. This is the result of preaching where the message is governed by the needs of the audience—a factor which affects (albeit to a lesser degree) the whole of the Gospel message. The real question, however, is whether behind the redirected Gospel explanation as it now exists there lay an original and recognizable allegorical explanation of the parable by Jesus Himself. This question is not automatically solved by the presence of a vocabulary and a mentality proper to the early Church, for such vocabulary and mentality could have been introduced in the redirection of the original explanation. We shall proceed verse by verse (in Mk 4).

In v. 14 Mk tells us, "The sower sows the word." Lk 8:11 is more explicit in its identification: "The seed is the word of God," while Mt 13:19 simply introduces the identification in passing: "When any one hears the word of the kingdom . . . that is what was sown along the path." As the Gospel explanation now stands, "the word" here seems to refer to the Christian Gospel. Jeremias[22] assures us, "The use of ὁ λόγος absolutely is a technical term for the gospel coined and constantly used by the primitive Church." Nevertheless, could "the word" have been used at an earlier stage by Jesus Himself to refer to His preaching of the kingdom? A background for such usage would be the prophets' employment of *dabar* (*logos*) for the divine message entrusted to them. There is some evidence that Jesus may have used the term. In Mk 2:2 we hear that Jesus, in the house, spoke "the word" (*logos*) to them. Now this is editorial narrative, but it may well stem from the actual usage of Jesus (as in Lk 11:28: "Blessed rather are those who hear the word of God and keep it."). Taylor maintains that in Mk 2:2 (and in Mk 4:14) "the word" means "the Good News"; later on it came to mean the Christian message, but there is no reason to find this meaning here.[23]

[22] *Op. cit.,* 61.
[23] V. Taylor, *op. cit.,* 193.

Thus there is no great difficulty in Jesus' having used the Semitic equivalent of *logos* to refer to his preaching of the kingdom (which is what Mt has).

As for sowing the word, the idea has a parallel in Jewish literature. 4 *Ezra* 9:31 says: "For, behold, I sow my Law in you, and it shall bring forth fruit in you, and you shall be glorified in it forever." Just as Jesus' message is sowed among men, so also the Law. On the other hand in 4 *Ezra* 8:41–44 there is a parable of how the farmer sows much seed on the ground and plants many seedlings; yet not all the sown shall be saved. Here men are the seed sown by the farmer. And so 4 *Ezra* has the same variation as the Gospel explanation: in one case the message is sowed; in the other, men are sowed. That 4 *Ezra* is the source of the whole Gospel explanation is highly improbable. However, if the parable of 4 *Ezra* 8 was ancient and well known, it could have influenced the final shaping of the Gospel explanation and have been responsible for the shifting from the seed's being equivalent to the message to its being equivalent to men.[24] In any case, the metaphors involved are not strange to the Jewish mind.

In v. 15 the birds are implicitly identified with Satan (Mk), the Evil One (Mt), the devil (Lk).[25] Many find this metaphor very artificial, and Cadoux[26] points out that the fault should be attributed to the soil and not to the birds. The latter objection is not insuperable, however, since Jesus certainly regarded Satan as a contributing cause to the ruin of many. And no matter how artificial the metaphor might seem, it is a metaphor that is known in intertestamental literature. *Jubilees* 11:11 reports. "Mastema sent ravens and birds to devour the seed which was sown in the land. . . . Before they could plow in the seed, the

[24] Nevertheless, there is Old Testament background too for the picture of God's sowing men; in Jer 31:27 God sows the house of Israel with the seed of man. Also Hos 2:23; Is 5:2.

[25] Jeremias, *op. cit.,* 64, maintains that the *diabolos* of Lk is the late form.

[26] *Op. cit.,* 48.

ravens picked [it] from the surface of the ground."[27] Not only do we have here the same type of farming (sowing before plowing) as in the Gospels, but also the birds are the instruments of Satan or Mastema. Thus there is no real reason to think that the basic imagery of this part of the Gospel explanation would not have been intelligible to Jesus' hearers, and the opposition of Satan to the kingdom seems to be a perfectly authentic echo of Jesus' ministry.

In vv. 16–17 the seed that fell on rocky ground is identified with people who have no roots and fall away in *thlipsis* and *diōgmos* (Lk uses *peirasmos*). Obviously the Gospel explanation may very well refer to the persecution of the infant Church; and in v. 17 we find the adjective *proskairos* which Jeremias,[28] following Jouon, characterizes as a Hellenism for which there is no corresponding adjective in Aramaic. But granting that there has been an adaptation to the situation of the Church, need we deny the possibility of Jesus' own reference to tribulation? Cadoux[29] objects that there is no evidence that Jesus' followers were persecuted during his ministry, but here we have a question of the preaching of the kingdom which is not totally a present reality. The kingdom involves the eschatological period, and Jesus may have been talking about that tribulation that would precede the full coming of the kingdom. Elsewhere he foresaw that this final tribulation would cause many to fail (Mk 13:19–20). The Qumran material has shown us how much a living concept was this final trial during the New Testament period. The very word that the Gospel uses to describe this tribulation is *thlipsis* which the Greek (Th) used as a translation for the time of eschatological tribulation referred to in Dan 12:1 (Ap 7:14). Cerfaux[30] maintains that this eschatological tribulation is lost

---

[27] W. G. Essame, "Sowing and Ploughing," *Expository Times,* lxxii, 1960, 54.

[28] *Op. cit.,* 61.

[29] *Op. cit.,* 24.

[30] In the article *Fructifier* (see n. 18).

sight of in Lk's *peirasmos* which, in its present context
refers to daily trial. Yet *peirasmos* too may have origi
nally connoted the eschatological trial as in the PN.[31] Thus
once again, behind the Gospel explanation we can trace
ideas that are perfectly at home in Jesus' ministry.

V. 18 identifies the seed which fell among thorns with
people who are choked by:

a) Worldly cares (*merimnai*)—all three Synoptics
b) The glamor of wealth (*apatē tou ploutou*)—Mk, Mt
c) Other sorts of desires (*epithymiai*)—Mk
d) The pleasures of life (*hēdonai*)—Lk

Many of these words are more at home in the Greek of
the epistolary literature of the New Testament than in the
Gospels, and so the retouching here may be quite exten
sive. But this is indicated in the text itself, for only in (*a*)
do all three agree. Otherwise the Evangelists show a real
freedom of expressing the basic idea in different terms.
More germane to our purposes is the question of whether
the basic idea is foreign to Jesus' ministry. In Jn Jesus fre
quently warns against the world and its powers of corro
sion. In the Synoptics too we find a distrust of worldly
preoccupations, e.g., Mt 6:25–33; Lk 12:13–21; 16:19–
25. There is no doubt that for Jesus wealth and luxury
presented an obstacle to inheriting the kingdom, as the
beatitudes state explicitly. This basic idea may be expanded
in the Gospel explanation of the parable in order to fit the
situation of the Church, but the fundamental identification
of worldly cares as one of the obstacles to the preaching
of the kingdom is not unworthy of Jesus.

We have now examined the main allegorical identifica
tions that constitute the Gospel explanation of the parable
behind each of them we have seen the possibility of origina
identifications offered by Jesus Himself. The parable was
designed to answer the question of failure and success en
countered in Jesus' preaching of the Good News of God

[31] See above, Chap. XII, under the Sixth Petition.

kingdom. The main point is the ultimate eschatological success of the kingdom. Its failure to succeed completely among certain groups gives background for the final overwhelming victory. Those who fail to heed the Good News include: (1) the hard of heart, like the Pharisees, who supply Satan with his opportunity to work against the kingdom; (2) vacillating would-be disciples (cf. Jn 6:66) who withdraw or will withdraw because Jesus' teaching provokes opposition on the Pharisees' part; ultimately this will culminate in the eschatological tribulations prefacing the full establishment of the kingdom; (3) those, like the rich young man, whose worldly interests turn them away from the stark demands of Jesus; these turn back after putting their hand to the plow. These three groups are contrasted to the true disciples who leave all things for the sake of the kingdom and whose reward will be great.

The reapplication of this explanation in the Gospels to the situation of the primitive Church simply reflects the continued validity of Jesus' teaching in the minds of His followers. Their word (the Gospel) was, after all, the extension of his word; therefore it encountered a similar fate. Such a rooting of the explanation of the parable in Jesus' ministry and words is, we believe, far more plausible than the theory of spontaneous introduction of allegory by the Church.

XIV

The Beatitudes According to Luke

Blessed are you poor, for yours is the kingdom of God.

But woe to you rich, fc you have had your cor solation.

Blessed are you who are hungry now, for you shall be satisfied.

Woe to you who are fu now, for you shall be hur gry.

Blessed are you who weep now, for you shall laugh.

Woe to you who laugh now for you shall mourn an weep.

Blessed are you when people hate and persecute you . . .
for behold, your reward is great in heaven.

Woe to you when every body speaks well c you,
for their fathers acte thus to the false propl ets.

Every schoolchild who knows his catechism knows th beatitudes according to Mt; few would know that there a special set of beatitudes in Lk, and almost no one woul know their wording by heart. Mt's beatitudes differ from Lk's in number and in significant wording. Mt is concerned with "the poor *in spirit*," with those who are "hungry and thirsty *for justice*." The Matthean beatitudes have been the subject of innumerable spiritual commentaries. A few pages here dedicated to the Lucan beatitudes may help to make them less unfamiliar.

THE SETTING OF THE BEATITUDES

The explanation that Jesus spoke the beatitudes on two different occasions and that Mt records one occasion and Lk another, has been abandoned by most modern Catholic scholars. The opinion has gained ground that Mt's Sermon on the Mount in chaps. 5 to 7 (which is the setting of the beatitudes) and Lk's Sermon on the Plain in 6:17–49 are basically the same scene and drawn from the same source, i.e., a collection of Jesus' teaching. The two Gospels, however, have handled the source quite differently.

In Matthew's Gospel we find that Christ's teaching has been collected and arranged under subject headings. For instance, the main theme of the Sermon on the Mount is that of the New Law replacing the Old. This mount becomes the Mount Sinai of the Christian dispensation, as Jesus in the role of a new Moses gives new laws for the new people of God. Again and again we hear, "You have heard that it was said . . . but I say to you." (Against this background, the beatitudes are the Christian equivalent of the commandments.) To the basic outline of this Sermon (which he found in his source), the Evangelist has added material found elsewhere in the source, material which could harmoniously expand the general theme. Thus the Sermon on the Mount becomes the great collection of Christ's teaching in Mt.

Lk seemingly prefers to keep somewhat closer to the order of the Sermon found in the source; hence his Sermon on the Plain is shorter than Mt's Sermon on the Mount. Elsewhere in his Gospel Luke has much of the material that

the author of Mt places in the Sermon on the Mount. Thi
different ordering of the material offers no real difficulty
The Gospel material was preached and taught, and th
needs of this preaching and teaching guided the Evangelists
ordering of the material.

THE BEATITUDES IN MATTHEW AND LUKE

When scholars turn to the beatitudes which are found i
the Sermon on the Mount and the Sermon on the Plain
they use the same approach which governed their study o
the Sermon. With its eight beatitudes (or really nine, fo
Mt 5:11 should be included), St. Matthew's Gospel give
us a collection of beatitudes spoken on this occasion an
on other occasions. The beatitude was a common speec
pattern used by Jesus, and Mt's collection is by no mean
exhaustive (see, for example, Mt 11:6; Lk 11:28, 12:37
Jn 20:29). It is interesting to notice that the additiona
beatitudes in Mt's collection of eight (or nine) concer
spiritual qualities: Blessed are the meek . . . the mercifu
. . . the pure in heart . . . the peacemakers. To corre
spond with this, we find a spiritual outlook in the beatitude
Mt shares with Lk. In Mt we are not dealing with the poor
but with the poor *in spirit;* not with the hungry, but wit
those who hunger *after justice.* Thus the end product o
Mt's collection is a moral instruction on the spiritual need
of the Gospel message—the classical guide to the newnes
of the spiritual life preached by Jesus.

Lk's beatitudes are emphatically not primarily on th
spiritual plane. His poor are the real have-nots of thi
world; his hungry know the misery of an empty stomach
his unfortunate are weeping *now.* And just so that we d
not miss the realism of his beatitudes, Luke narrates a serie
of corresponding "woes": stark anathemas hurled agains
the rich and the content who do not know the meaning o
need.

THE IDEAL OF POVERTY IN LUKE

St. Luke's Gospel is the Gospel preached in the Gentile churches of Asia Minor and Greece, the churches evangelized by St. Paul. Here the majority of those converted to belief in the Jesus of faraway Nazareth were not the wealthy and the powerful but the poor, the downtrodden, the outcasts. It was among the lower classes of society that the radical novelty of the new religion made its most profound impression. Into the midst of their drudgery, slavery and poverty there had come the sweetness of hope, a hope enshrined in the words of the carpenter's Son who had not a place to lay His head, who had by choice lived among the sick, the poor, and the sinners, who had known pain and thirst, who had taken to Himself the role of a slave.

It is by no accident, therefore, that Luke's Gospel highlights that aspect of the teaching of Jesus which shows His love for the poor of this world. In the very opening of Luke's Gospel, Mary's *Magnificat* extolls the God who, through the coming of Jesus,

> "has put down the mighty from their thrones
> and raised up those of lowly state;
> has filled the hungry with good things
> and has sent the rich away empty."

Of course, all the Gospels agree that Jesus stood in opposition to wealth. After all, the prophets of Israel like Amos and Isaiah had savagely denounced the wealthy with their houses adorned with ivory and their wives bedecked in expensive clothes and jewels. Jesus was only being true to the prophetic tradition in saying: "How hard it is for those who have riches to enter the kingdom of God." So hard that it is easier for a camel to go through a needle's eye; so hard that it is impossible, humanly speaking, without God's mercy (Lk 18:25–27).

But it is in Lk that we find this theme expanded in detail. Only Lk (12:15–21) gives us the parable of the man who sinks his wealth into the building of barns. For one standard of life this is only common sense, a reinvestment of capital. But in Jesus' eyes the man is a blasphemous fool for he had laid up treasure for himself (12:21). Often we comfortably explain away Lk's passages as tantamount to a condemnation of too much concentration on wealth. But if we read carefully, we see that Lk is reporting an attack on wealth itself. Wealth gives happiness in this life, and according to the contrast explicit in Lk's beatitudes we cannot have our cake and eat it too! Those who are content here have already had their share of contentment.

We might recall the parable of Lazarus and the Rich Man, reported only in Lk 16:19–31. It gives a simple contrast: a rich man with fine clothes and plenty of food, and Lazarus who is poor, sick, and hungry—a living exemplification of the Lucan beatitudes. The suggestion that the rich man was leading a dissolute life has no foundation; the story tells us simply that he enjoyed his wealth. And when he later cries out from Hades for help, hear what he is told: "Son, remember that you in your lifetime received good things, while at the same time Lazarus received evil; but now he has comfort here, and you are in torment" (Lk 16:25).

In the spiritual outlook of St. Luke's Gospel, the only proper use of wealth is to get rid of it, to give it to the poor. This is the correct meaning of that badly misunderstood verse: "Make friends for yourselves by means of wicked wealth [the mammon of iniquity], so that when it gives out you may be received into the eternal dwellings" (Lk 16:9). Again, Mt 6:19–20 tells us, "Do not lay up for yourselves treasures on earth . . . but lay up treasures in heaven for yourselves." But notice Lk's form (12:33) of this saying: "Sell your possessions and give alms; provide yourselves . . . with a treasure in heaven that does not fail." It is in this same light that Lk 14:13 preserves Christ's words that in giving a banquet, the only fit guests to invite are the poor, the maimed, the lame, and the blind.

How demanding the emphasis on such renunciation of wealth is, we see in the answer given to the rich young man. In Mk 10:21 and Mt 19:21 he is told, "Go, sell what you have, and give to the poor." Only Lk 18:22 has "Sell *all* that you have." Again, in the call of the first disciples, Mk 1:20 and Mt 4:22 tell us that they left their father and their boat and followed Jesus. But Lk 5:11 says they left *all* and followed him. In the sending out of the disciples on a trial mission, Mk 6:8, while instructing them to have no bread, nor money, allows them to have a staff. Lk 9:3 denies even this convenience. Another example is Mt 5:42: "Give to him who begs from you and do not refuse him who would borrow from you." Lk's form (6:30) is even more drastic: "Give to *everyone* who begs from you, and do not ask your goods back from the man who takes them away."

The ideal realization of Christ's stringent demands is described by St. Luke in Acts 2:44–45; 4:32–35 in the communal living of the early Church where members sold all they had to follow the master.

APPLICATION OF LUKE'S BEATITUDES

With this background, the meaning of Lk's beatitudes is clear: they concern the privileged role of the physically poor and needy in Jesus' evaluation of men. We might clarify this by emphasizing that when we hear of poverty, suffering, and hunger here, the whole religious outlook of the New Testament requires us to supply the clause "accepted for the love of God." No one could suggest that Jesus is praising poverty as a social phenomenon without religious overtones. The poor or the hungry who blame God for their suffering would not be included in Lk's beatitudes. The poverty that is blessed is one which leads men to place their whole trust in God. The rich are cursed because they are self-sufficient and do not need God; the greatness of the poor lies in the need which makes them dependent on God.

Again we might point out that in analyzing the poverty and hunger which Jesus blesses, we must distinguish between that need which allows men to turn to God and that grinding misery and abject destitution which gives men no time and no energy for anything but bare survival. The latter is far from the Christian ideal, and should be effaced from the earth.

However, in making these distinctions, we must not go to the other extreme of spiritualizing Lk's poverty and hunger and equating them with Mt's poverty in spirit and hunger after justice. Lk's beatitudes and Mt's beatitudes bring out two different but perfectly valid aspects of our Lord's teaching, each a completely homogeneous echo of Christ's intentions.

In the spirituality of Mt's beatitudes, Christianity has place for those who are comfortable and wealthy in this world if they preserve a spirit of detachment in relation to their goods, and do not allow their wealth to choke off the vitality of God's word (Mt 13:22). Nevertheless, theirs is not the virtue extolled in Lk's beatitudes. There is a unique blessing within Christianity for those whose physical needs and sufferings lead them to place all their hope in God, for those who do not have the comforts of this life and yet accept their state for the love of God. If this were not so, God's Son would not have come to us in the tattered mantle of poverty and hunger and suffering.

Practically, is the ideal of Lk's beatitudes impossible in a world where a man's worth is frequently measured by standards of salary, home, car, and TV? Before we would answer too pessimistically, we might think of those Christian parents who bring into the world large families, despite the knowledge that each child means more privation of clothing, amusements, leisure. The Sermon on the Plain finds its hearers even in the twentieth century.

As for priests and seminarians, we would refrain from sermonizing. In face of the inevitable temptation to enjoy this world's goods, sometimes we justify ourselves by a too free use of Mt's beatitudes, and tell ourselves that regardless of our possessions, we are "poor in spirit." Perhaps the more stark standards of Jesus as presented in St. Luke may serve as a reminder of truth.

In his eloquent denunciation of Communism, Bishop Fulton Sheen has said that the Reds are substituting the gospel according to Marx for the Gospel according to Mark. While the play on words might not be so elegant, we suggest that the more precise opponent to the gospel according to Marx is the Gospel according to Luke. Karl Marx is called a revolutionary because the Communist Manifesto urged the workers of the world to unite since they had nought to lose but their chains. This was not revolutionary, but simply the age-old incitement of the poor against the rich—incitement used by every demagogue since the dawn of society. The genuine Revolutionary stood on a plain in Galilee and dared to proclaim, "Blessed are you who are poor."

AUTHOR INDEX

(*This index does not include all the places an author's name is mentioned. It includes the places where bibliographical information is given, or where there are important discussions of an author's views.*)

INDEX OF PASSAGES IN JOHN

(The Fourth Gospel is the subject of more than half the essays in this book; the following index covers the principal references to the Gospel.)

GENERAL INDEX

OTHER IMAGE BOOKS

hese prices subject to change without notice

OTHER IMAGE BOOKS

These prices subject to change without notice

OTHER IMAGE BOOKS

hese prices subject to change without notice

OTHER IMAGE BOOKS

These prices subject to change without notice